Date Due

OCT 1 0 '59		
DEC 1 4 '59		
DEC 1 5 '61		
OCT 1 1 '63		
DEC 4 '68		
⑯	PRINTED	IN U. S. A.

HOLY MASS AND LIFE

"*He who eats My flesh and drinks My blood has life ever-lasting and I will raise him up on the last day.*" I Cor. 15:55

HOLY MASS AND LIFE

By

REV. A. BISKUPEK, S.V.D.

SOCIETY OF SAINT PAUL
NEW YORK — CANFIELD — DETROIT — DERBY

FOREWORD

ALTHOUGH *he is dead, the author of these plain but practical pages still speaks to us; his work follows him. And this is what he says to each one of us:*

Place together the merits of the Blessed Virgin Mary, the adoration of the angels, the labor of the Apostles, the sufferings of the martyrs, the austerities of the anachorets, the purity of virgins, the virtues of confessors, in a word, the good works of all the saints from the beginning to the end of the world; add to all these the merits of the saints of a thousand worlds more perfect than ours: it is of faith that you will not have the virtue of a single Mass. The all-sufficient reason is that the Mass is identical with Christ's oblation on the Cross.

Oh, the infinitude of the riches enshrined in the sacrifice of Golgotha as re-enacted on the Altar! Oh, the supreme efficacy of that Prayer of the Eternal Son to the Eternal Father—the Prayer which because of His divine reverence and respect for His co-eternal, co-equal Son, (Hebr. 5:7) the Father must hear and answer.

Such is the summary of the last book which Father Biskupek has left us, a book which, we make bold to say, is redolent of and remindful of the Imitation of Christ: same simplicity, same profundity. There is no doubt that those who will use it will find it both immediately and permanently helpful as an aid to their devotion to Holy Mass.

REV. JOSEPH LELEN, PH.D.

CONTENTS

PAGE

FOREWORD 7

INTRODUCTION 11

CHAPTER

I—*From the Beginning of the Mass to the Kyrie*   13
    1. Unto the Altar of God 14
    2. I Have Sinned 18
    3. Life, Salvation, Joy 25
    4. Into the Holy of Holies 27
    5. Have Mercy 31

II—*From the Gloria to the Credo* 35
    1. Gloria 36
    2. Prayer 38
    3. The Epistle 43
    4. The Gospel 48

III—*From the Offertory to the Canon* 55
    1. Oblation of the Host 56
    2. Wine and Water 60
    3. The Chalice of Salvation 65
    4. Humble and Contrite 67
    5. Blessed by the Holy Spirit 70
    6. Among the Innocent 72
    7. Commemoration, Honor, Salvation 77
    8. Preface and Sanctus 82

IV—*The Canon before the Consecration* 87
    1. Offering and Petition 88

CHAPTER   PAGE

    2. Memento for the Living _____ 90
    3. In Union with the Church Triumphant   95
    4. Peace and Salvation _____ 97
    5. Consecration _____ 101

V—*The Canon after the Consecration* _____ 111
    1. Commemoration and Fulfillment _____ 112
    2. Abel, Abraham, Melchisedech _____ 115
    3. Angel and Altar _____ 118
    4. Refreshment, Light, Peace _____ 121
    5. Heaven our Goal _____ 126
    6. Christ our Mediator _____ 131

VI—*From the Pater Noster to Holy Communion*   135
    1. Our Father _____ 136
    2. Free and Secure _____ 140
    3. Breaking, Mingling, Consecrating _____ 142
    4. Agnus Dei _____ 146
    5. Peace and Unity _____ 149
    6. Union Inseparable _____ 153
    7. Protection and Healing _____ 156
    8. Before Holy Communion _____ 159
    9. O Lord, I Am not Worthy _____ 161
    10. The Body of Our Lord Jesus Christ _____ 166

VII—*The Closing Parts* _____ 171
    1. May It Cleave to My Soul _____ 172
    2. The Final Oblation _____ 176
    3. God Bless You _____ 181
    4. The Last Gospel _____ 182

CONCLUSION _____ 187

Introduction

READING the New Testament attentively, one cannot but be impressed with the high degree of Christian perfection placed before the faithful as their ideal. Our Lord wants all to be perfect as their Father in heaven is perfect, to learn of Him to be meek and humble of heart, to love one another as He has loved them. These are the fundamental principles; He gives definite details in many places throughout the Gospel, especially in the Sermon on the Mount. The eight beatitudes are, what we might call, a pattern for heroic sanctity; yet they are meant for all. Purity of intention that excludes all selfishness, continuous prayer, forgiving charity, unbounded trust in Providence, unceasing work for God and heaven, are all things expected of the disciple of Christ. The apostles echo the spirit and the words of Jesus. For St. Paul, the Christian is a temple of the Holy Spirit, a member of Christ's body; the very idea of it excludes sinful and worldly desires, and calls for love of God and neighbor that makes of life a living and holy sacrifice. St. Peter reminds the faithful of their dignity; they are partakers in the divine nature and life, a priestly nation, a holy priesthood. Therefore they are expected to follow in the footsteps of Christ, be holy as He is holy, and consider themselves as strangers and pilgrims in this life, ever moving onward to their undefiled and unfading heavenly inheritance. St. James insists upon active, living faith, which means, of course, the doing of all things proposed in the commandments and the teaching of Christ; in particular, he warns against the sins of the tongue; yet such is the significance of the proper use of speech, that he who does not fail by his tongue is a perfect man. St. John is the apostle of charity; we must lay down our lives for our brethren, and he who hates his brother is a murderer and the love of God is not in him. Charity is the fulfillment of the whole law.

The ideal of Christian perfection has not changed. It is proposed to us not only in the sacred writings but in living reality. Jesus our divine Teacher and Model continues to live in our midst as our pattern of a holy life in the Blessed Eucharist, the memorial of all His wonderful works. In the Holy Sacrifice of the Mass, prayers, instructions, and ceremonies, holy Church places before the faithful the ideal of Christian perfection as taught and exemplified by our Blessed Savior. Holy Mass thus becomes a real school of perfection. It can easily be seen what an important part this aspect of Holy Mass must hold in the life of the Church. If properly understood by the faithful, every Holy Mass becomes for them a lesson in Christian living, a source of inspiration and grace. The following reflections on the Ordinary of the Mass endeavor to present the Holy Sacrifice as the pattern of Christian perfection.

I

From the Beginning of the Mass to the Kyrie

HOLY MASS is the unbloody re-enactment of the bloody sacrifice of our salvation, Jesus our peace and reconciliation. The only obstacle to making salvation, peace, and reconciliation our own is sin. Sin therefore must be removed, and it can be removed only by repentance. God who is offended by sin is appeased by penance; in His infinite mercy He promises forgiveness to the sinner, "If the wicked do penance for all his sins which he hath committed, and keep all my commandments, and do judgment and justice, living he shall live and shall not die. I will not remember all his iniquities, that he hath done; in his justice which he hath wrought he shall live." (Ezechiel 18:21ff) Hence we must hope in God, repent our sins, and ask forgiveness, if we wish to share in the fruits of Holy Mass. These are precisely the thoughts and sentiments expressed in the opening prayers of holy Mass.

1. UNTO THE ALTAR OF GOD

HOLY MASS ordinarily begins with the recitation of the forty-second Psalm at the foot of the altar. The place, which this Psalm has been given in Mass, suggests that it was composed by David during the rebellion of Absalom. A great part of the people, the unholy nation, had joined the rebel; one particular individual, the unjust and deceitful man, must have caused the psalmist extraordinary grief by his treachery and injustice. Away from Jerusalem and its sanctuary on the holy mountain, the psalmist finds his consolation in prayer and is certain of eventual victory and return to the temple for glad thanksgiving. Bearing in mind this historical background of the psalm, its application to the Christian life offers no difficulty.

Render me justice, O God, and defend my cause against an unholy nation; deliver me from the unjust and deceitful man. For Thou, O God, art my strength. Why hast Thou forsaken me, and why do I live in sorrow, afflicted by the enemy?

Unholy nations have risen against Christ and His Church in our days; evil spirits roam through the world seeking the ruin of souls. And the unjust and deceitful man is right within us, that is, corrupt nature with all its evil lusts. We have greatly suffered from these our ene-

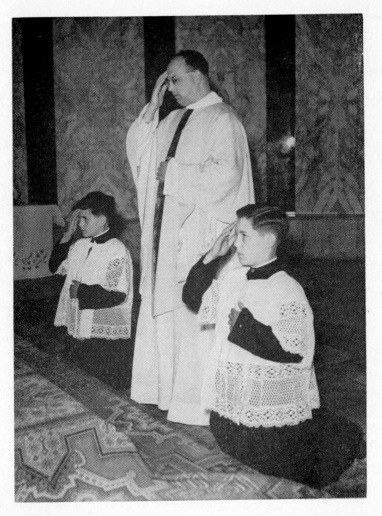

The priest marks himself with the sign of the Cross

mies in the past and we are fully aware of their cunning and malice. We take our case before God; He is our Creator and Lord. Despite our faults and failings we are conscious of His sovereign rights over us and we want to render Him loyal service. Interference with this service on the part of our enemies is also injustice against Him. In our helplessness we turn to Him, praying that He may take our case into His hands. We trust in Him, though we do not understand the mysteries of His providence—why He acts as if He had forsaken us, why He allows the powers of darkness to triumph and to inflict such harm on souls.

Send forth Thy light and Thy truth; may they guide me and conduct me to Thy holy hill and into Thy tabernacle. And I will go in to the altar of God, the God who fills me with joy and exultation.

The teachings of the faith are our light, the faithfulness of God is our hope. Faith and hope lead us to Calvary, the holy hill, on which was offered the sacrifice of our salvation; they lead us to the altar, because on it will be re-enacted in a mysterious manner the sacrifice of Calvary. Here darkness is changed into light, sorrow into joy, here invincible courage is instilled into the soul, so that we can take up anew the struggle against unholy nations and the unjust and deceitful man with the certainty of final victory.

And to Thee, O God, my God I will give praise upon the harp. Why art thou sad, O my soul? Why art thou troubled within me? Hope in God, for I will again give praise to Him, my Savior and my God.

As in past, so also in present and future afflictions, God will come to our assistance; there is no reason for yielding to sadness or despondency. So I, too, will rejoice. My soul shall be the harp on the strings of which I will sing the praises of God and give thanks to Him for the great things He has done for me. Those who trust in God shall never be disappointed.

2. I HAVE SINNED

Sin was and is the principal obstacle to joy in the Lord; it must be given no place in the Christian life. If we have sinned we must seek forgiveness. We do it in the Confiteor and the prayers which follow it. And "If we acknowledge our sins, he is faithful and just to forgive us our sins and to cleanse us from all iniquity." (I John 1:9)

The structure of the Confiteor is dramatic. We are to see ourselves as defendants in a court trial. God presides; angels, saints, and the faithful assist; in their presence we plead guilty and ask for mercy.

I confess to almighty God—We would expect this confession of our guilt to be directed to the all-knowing God who has witnessed our sins, or to the all-merciful God from whom we hope to obtain mercy and forgiveness. Yes, we turn to the almighty God, because forgiveness of sin implies a restoration or increase of the life of grace, which is a participation in the divine life, and God alone can give it in virtue of His almighty power.

Bowing profoundly the priest recites the Confiteor

To blessed Mary, ever virgin—The Mother of our Savior and Judge, our Mother and the Mediatrix of all grace, the Virgin merciful.

To blessed Michael, the Archangel—Leader in the warfare against Satan; we want to break with Satan and rejoin the heavenly armies.

To blessed John the Baptist—Preacher of penance, who prepared the way for the Savior and led the people to Him, the Lamb of God, that takes away the sins of the world. We wish to follow his directions.

To the holy apostles Peter and Paul—Peter, who holds the keys of the kingdom of heaven; Paul, who is the herald of God's mercy.

To all the saints—All of whom owe their salvation to the mercy of God.

To you, brethren; to you, Father—This is a most touching feature in the Confiteor. The priest is human; he may and he does fall. He may have scandalized the faithful; he may have been an obstacle to the growth of the kingdom of Christ. But notwithstanding all this, the people have no reason to despise him or think themselves better. They, too, have sinned, and the priest has given them absolution; he has looked into the depth of their weakness. It behooves both, priest and people, humbly to admit their guilt and to beg for forgiveness. It is the best way to repair the wrong of the past.

I have sinned exceedingly in thought, word, and deed—Sin is the greatest evil in the world; it exceeds all measure of the excusable or allowable. It is an abuse of the most precious faculties with which God has endowed man: reason and free will. The sinner defiled the sanctuary of his mind with evil thoughts and intentions; their malice was carried into the minds of others by means of speech and thus the evil spread. Deeds followed and brought to completion the evil of sin.

Through my fault, through my fault, through my most grievous fault—That which makes sin to be what it is, is my free will. Only in as much as thoughts, words, deeds are imputable to me can they be sinful. Sin is all my fault, all my own. True, often sin was committed through weakness. But, that I was so weak was my fault. I did not flee the occasion of sin, I did not seek strength in prayer and the sacraments, I did not keep in close touch with our Blessed Lord and our heavenly Mother. Hence I confess, I do not deny, I do not excuse myself; I have sinned through my most grievous fault.

Therefore I beseech the blessed Mary ever virgin, blessed Michael the Archangel, blessed John the Baptist, the holy apostles Peter and Paul, all the saints, and you, brethren; you, Father; to pray to the Lord our God for me—The saints will intercede for us; they cannot resist the appeal of such a humble confession. In the repentant sinner they see souls redeemed by the blood of Christ and their own future companions in eternity.

Thus, united in humility and sorrow for their sins, priest and people stand before the altar of sacrifice. They are asking for things which the loving Heart of Jesus is most eager to give—forgiveness of sins for which He shed His most precious blood. They receive what

*The priest prays for pardon as he ascends the
altar-steps and approaches the Holy of Holies*

they ask through the mouth of the priest as he pronounces the words of absolution:

May almighty God have mercy on you, forgive you your sins and lead you to life everlasting. May the almighty and merciful God grant us pardon, absolution and full remission of our sins. Amen.

3. LIFE, SALVATION, JOY

Implied, though not expressed in the Confiteor, is the petition for restoration of the things lost through sin and protection against future falls. This petition is now stated explicitly and in a manner which demonstrates the unspeakable malice of sin and its terrible effects.

Turn to us, O God, and give us life, and Thy people shall rejoice in Thee.

This is the human way of expressing ourselves. We naturally turn away from a disgusting and repulsive sight. Sin is the most repulsive sight for the infinitely holy God, and makes Him, so to say, turn away from the sinner in disgust. If we could see a soul in the state of mortal sin and behold the death and desolation sin has brought to it, we would be horrified. But we believe what faith teaches about the effects of sin, and faith inspires this ardent petition that God will turn to us again, restore to us His life and love, for then only shall we be able to rejoice again and be happy.

Show us, O Lord, Thy mercy and grant us Thy salvation.

The appeal is made to the mercy of God, for we have no claim of justice to forgiveness and grace. We stand before God as debtors unable to pay their debts, as beggars with nothing to call their own, as traitors deserving death, as sick and afflicted with an incurable disease, as prodigals, who have squandered their Father's substance and are not worthy to be called His children. But God is infinitely merciful; neither the malice of sin nor their number can exhaust His mercy. Blessed Henry Suso has strikingly illustrated the wonderful mercy of God, when he compared it to a fiery ball as large as the sun, and all the sins of men to a handful of straw. Throw that handful of straw into that immense ocean of fire and see how it is burned up instantly. So our sins shall be burned away in the infinite mercy of God and we shall be saved.

O Lord, hear my prayer, and let my cry come unto Thee.

A man lost in a forest will shout for help, hoping that some one will hear him; people caught in a burning house frantically call for means of escape; sick persons suffering from intense pain may scream and moan aloud. The sinner is lost in the dark thickets of the world, caught in the snares of burning passions and cannot find the way out; he is afflicted with a disease which no human physician can heal. What wonder that he cries out in horror at the realization of his condition and calls for help. However, our prayer for help need not be shouted out in a loud voice, but it must be the soul's sincere appeal to the merciful God. The cry of the soul goes farther than the cry of the mouth. United to the prayer of our divine Mediator, who "in the days of his earthly life, with a loud cry and tears, offered up prayers and supplications to him, who was able to save him from death and was heard because of his reverent submission" (Hebrews 5:7), it penetrates the clouds and reaches the throne of God's mercy, and the answer will be: mercy, life, salvation, joy.

4. INTO THE HOLY OF HOLIES

The priest now ascends the altar steps. In the prayer which he recites at the same time, the altar is spoken of as the holy of holies. The altar, upon which the Holy Sacrifice is offered, is indeed the antitype of the holy of holies in the tabernacle of old. In that holy of holies was kept the ark of the covenant, which contained the tablets of the law, given to Moses on Mount Sinai, and a vessel with manna, the tokens of God's merciful love for His people. Only once a year, on the day of atonement, the high priest alone was allowed to enter it, and that only after a long preparation and the performance of impressive rites. The Holy Spirit signified by this that the way into heaven was not yet thrown open, inasmuch as the Jewish material sacrifices could not perfect the worshipper in conscience. This could be done and was done by our eternal High Priest, Jesus Christ, by virtue of His own blood. He, who offered Himself through the Holy Spirit unblemished unto God, can and will cleanse our conscience from the dead works of sin to serve the living God. (Hebrews 9:8ff)

Take away from us, we beseech Thee, O Lord, our iniquities, that with pure minds we may enter the holy of holies.

The shadow of the Old Testament has given way to the full light of the revelation, the type to reality. Our altar is the true holy of holies. The divine High Priest will re-enact on it His bloody sacrifice of atonement in an unbloody manner, just as He anticipated it at the Last Supper. So much greater is, therefore, our obligation to approach this holy of holies with pure minds, purified in the fire of repentant love and the desire to please God.

We beseech Thee, O Lord, through the merits of Thy saints, whose relics are here, and of all the saints, that Thou wouldst vouchsafe to forgive all my sins.

This prayer is said by the priest standing inclined in the middle of the altar; when mentioning the relics he kisses it. Relics of at least two martyrs must be enclosed in the altar stone; relics of other saints may be added. The martyrs died for the love of God; it is fitting that love unto death should be close to the mystery of love. However, the essential factor in the martyr is not the endurance of death as such, but his love unto the shedding of his blood. Many other saints loved God with an equal love and would have gladly laid down their lives for Christ, had they had the occasion for it. Therefore, relics of saints, not martyrs, are also put

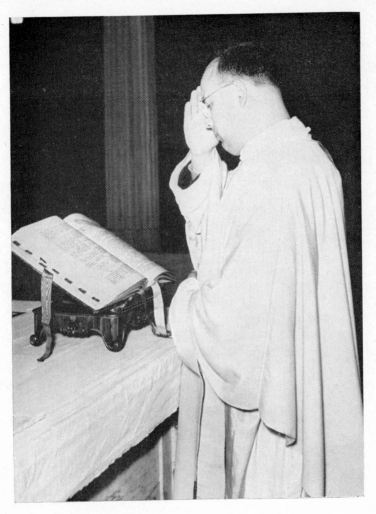

The priest recites the Introit—an entrance hymn
—says the Kyrie Eleison alternately with his
servants, and intones the Gloria in Excelsis

into the altar stone. Such love can also be ours; it should be the object of our desires and efforts. Such love infallibly secures forgiveness and is the surest protection against sin. We can become martyrs, if not of blood then of love, through the slow and continuous spending of life and energy in the service of God. St. John Chrysostom says, "There is with us the most merciful God, who will grant to them that long for Him either martyrdom, or, without a martyr's death, the divine reward of the saints."

5. HAVE MERCY

The climax of the prayers for forgiveness is reached in the heart-stirring Kyrie eleison. The cry for mercy is addressed three times to each of the three divine Persons, and in this threefold repetition we can easily see the particular relations which we attribute to the three divine Persons in our regard, that is, the special gifts and blessings which we have received or hope to receive from them. These petitions, therefore, also throw more light on the injustice and malice of sin, arouse more profound sorrow, and enkindle stronger hope and love.

Lord, have mercy!

I address myself to the first Person of the most Blessed Trinity. He is my Creator. All that I am and all that I have, in body and soul, is His gift. All my faculties of body and soul, therefore, must be used according to His will. In sin I have refused to do so; I have abused

His gifts to offend Him. My Creator is also my Father, for He has created me according to His image and likeness, and with fatherly love He has provided for all my needs. But in sin I have proved myself to be an ungrateful child that left the happiness of the paternal home and sought his happiness in moral degradation. Yet, this heavenly Father has not ceased to love me. Like the father of the prodigal He is waiting for my return, and longing for the moment when He can clasp me again to His Father's bosom. For He is and must be of necessity also man's last end. He has created us for Himself, and restless is our heart unless it rests in Him. Eternal happiness in heaven is eternal rest in God. God is the all-important and all-decisive end of life; all other ends must be subordinated to it. To miss this end means to be lost forever, eternally unhappy. Lord, have mercy! Let not the work of Thy hands be lost forever; let not Thy child be forever separated from the Father; let not him, whom Thou hast created to be happy with and in Thee forever in the heavenly kingdom, be among those cursed ones condemned to that eternal fire, where there shall be weeping and gnashing of teeth.

Christ, have mercy!

Christ is our Redeemer. "You know that you were redeemed . . . not with perishable things, with silver and gold, but with the precious blood of Christ, as of a Lamb without blemish and without spot." (I Peter 1:18) So wonderfully rich in blessings is this redemption that holy Church on Holy Saturday night sings of the "blessed guilt" that has brought us so great and so good a Redeemer. Yet, in sin we reject this good Redeemer and His blessings, and, as far as lies in us, crucify Him again. Having redeemed us, Jesus became our King and Leader, that having died to sin we might follow in His steps, learn of Him who is meek and humble of heart and live to justice. However, through sin we have deserted Him and joined His enemies. Because He is our Savior and King, He is also our Judge; He is divinely competent to act as such. He knows all things and cannot be deceived; He is all-just and with Him there is no acceptance of persons; He is all-powerful and there is no power on earth or in hell that could interfere with the execution of His sentence. Jesus Himself has described in grand style His coming for judgment and made known to us the final sentence, "Come, blessed of my Father, take possession of the kingdom prepared for you from the foundation of the world." "Depart from me, accursed ones, into the everlasting fire, which was prepared for the devil and his angels." (Matthew 25:34ff) Through sin I recklessly exposed myself to the sentence of eternal damnation. But:

> Thou, who Mary didst forgive
> And who badst the robber live,
> Hope to me dost also give.

Lord, have mercy!

The Holy Spirit is the Spirit of love, for the charity of God is poured out in our hearts through the Holy Spirit who has been given us. He has made us children of God, when we were born again of the water and the

Holy Spirit in baptism. We were made partakers in the divine life, and as Consoler and Comforter He continually assists us with His light, inspiration, strength, and consolation to further develop this life. The sanctity of the saints is the work of the Holy Spirit. And what this Spirit of love has begun, He will also bring to perfection in eternity. The grace of perseverance is His special gift. And what will be the final consummation of His work? "Eye has not seen nor ear heard, nor has it entered into the heart of man, what things God has prepared for those who love Him." (I Corinthians 2:9) Faith shall pass into vision, "We shall be like to Him, for we shall see him just as he is." (I John 3:2) Hope will enter upon the possession of all things that had been promised us and for which we prayed and worked. Love enters its final stage in the beatific vision. At last, on the day of the Last Judgment, the glory of the soul shall be communicated also to the body, for "If the Spirit of him who raised Jesus from the dead dwells in you, then he who raised Jesus from the dead, will also bring to life your mortal bodies because of the Spirit who dwells in you." (Romans 8:11) If we consider sin in this light it must appear to us as criminal blindness, basest ingratitude, incomprehensible folly. However, the love of the Holy Spirit is infinite. He calls to repentance, and, as long as life lasts, offers grace and forgiveness, and so also the greatest sinner has reason to pray:

> Here Thy grace and virtue send,
> Grand salvation in the end
> And in heaven felicity.

II

From the Gloria to the Credo

CONSIDERATION of the awful malice of sin and its consequences has confirmed our determination to break with it definitely and irrevocably. We want to follow Christ, our Leader, with the sentiments expressed by David's faithful friend, "As the Lord liveth and as my lord, the king liveth: in whatever place thou shalt be, my lord, O king, either in death or in life, there will thy servant be." (II Kings 15:21) Henceforth we want to follow Christ, be true Christians. How we are to follow Him is shown in the Gloria, the Epistle, and the Gospel. To reflections on these parts of the Mass we add prayer for grace since without grace we can do nothing.

1. GLORIA

THE GLORIA begins with a summary statement of the Christian's program of life and its principal features. There follow three petitions to Jesus, the Lamb of God, and three motives because of which we hope to see the petitions granted.

Glory to God in the highest and on earth peace to men of good will.

This is the message of the angels during that silent, holy Christmas night. No clearer statement could be given of the purpose for which the Son of God came into the world. So it is our task to give glory to God; it is the only way to secure for ourselves the peace of Christ.

We praise Thee; we bless Thee; we adore Thee; we glorify Thee; we give thanks to Thee because of Thy great glory, O Lord, God, heavenly King, God the Father almighty, O Lord, Jesus Christ, the only-begotten Son.

Praise is the first reaction of the believing heart as we behold the grandeur of God's works surrounding us, "The heavens show forth the glory of God, and the firmament declareth the works of His hands." (Psalm 18:1) On earth mountains and valleys, lakes and rivers, fields and forests, flowers and trees, birds in the air and fishes in the water, and all the living and moving things on the face of the earth, all declare the wonderful wisdom and power of God. Immeasurably greater yet are the works of God in the economy of our salvation: the Incarnation and Passion, the Blessed Eucharist, the indwelling of God in the soul of the just. "Oh, the depth of the riches of the wisdom and of the knowledge of God." (Romans 11:33) Since all these works of God are meant for our salvation, we cannot but bless Him as our greatest benefactor. We recognize Him as the almighty Creator, as God, whom we must adore and, through humble submission to His will and faithful service, glorify. And since the manifestation of His wisdom and power in the universe and in His works for men impress upon us His majesty and love, and prompt us to render Him loyal service, we thank Him for the lessons and the inspiration of His glory.

O Lord God, Lamb of God, Son of the Father, who takest away the sins of the world, have mercy on us. Who takest away the sins of the world, accept our prayer. Who sittest at the right hand of the Father, have mercy on us.

Sin is the only obstacle to the loving designs of our Savior. May He, the Lamb of God, that has taken away the sins of the world, grant us forgiveness and accept our prayer for unwavering loyalty in His service. Loving service is the only way to Him, sitting at the right hand of the Father. Therefore, "Let us mind the things that are above, where Christ is seated at the right hand of God. Mind the things that are above, not the things that are on earth." (Colossians 3:1ff)

For Thou alone art holy, Thou alone art Lord, Thou alone the highest, O Jesus Christ.

The preceding petitions are prayers for sinlessness, a virtuous life according to the will of Christ, holiness and heaven. Jesus has the power to grant all these petitions. He is the Holy One, the brightness of His Father's glory and the image of His substance; He is the author and source of all grace that renders possible the practice of virtue. He is the abyss of all virtues, and therefore the model for all holiness. Men may reach astounding heights of sanctity, as exemplified in the Blessed Mother of Jesus and the saints, but, above them all stands Jesus in unapproachable distance. He is the highest and therefore can lift us up, no matter how high may be our aspirations in the spiritual life.

The Gloria is like a beacon light showing us the way to the goal of our life. We must walk in this light. "O almighty God, we beseech Thee, grant us, who are enlightened by the new light of Thy Word made flesh, that the light which shines in our minds may be reflected in our works." (Collect, second Mass of Christmas) Thus we will give glory to Christ our Lord and Savior,

Together with the Holy Spirit in the glory of the Father."

2. PRAYER

The celebration of holy Mass proceeds amid prayer. At repeated times the prayers of the Mass are preceded by the Dominus vobiscum, begun with the Oremus, and

The priest recites the Collect, the chief prayer of the day
in which are gathered the petitions of priest and people

closed with a reference to Jesus Christ, our Lord and Mediator. All these features have a definite, practical significance.

Priest and People

Eight times during the Mass do priest and people pray for one another explicitly. The priest says, "Dominus vobiscum—The Lord be with you," and the people, usually through the server or the choir, reply, "Et cum spiritu tuo—and with your spirit, i.e., and with you." The tremendous mystery that will be enacted upon the altar calls for concentration of mind. God must fill the minds and hearts of the faithful assisting to the exclusion of all earthly thoughts; their own interests, temporal and eternal, will be most deeply affected by what is going on at the altar. For the priest himself, the manner in which he says Mass is a matter of life or death. He stands at the altar as another Christ; let him also act as such. This is precisely the meaning of the answer of the people: "And with you." May the Lord fill also your mind and heart, may He animate your priestly spirit, stir up the grace that is in you through the imposition of the bishop's hands. This is an excellent opportunity for the people to pray for their priests. If the priest at the altar is not such as he ought to be, may the Lord be with him, so that he may become a better priest and realize more fully his obligation to strive after holiness. If he is a good and holy priest, let the faithful pray that he may persevere and increase ever more in priestly perfection. Good priests are an incalculable blessing for the people and the faithful ought to show their interest and gratitude by praying for their priests.

LITURGICAL PRAYER

Oremus, let us pray, is an invitation to the people to join in the prayers of the priest. The faithful too have a share in the offering of the holy Sacrifice, as stated in Mediator Dei, "Now the faithful participate in the oblation . . . after their own fashion and in a twofold manner, namely because they not only offer the sacrifice through the hands of the priest, but also to a certain extent in union with him . . . the people unite their hearts in praise, impetration, expiation and thanksgiving with the prayers or intentions of the priest, even of the divine High Priest Himself, so that in the one and same offering of the Victim and according to a visible sacerdotal rite, they may be presented to God the Father." The faithful will join the more readily in these prayers of the Mass if they consider the excellence of liturgical prayer.

Liturgical prayer is the prayer of many. Unity makes strong. Many threads make a strong rope, many drops a mighty river, many soldiers a powerful army. So the prayer of many multiplies the praise and thanksgiving, the power of atonement and the efficacy of petitions, addressed to God during the Holy Sacrifice of the Mass. Prayers of the Mass are, moreover, prayers of Christ and the Church. Christ, always making intercession for us in heaven, prays on earth through the Church, and that most eminently at Holy Mass, in which He re-enacts in an unbloody manner His bloody sacrifice. The part which Christ holds in these prayers is impressed upon the faithful by their conclusion, which always refers to Him as Jesus Christ, the Son of God and our Lord, who together with the Father in the unity of the Holy Spirit lives and reigns forever and ever. The Father cannot deny what is asked of Him in the name of His well beloved Son; the Son is Lord and Himself can grant our petitions; the Holy Spirit sees in the gifts granted by Father and Son the outpouring of His love bringing ever closer the consummation of the eternal decrees of God: the everlasting kingdom of God in heavenly glory.

Liturgical prayer by its very nature is the most perfect prayer. The wonderful forms, which holy Church has given her prayers, add to their excellence and make them so much the more appealing. Well, then, Oremus —let us pray.

3. THE EPISTLE

The program of the Christian life, laid down in its broad outlines in the Gloria, receives official interpretation in the Epistle. Here divinely inspired teachers speak to us. The work of these sacred writers has been taken over by the Catholic Church, founded by Christ for the purpose of teaching all nations and guiding them along the ways of salvation. But the faithful must cooperate. As St. Gregory the Great says, "We have departed from our homeland by pride and disobedience, by seeking the things that strike the eye, by tasting the forbidden fruit; hence, it needs must be that we return to it by sorrow and obedience, by despising externals and subduing the desires of the flesh." (Fourth Sunday within the octave of Epiphany) The significance of the Epistle for the Christian life is aptly character- ized by its very names and by some features connected with its reading.

Epistle means letter. The sacred writers were in- spired by the Holy Spirit, and so the Epistle is a letter sent by God to His children on earth. It brings good news about our heavenly home, words of instruction, encouragement, and warning, and the promise of help. Children far away from home are glad when they re- ceive a letter from home and eagerly read it. Such would be the attitude of the faithful towards the Epistle, if they with living faith saw in it a letter from their heavenly home. The Epistle is also called lesson or reading, something that must be read and studied. In- terest in reading and studying a subject is proportionate to the advantages expected from its knowledge. No human knowledge could ever be as useful to us as the divine lessons given us in the Epistle.

In the Epistles of St. Paul the faithful are com- monly addressed as "Brethren." So we are not strangers, whose presence would be merely tolerated, but we are the brothers and sisters of Christ, children of God. Men with worldly ambitions seek admission into select society; association with distinguished men and women means much for their advancement. No human associa- tions can compare with the nobility and the advantages of associating with children of God and saints of heaven. "Dearly Beloved" is the address used in the Epistles

The priest reads the Epistle, the lesson taken from the Bible, the letter sent by God to His children

taken from the writings of Sts. Peter, James, and John. So we are the beloved of God and the Church. But where love is, there is also the desire to help. God and the saints are ready to help us, because they long for our salvation and company in heaven.

While the priest reads the Epistle he lays his hands upon the missal. This is a beautiful symbol of our readiness to grasp the hand of the Church and to follow her guidance. The teaching of the Church is not a lofty theory or interesting story for our entertainment; it is a call to action and implies tremendous consequences, for, "Not every one who says to me, Lord, Lord, shall enter into the kingdom of heaven, but he who does the will of my Father in heaven shall enter the kingdom of heaven." (Matthew 7:21)

The response at the end of the Epistle is "Deo gratias," Thanks be to God. Gratitude implies appreciation and guarantees good use of the gifts received. Knowledge of religion is the most noble and most necessary knowledge, yet it is little appreciated among men. Men will pay heavily for cultural and scientific education, but will think that they do God a favor, if they accept religious instruction. God does not expect material remuneration for the knowledge He offers, but He expects gratitude; gratitude which consists not in mere words, but in acting according to this knowledge. "Be doers of the word and not hearers only, deceiving yourselves." (James 1:22)

4. THE GOSPEL

The Gospel gives us the life story of Jesus Christ, the Son of God and Savior of the world. It is not fiction; it is all truth and reality. No other life story can compare with it in grandeur and beauty, in fruitfulness and significance for time and eternity. Jesus is our Savior and we must accept Him as such, for there is no other name given to men by which we could be saved. But Jesus does not expect blind and unreasonable faith. He proves Himself to be the almighty God who can save the world, the all-loving God who longs for men's salvation. All His miracles and teaching serve this purpose. Water is changed into wine by His mere will. He lays His hands upon the sick and they are healed, they touch His garments and feel the effect of His power; His word heals even those who are not present. He commands the winds and the waves and there follows a great calm; He blesses the loaves and they multiply while they are distributed. He raises the dead to life; He allows Himself to be crucified, but rises from the tomb in immortal glory. Truly, this man is the Son of God. Divine power stands in the service of divine love. All miracles of our Lord are wrought in behalf of poor and suffering mankind. It is this love that draws all hearts to Him. He invites all who labor and are burdened to come to Him; with Him they will find rest for their souls. Love will make sweet His burden and light His yoke. The Savior's love goes out in a special manner to the poorest of the poor, the sinners; words of forgiving love flow from His lips when He speaks

The priest reads the Gospel of the day, "the heaven-drawn pen-picture of Christ, the Living God"

to them. He does not condemn the adulteress, nor withdraw His feet from being anointed by a sinful woman; He offers forgiveness to Judas, has a look of tender pity for Peter, the promise of paradise for the repentant thief.

Such is the life of Him of whom the Gospel speaks. Jesus is the Way, the Truth, and the Life, and, as St. Hilarion says, there is nothing more dangerous for the world than not to know Christ. What the attitude of the Christian should be toward the Gospel is pointed out in the prayers and ceremonies which precede, accompany, and follow the reading of the Gospel. Before reading the Gospel, standing in the middle of the altar and making a profound inclination, the priest prays:

Cleanse my heart and my lips, O God almighty, Thou who hast cleansed the lips of the prophet Isaias with a burning coal; vouchsafe so to cleanse me in Thy gracious mercy, that I may be able to announce Thy holy Gospel in a worthy manner. . . . The Lord be in my heart and upon my lips, that I may announce His Gospel with dignity and competence.

The first part of this prayer is based on the vision of God related in the sixth chapter of the prophet Isaias. The prophet considers himself a man of unclean lips, not worthy to be a messenger of God. Only after his lips have been touched by an angel with a burning coal taken from the altar does he feel confident to accept the mission. How pure and holy must be the lips that announce the words and works of our Savior Jesus Christ. But not only priests are the heralds of the word of Christ; all the faithful are to spread the knowledge of Christ in a world that to such a large extent is hostile to Christ. Their words, however, will produce little effect unless they are inspired by sincere love and supported by blameless lives.

Before reading the Gospel the priest makes the sign of the cross on the missal, and then he signs himself with the sign of the cross on the forehead, mouth, and breast. The faithful do the same. The meaning to be conveyed by this act is that the Gospel is the word of the cross, the word of Christ, who died on the cross and accepts as His disciples only those who are willing to carry the cross after Him. Therefore, the cross must be in our minds so that we may judge all the affairs of this world in the light of the cross; it must be in our mouths, courageously professing our love and loyalty to the Crucified; in our hearts, ready to live and to die for Him. We declare our readiness to accept these conditions and to devote our lives to the Crucified by answering at the beginning of the Gospel, "*Glory be to Thee, O Lord,*" and at the end, "*Praise be to Thee, O Christ.*" The holy lives of the faithful shall be the glory of Christ. The faithful stand while the Gospel is read. This is a sign of reverence, but also of our determination to follow Christ and to stand by Him in life and in death.

In the Credo that follows we give renewed expression to our faith, hope, love, and loyalty. After all the preceding reflections our sentiments should be those of St. Peter, "Lord, to whom shall we go? Thou hast words of eternal life and we have come to believe and to know that Thou are the Christ, the Son of God." (John 6:70)

The priest recites the Creed, the flag of his Faith,
his Hope, his Love, his loyalty

III

From the Offertory
to the Canon

THE very idea of sacrifice implies that we offer to God a visible gift in order to acknowledge Him as our Creator and Giver of all things we possess, and to worship Him as our Lord and Master. In the present order of things there is but one sacrifice which is accepted by God as such, and that is the Holy Sacrifice of the Mass. It is in substance identical with the sacrifice of the cross, since the priest and victim in both are the same, Jesus Christ, and differs from it only in the manner of being offered. Even though Jesus is visible neither in His divinity nor humanity, nevertheless the appearances of bread and wine under which He is present are visible. We have furnished the bread and wine, they are our sacrificial gifts; however, their oblation is not the sacrifice. They will be changed into the body and blood of Jesus Christ and be the medium by which Jesus offers Himself in sacrifice. Furnishing the sacrificial elements we express our desire to have a share in this sacrifice and to offer ourselves through Him and in Him. These ideas are admirably expressed and developed in the prayers and ceremonies of this part of the Mass.

1. OBLATION OF THE HOST

ACCEPT, *holy Father, almighty and eternal God, this spotless host which I, Thy unworthy servant, offer to Thee, my living and true God...*

The bread which is used for the Holy Sacrifice is called host. The word is derived from the Latin hostia, victim, which was the name for the animal slaughtered in a bloody sacrifice. We are therefore reminded of our Savior's bloody sacrifice, of which Holy Mass is the unbloody re-enactment. However, when we speak of the host we think in the first place of the altar bread that will be changed into the body and blood of Jesus Christ; after the consecration we call it the sacred host. As such it is also the bread of life which we receive in Holy Communion. Natural bread sustains our natural life by being changed into our substance; Holy Communion is the food for our supernatural life, not however by being changed into our substance, but by making us partakers in the divine life.

Now we offer this host to the living God; living, because continually active in our behalf. He is active in every breath of the mouth and every beat of the heart, in every act of seeing, hearing, and speaking, in every movement of hands and feet, in everything that in one way or other serves the sustenance of our lives; nothing could exist without this activity of God.

The priest offers the bread which is to be transubstantiated into the Body of Christ

By this energizing and life-giving activity God proves Himself to be the true God; the gods and goddesses of the pagans have neither life nor activity, being but fictions of the mind. And thus we offer sacrifice to the almighty Father as the author of all life; to the eternal Father, who from all eternity called us to life everlasting in His beloved Son, our Savior; to the holy Father who wants us to be His holy children; to the living God who wants us to live for Him; to the true God who must be served in spirit and in truth, not by eye service but in sincerity of heart.

For my innumerable sins, offenses, and negligences, for all here present, and for all the faithful Christians, living and dead, that it may avail to me and to them unto salvation in life everlasting.

Holy Mass is the sacrifice of atonement, Jesus the Victim of sin, the propitiation for our sins, our peace and reconciliation. Where sin has abounded, grace has abounded more. In Holy Mass we have atonement full and adequate for our individual sins, for all those offenses by which we have become the cause or occasion of other men's sins, for all our omissions and negligences in the service of God. It remains for us to make use of these treasures of atonement for ourselves and for the world. We can do it by making the toil and labor of our vocational duties and all other hardships that may fall to our lot part and parcel of our Mass offering. This is strongly suggested by the very choice of the sacrificial element of bread. Does it not remind us of the sentence pronounced on our first parents in Paradise that, in punishment of their sin, they would have to eat their daily bread in the sweat of their faces? But as Jesus labored and died for the salvation of all men, let us think in our daily atonement not only of ourselves but of all mankind, since it is the ardent desire of the Savior's sacred Heart that all men should be saved.

2. WINE AND WATER

After the oblation of the host the priest pours wine into the chalice, adding a few drops of water. It is believed that was done also by Jesus at the Last Supper. The wine symbolizes the divine, the water the human nature, and the mixing of wine and water recalls the mysteries, by which human nature, created in wonderful dignity, was restored more wonderful after the Fall.

O God, who didst create human nature in wonderful dignity and even more wonderfully hast renewed it...

Man is the masterpiece of creation, a compendium so to say of all created orders, material as well as spiritual. As St. Gregory the Great says in his homily for the feast of the Ascension, man has something in common with all orders of created beings; with lifeless matter he has in common existence, life with plants, sensation with animals; like the angels he is endowed with a mind and will, and through grace he even shares in the divine life. Before the Fall these perfections of human nature were further enhanced by the so-called preternatural gifts; immortality of the body, freedom from inordinate passions, a penetrating mind and powerful will, undisturbed happiness. This marvelous state of man came to an end through sin. Grace and the preternatural gifts were lost, evil concupiscence, that is, the rebellion of the material nature in man against the spiritual was unleashed.

Through Jesus Christ the damage done by sin was fully repaired, and human nature restored to a dignity even more excellent than before sin. We are again sharing in the divine life through sanctifying grace and are placed into another paradise more beautiful than the first. It is the Catholic Church. Here grows the tree of life, the cross bearing the bread of life, here flow the rivers of grace in the Holy Sacrifice of the Mass and the sacraments. The original Paradise with all its enchanting beauty and happiness had no Mass, no Holy Communion, no tabernacle harboring the God-man. True, the preternatural gifts have not as yet been restored to us, but they will be ours in even greater perfection in heavenly life. All this wonderful change has been accomplished through the mysteries symbolized by the mixing of wine and water.

Grant us by the mystery of this wine and water to be partakers in the divine nature of Him who deigned to assume our human nature, Jesus Christ, Thy Son, who lives and reigns with Thee in the unity of the Holy Spirit, God, forever and ever. Amen.

A mystery is the Incarnation, the assumption of human nature by the Son of God and our Savior. Without ceasing to be what He was, He begins to be what

He was not; the God-man, God, capable of suffering
and dying for our salvation. This is a tremendous mystery of which St. Leo the Great says, "Unless faith accepts it, language cannot explain how both natures
have united in one Person." The Son of God became
man "for us and our salvation," as the Nicene Creed
puts it. It is the mystery of God dying for men that
men might live. "One of the soldiers opened His side
with a lance and immediately there came out blood
and water." (John 19:34) From this His pierced heart
He now offers us the blood of redemption and the
water of our sanctification. The mysteries of the Incarnation and redemption find their consummation in
the mystery of grace, that marvelous participation of the
soul in the life of God, its incorporation into the God-
man. This mystery is well illustrated by the mixing of
wine and water. No chemical change is effected by this
mixing; the wine remains wine and the water remains
water. But where is the water? It cannot be seen nor
tasted; it shares in the appearance and taste of wine.
So does the soul, united with God through grace, remain a human soul; neither is the divine substance
changed into the human substance. Yet, there is such
an intimate union between God and the soul that Jesus
compares it to the union of stem and branches in the
vine, and St. Paul can say, "It is no longer I that live,
but Christ lives in me." (Galatians 2:20) There can be
no grander conception of the dignity of man, no higher
exaltation of his nature, than that spoken of in this
prayer. As St. Augustine puts it, God has become man,
that man might become divine. Clearly, the application
of this truth to life means that it must be the Christian's

*The priest offers the wine to be transubstantiated
into the Blood of Christ*

ambition first and foremost," to be found in the form
of Him, in whom our nature has been united with God."
(Secret, first Mass of Christmas)

3. THE CHALICE OF SALVATION

The wine mixed with a few drops of water will be
changed at the Consecration into the blood of Christ
that was shed for us on the cross. For this reason the
chalice is called the chalice of salvation.

*We offer to Thee, O Lord, the chalice of our sal-
vation, beseeching Thy clemency that it may ascend
before Thy divine majesty with the odor of sweetness,
for our salvation and that of the whole world.*

Bread and wine are offered separately, and separately they will also be consecrated. Thus we are
reminded of the separation of the body and blood
of Jesus in His Passion and Death. His was a violent
death, and the violent shedding of His blood is the
most appropriate atonement for sin. Nothing could
bring home to us more impressively the violent separation of the soul from God in sin. What must be the
malice of sin if God thus punishes it; God, who is infinitely just and cannot punish sin more severely than
it deserves. If mortal sin in each case were punished
with immediate violent death, few sins would be committed.

The choice of wine as a sacrificial element also

conveys a practical lesson. Wine is an intoxicating
beverage; the intemperate use of wine deprives a man
of the use of reason and makes him act foolishly. So
is sin an intoxication caused by the intemperate use
of creatures, the greatest folly of which man is capable.
Is it not incomprehensible folly to rise in rebellion
against the almighty God and expose oneself to the
danger of eternal damnation for a low and transitory
pleasure?

Against this intoxication of sin stands the intoxication of love by which sin is atoned. To be drunk with
love is a common figure of speech. The love of Christ
in His Passion and Death was a scandal to the Jews
and folly to the Gentiles. The folly of love atoned for
the folly of sin. Indeed, this is an astounding manifestation of divine love and "the sensual man does not perceive the things that are of the Spirit of God, for it is
foolishness to him." (I Corinthians 2:14)

On the other hand, wine is one of the blessings
which God promised to His people in the Old Testament in reward for faithful service. The psalmist gratefully speaks of its effect, "that wine may cheer the
heart of men." (Psalm 103:15) Did not our Lord
work His first miracle by changing water into wine at
the wedding feast of Cana to make His friends and
their guests happy and cheerful? No less an authority
than the Angelic Doctor finds in the exhilarating effects
of the moderate use of wine the reason why it is the
proper matter for the Eucharist, "Wine from the grape
is more suited to express the effect of the sacrament,
which is spiritual joy." The Holy Sacrifice of the Mass,
Holy Communion, and the presence of Jesus in the

tabernacle are ever flowing fountains of spiritual joy and peace, such as the world cannot give. And the joy of the Christian heart in this life will in due time blossom forth into the joy of life everlasting.

Wine is the product of crushed grapes and this crushing of the grapes is in holy Scripture the symbol of humiliation, sorrow, and suffering. Pride, the root of all sins, must be crushed and there is nothing that does it more thoroughly than suffering and humiliation. It is something like a violent death inflicted upon self-love, and its patient endurance is folly in the eyes of the world. We need more of the intoxication of divine love in order to love sufferings and humiliation, which so often accompany the loyal service of Christ. For such love we pray in the words of St. Ignatius, "Blood of Christ, inebriate me." The blood that will be in the chalice is the wine, that enraptures the soul with the folly of divine love. From hearts filled with such love this oblation of the chalice will ascend before the throne of God with an odor of sweetness.

4. HUMBLE AND CONTRITE

"In order that the oblation by which the faithful offer the divine Victim in this sacrifice to the heavenly Father may have full effect, it is necessary that the people add something else, namely, the offering of themselves as a victim." (Mediator Dei) Precisely this is the object of the prayer which follows the oblation of the sacrificial gifts.

In the spirit of humility and with a contrite heart may we be received by Thee, O Lord.

God is truth and only truth can please Him. Reason and faith tell us that our life's task is to glorify God by the use of His gifts according to His will. This we have not done. We have used God's gifts against His will; we have sinned. God's will aims at our sanctification, our exaltation, and eternal happiness; acting against the will of God we have, therefore, degraded ourselves and acted against our best interests. With all the wisdom and judgment of which we boasted, we have acted recklessly, foolishly, and found it out to our regret. We sought pleasure and found pain, we sought rest and found labor, we sought peace and were tortured by qualms of conscience. Disillusioned we acknowledge our mistake; we feel sorry, humbled, crushed. But a humble and contrite heart God will not reject.

And may our sacrifice be so offered in Thy sight today, that it may be pleasing to Thee, Lord, God.

This renewed oblation of ourselves will have value only if it is sincere and offers the complete, unconditional, and permanent surrender of our will to God. There must be no exception or reservation, no division in our love and loyalty. It will not do to act as a servant of God in church and in religious exercises, and follow the principles of an unchristian philosophy in work and business, in family and social relations, in worldly ambitions and pursuits. The completeness of our surrender to God implies that it be unconditional.

Ever so often we attach, even though only implicitly, conditions to our service of God. We want to work for Him but only in the place of our choice, in the manner that appeals to us, in the company of such as are agreeable to us. We are willing to carry the cross provided it is not too heavy, to do penance provided it does not hurt. We forget that the very idea of cross and penance is pain and discomfort; spiritual anesthetics have not as yet been invented. And, lastly, our surrender to God must be permanent, definite, and final, for the simple reason that our fundamental relation to God as our Creator, Lord, and last end can never change. Hence our whole life, all our work, all our crosses must be included in the sacrifice offered to God; not one particular act or day, but the long-drawn-out series of days and months and years which He may grant us. Because of the fickleness of our nature it is necessary that we renew these sentiments again and again, and unite ourselves with the divine Victim, who at the end of His life could say that He had accomplished the task which His Father had given Him to do.

Acting in harmony with the sentiments expressed in this little prayer will be a source of incalculable blessings. There will be consistency in our lives, trustful submission to God's holy will, daily growth in the love of God and heavenly riches, profound and undisturbed peace. Hours and days with all their toil and labor, their hopes and disappointments, their sorrows and joys, are drawn into the sanctifying contact with the Holy Sacrifice; life becomes a continuous self-immolation which cannot but be pleasing to God.

5. BLESSED BY THE HOLY SPIRIT

Bread and wine have been blessed and prepared for their high purpose; in their offering was included the oblation of ourselves. There follows now a striking invocation of the Holy Spirit that He may bless this sacrifice, which is said to have been prepared for His holy name.

Come, Sanctifier, almighty and eternal God.

To sanctify is to dedicate to God, to make sacred and pleasing to God, to unite with God. We attribute all sanctification to the Holy Spirit, because He unites Father and Son in His eternal love. And so we find the Holy Spirit active in the work of our redemption, which has for its purpose the reconciliation of men with God. He acts as Sanctifier in the life of Jesus our Savior as well as in the life of the redeemed. It is of the Holy Spirit that Jesus is conceived by the Blessed Virgin Mary, and therefore, "The Holy One to be born shall be called the Son of God." (Luke 1:35) Again, it was when the Holy Spirit came down upon Jesus at His baptism, dedicating Him to His public ministry, that the voice of the Father was heard, "Thou art my beloved Son, in Thee I am well pleased." (Luke 3:22) And, in the synagogue of Nazareth, Jesus Himself testified that the Holy Spirit was upon Him, anointing and equipping Him for His mission. As to the Christian who is incorporated into Christ's mystical body and shares in His life, the Holy Spirit plays a most prominent part. It is through water and the Holy Spirit that we are born again and made partakers in the life and holiness of God; the sanctifying power of the Holy Spirit is active in all other sacraments, particularly in the sacrament of penance and in Holy Commuion, the body and blood of Jesus Christ, formed by the Holy Spirit in the womb of the virgin Mother. Is it not logical that we should invoke the Holy Spirit to bless this bread and wine and us, in order to prepare us for a more perfect and fruitful participation in the Holy Sacrifice?

And bless this sacrifice.

This blessing of the Holy Spirit will definitely dedicate the sacrificial elements to their sacred purpose; it will bestow upon them mysterious power by which after the Consecration they will be able to arouse in the faithful sentiments of faith and hope, a tender love for Jesus, and an ardent desire for the abundance of His gifts. As to ourselves this blessing will secure greater purity of conscience, more light to understand what we are doing, a more profound appreciation and love for the Holy Sacrifice.

Which has been prepared for Thy holy name.

Holy Mass is the sacrifice of divine love. Yet, the Holy Spirit is the Spirit of love, and His love celebrates its greatest triumph in the Eucharistic Sacrifice. In Holy Mass Jesus continues His mission of love. Through Holy Mass He is sacramentally present in our midst and to the end of time will extend to men His loving invitation, "Come to me, all you who labor and are burdened, and I will give you rest. Take my yoke upon you...and you will find rest for your souls. For my yoke is easy and my burden light." (Matthew 11:28) Through Holy Mass we ourselves are drawn into the Savior's mission of love. Here we are strengthened to love God with our whole heart and with all our strength, to render Him the daily homage of our adoration and service, of thanksgiving and atonement. Here we learn true love of our neighbor, seeing how Jesus has loved men and laid down His life for them. Those whom He has loved unto death surely deserve our love. The great works of the saints in behalf of men, their apostolic zeal, their self-forgetting service of the poor and needy, their silent prayer and self-immolation in the austerities of cloistered life, all draw their inspiration from this sacrifice of love.

Holy Mass, as it is the greatest manifestation of God's love for men, so it is also His most effective glorification. It is in every way the triumph of divine love. Therefore, Holy Mass must be said to be prepared for the glory of the Holy Spirit's name; His name is Love.

6. AMONG THE INNOCENT

The priest now washes his hands, reciting at the same time the twenty-fifth Psalm. This psalm may have been composed by David at about the same time as the forty-second Psalm that was recited at the beginning of the Mass. At all events, it is the prayer of one greatly troubled by malicious enemies. The psalm-

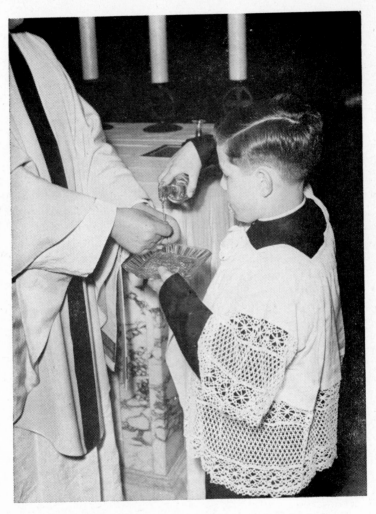

*The priest washes his finger-tips—a symbol of the
purity of soul required for offering the Sacrifice*

ist protests that he has not provoked the trouble; suffering unjustly, he feels so much the more drawn to God's sanctuary and its peace. The temporary success of his enemies does not shake his confidence in God. The thought of their ultimate punishment and his vindication confirms him in his determination to follow the straight path of the commandments, and by word and example to lead the people along the same road. These should be our sentiments as we proceed with the sacred action.

I will wash my hands among the innocent.

Hands are the symbol of work; the washing of hands symbolizes the avoidance of evil and the consecration of our work to God. Union with Jesus in His Holy Sacrifice calls for sinlessness. It would be an affront to the divine High Priest and in glaring contrast to the Sacrifice of atonement, if we were not determined to lead sinless lives. There can be no partaking in the fruits of the Sacrifice of atonement, where there is attachment to sin and unchristian principles.

I will be around Thy altar, O Lord, that I may hear the voice of praise and tell of all Thy wondrous works.

I will press close to the altar and with the eyes of faith look upon the mysteries enacted there. I will listen and endeavor to understand the prayers and hymns of praise that fill the house of God, those divinely inspired texts and stirring melodies, that have echoed through the churches of the New Testament from the beginning, and will continue to the end of time, then to be taken up and continued for all eternity by the blessed in heaven. Having seen and heard I will spread abroad the wondrous works of God. Of what the heart is full, the mouth flows over.

I have loved, O Lord, the beauty of Thy house and the place where Thy glory dwells.

The essential beauty of the house of God is that it is the dwelling place of God. If we love God we will seek to be in His presence, not only when duty compels us to be there, but as often as time and circumstances allow. This divine beauty of the house of God must be surrounded by created beauty. All that human art and wealth can furnish should be there; the beauty of architecture and ornamentation, of vestments and vessels, the splendor of ceremonies and sacred chants. Such beauty will be a faint reflection of the heavenly holy of holies; it cannot fail to attract even non-Catholics to the Church.

Take not away my soul, O Lord, with the wicked, nor my life with the men of blood, in whose hands are iniquities and whose right hand is filled with gifts.

The dreadful possibility that we might yield to sin inspires this petition. Man is weak; even the apostles were warned to watch and to pray lest they fall into temptation. The punishment of the wicked and the men of blood will be terrible. But in a certain sense all men are men of blood, since all have contributed to the death of Christ by their sins; many have done so by their oppression and exploitation of the poor. May God preserve us from sin and its punishment.

As for me, I follow the way of innocence; redeem me and have mercy on me. I keep my foot on the straight way. In the assemblies of men I will bless Thee, O Lord.

Following in the footsteps of our Savior we follow the straight way and stand on firm ground, which does not give way and on which we do not slip. Out of gratitude for all these blessings I will spread the knowledge of God among men, that they too may know and serve Him and thus save their souls. To do this on a large scale by speaking in the assemblies of men is the privilege of only a few. However, all can spread the knowledge of Christian principles and lead men to God and His Church in the daily contacts with their fellowmen by their words, but above all by their example of Christian living.

Christ, our God and Savior, must rule in the world, in public and private life, in politics and business and education. We are still far from this ideal state of things, and we freely dedicate ourselves anew to work for its realization in the surroundings in which God has placed us. Every Holy Mass, at which we assist in the spirit of this beautiful psalm, will ratify and strengthen this dedication through union with Jesus in the mystery of His body and blood.

7. COMMEMORATION, HONOR, SALVATION

In the prayer following the washing of hands we find a summary statement of the objects of the Holy

Sacrifice: Homage to the three divine Persons, commemoration of the mysteries of our salvation, honor for the saints, salvation for the faithful.

Receive, O Holy Trinity, this oblation which we offer up to Thee.

Since there is but one God, one divine nature, all three divine Persons were active in the work of our redemption. The Father gave us His only-begotten Son, "O wondrous condescension of Thy kindness towards us, O tenderness of love surpassing understanding, that to save a slave Thou gavest up the Son." The Son assumed human nature and in this nature suffered and died for our salvation. The Holy Spirit gave us the sacred humanity of our Savior, anointing and equipping Him for His mission, and brings the work of redemption to its completion by the sanctification of souls. Hence, this explicit oblation prayer addressed to the Holy Trinity.

In memory of the Passion, Resurrection, and Ascension of our Lord Jesus Christ.

St. Paul speaking of the Last Supper records these words of our Lord, "As often as you shall eat this bread and drink this cup, you proclaim the death of the Lord, until He come." (I Corinthians 11:26) The memory of the Passion stands in the foreground of Holy Mass, since it is the unbloody re-enactment of His bloody sacrifice. However, Holy Mass is not a mere commemoration of the Passion as is a passion play; it is real action, with Christ personally acting as priest and victim, though doing it through the instrumentality

In sacred silence the priest recites the Secret, a prayer inspired by the special day's sacrificial celebration

of the priest. But since Jesus, having died once dies no more, and is present in His glorified state as He is now in heaven, the memory of the Passion is inseparable from the memory of His Resurrection and Ascension.

In honor of Blessed Mary, ever virgin, blessed John the Baptist, the holy apostles Peter and Paul, of these (i.e., of the saints whose relics are in the altar) and all the saints.

The saints are the glorious fruits of Christ's redeeming death; it behooves us to give thanks to God for their holiness and glory. The honor of the saints is our honor, their remembrance a solemn call to holiness of life.

May it redound to their honor and to our salvation; and may they, whose memory we celebrate on earth, graciously intercede for us in heaven. Through the same Christ our Lord. Amen.

Every Holy Mass is to bring us closer to our final heavenly goal in a twofold way. In the first place, we join our divine High Priest in fulfilling the primary object of our lives, that is, to honor and adore God, to give thanks to Him, to atone for our sins. Uniting ourselves with the divine Victim we offer our lives to be spent completely in service for the glory of God. In the second place, we implore the intercession of the saints. They love us because they love Jesus who loved us unto death; they see in us their future companions and our salvation will be their delight for all eternity. Therefore, they rejoice in praying for us and helping us in many other ways. The ultimate object of their

intercession is that we too may become holy, "Be followers of us as we were followers of Christ."

The above prayer brings the Offertory proper to
a close. The Orate Fratres and the so-called secret
prayers which follow are prayers in support of the
ideas thus far presented.

8. PREFACE AND SANCTUS

The Preface is the solemn entrance into the grand
mysteries of the Canon, the joyous prelude which the
Church intones as we set out to meet our divine High
Priest in His heavenly glory. It consists of the so-called
responsories and a sublime canticle of praise and thanksgiving. All is calculated to fill us with holy awe and
reverence.

*Per omnia saecula saeculorum. Amen.—Forever
and ever. Amen.*

We hear the echoes of eternity, we feel its breath.
Our divine High Priest is the Eternal One, who lives
and reigns in His heavenly kingdom with the Father,
in the unity of the Holy Spirit forever and ever.

The Lord be with you—And with you.

If ever we need concentration of mind, it is now as
we are about to witness the tremendous mystery re-
enacted before our very eyes. Would it not be unbear-
able ingratitude, willingly to keep in our minds any
other thought than that of God and His love?

Lift up your hearts—We have lifted them up to the Lord.

Lift up your hearts to Jesus sitting at the right hand of the Father; lift them up from the cares and worries of this life, from the enticing allurements of the world to the delights of heaven, from the narrow horizons of human selfishness to the vast expanses of God's limitless love, from the treacherous instability of human friendships to the love unto death of your changeless friend.

Let us give thanks to the Lord our God—It is meet and just.

As the rays of the sun gather in the focus, so the rays of God's love gather in this eucharistic mystery, the memorial of all His wonderful works. Let us give thanks; but let us do so through Jesus Christ, who is our Eucharist, our thanksgiving.

It is truly meet and just, right and profitable unto salvation, that we should at all times and in all places give thanks to Thee, O holy Lord, almighty Father, eternal God, through Christ our Lord.

The tremendous mystery of the Eucharist reaches into eternity, embraces all times and all places. As we look into the past we behold the eternal love of God by which He decreed our salvation; as we turn to the future we gaze at the kingdom of glory, thrown open for the elect by the blessings of this Sacrifice. Holy Mass is the Sacrifice foretold by the prophet Malachy, that would be offered up from the rising of the sun to its going down, the clean oblation by which the name of God would be great among the Gentiles, and the sacrifice offered to Him in every place.

Through Him the angels adore Thy majesty, the Dominations adore, the Powers thrill with wonder.

Jesus, though not the Savior of the angels, is also their Mediator. They now behold Him, who was shown to them in a vision to test their loyalty. As then so now they praise and adore the infinite wisdom and power of God, that has raised a created nature to such glory. Dominations are probably spirits who rule over the laws and forces of nature active throughout the universe. These laws will be suspended when the Lord of lords becomes present under the species of bread and wine. The Dominations humbly adore, bowing before the all-controlling authority of God. Powers thrill with wonder. Display of power must have a special appeal for spirits distinguished by their capacity for doing great things. The grandest display of power is found in the eucharistic mystery, power so great as to make these powerful spirits thrill with wonder and reverent awe.

The heavens, the heavenly hosts, and the blessed Seraphim join in the celebration with jubilant accord.

The offering of Holy Mass is a celebration, a feast for those heavenly spirits. "Wisdom has built herself a house, has mixed the wine and set the table." Here infinite wisdom has enthroned infinite love through infinite power. We do not see as yet face to face as the angels do, but we believe, rejoice, praise, and give

thanks; we wish to join them in their praises of the
all-holy and merciful God, acclaim our divine High
priest and welcome Him in our midst.

*Grant, we humbly pray, that united with them
our voices too be given hearing as in praise and sup-
plication we cry out: Holy, holy, holy Lord, God of
hosts. The heavens and the earth are full of Thy glory,
Hosanna in the highest.*

These words are taken from a vision of the prophet
Isaias. The prophet beholds God sitting on a high
throne, His train filling the temple. Two Seraphim are
standing before Him, proclaiming throughout the heavens the holiness of God. Heaven and earth are full of
His glory. The visible universe unceasingly proclaims
the glory of the Creator, and in heaven angels and
saints in a yet more impressive manner give testimony
to the merciful love of Him to whom they owe all that
they are. But the wonders of the universe and the glory
of angels and saints pale into insignificance before the
majesty and splendor of the eucharistic mystery.

*Blessed is He who comes in the name of the Lord.
Hosanna in the highest.*

When on Palm Sunday Jesus solemnly entered
Jerusalem where a few days later He was to be crucified, crowds of people welcomed Him. They scattered
palm branches on the road, spread their garments in
His path, while their cries of joy rent the air, "Hosanna
to the Son of David! Blessed is He who comes in the
name of the Lord!" The same Jesus will soon be in our
midst to offer the same sacrifice which He offered in

Jerusalem. We welcome Him; for us, too, He is the One who comes in the name of the Lord.

He comes in the name of the Father who sent Him. Never has greater work been accomplished for the honor of God than by Jesus. Reparation full and adequate was made for the sins of the world; infinite honor was given to God by one, who, though man, was also God. He became obedient unto death, death on a cross. So He is blessed by the Father and the Holy Spirit. And blessed He is by the saints in heaven, for all of them owe their holiness and glory to Him. So He comes as the Blessed One also for us, for all those millions of men living on earth, for through Him alone can they be saved. Should we not welcome Him with holy enthusiasm and grateful love? Hosanna in the highest!

The coming of Jesus to earth in the form of a servant to die for us, and His eucharistic coming for the mystical re-enactment of His sacrifice, will be followed by His coming with power and majesty on the day of judgment. Then there will go up from the vast multitude of all the redeemed from all nations, tribes, and tongues, the last Benedictus, the thundering welcome, "Blessed is He who comes in the name of the Lord. Hosanna in the highest."

IV

The Canon before
the Consecration

THE MASS is a sacrifice, a gift to God. We now come to the heart and center of the Mass, to the very sacrifice itself, offered up to God at the Consecration. This is the whole point and purpose of the Mass—that we offer with Christ the same Sacrifice He offered on the Cross of Calvary. As Christ offered Himself, Body and Blood, to His Heavenly Father, so at Mass Christ's sacrifice is continued. Now Christ's work is accomplished in company with us, who are His faithful members.

1. OFFERING AND PETITION

THE FIRST prayer of the Canon bears striking resemblance with the prayer said by our Lord at the Last Supper. He then renewed the oblation of His life to His heavenly Father, prayed for the apostles and for all those who upon their word would believe in Him; He prayed for unity and peace and holiness among the members of the Church. In this prayer we do the same.

And now we humbly beseech Thee, most merciful Father, through Jesus Christ Thy Son, our Lord, that Thou wouldst accept and bless these gifts, these offerings. these holy and undefiled sacrifices.

The bread and wine upon the altar and all the other things required for the offering of Holy Mass are personal gifts: the contributions of the faithful through their support of the Church; they symbolize the oblation of their own persons. These gifts are moreover official gifts, accepted by the Church for an official public act of worship; they are sacrificial because they are destined for the offering of the Eucharistic Sacrifice. As sacrificial gifts they are said to be holy and undefiled. This statement had a very practical meaning for the faithful in the early times of Christianity, when pagan sacrifices were offered in great number. The offering of a gift to an idol would be a hideous defilement of the gift, whereas its oblation to the true God sanctifies it. Idol worship in the ancient form has practically disappeared, but every sin is idol worship in one form or other. It is the worship of self through pride and vanity, the worship of the flesh through intemperance and impurity, the worship of mammon through greed and avarice. Should we have become guilty of such idol worship, this prayer reminds us of the necessity of cleansing our souls from such defilements, if we wish to be united with the divine High Priest and Victim in this Holy Sacrifice.

Which we offer to Thee, in the first place, for Thy holy Catholic Church. Grant her in Thy mercy peace; guard, unite, and govern her throughout the world, together with Thy servant, our Pope N., and with our Bishop N., and with all who profess and propagate the Catholic and apostolic faith.

The Church is holy; should we not be her holy members? She is Catholic; what do we do to spread the faith and to bring non-Catholics into the Church: pray, give good example, support her missionary work? Even though times of persecution belong to the most glorious of the Church, nevertheless, generally speaking, the Church will be best able to accomplish her mission in times of peace, tolerance, and freedom of religion. The Church needs peace, not only from without but also from within. National and racial prejudice, vain ambitions of individuals and groups of members of the Church have only too often in the past torn asunder the unity of the mystical body of Christ and caused untold harm. Unity makes strong. The Church can flourish internally and externally only if the faithful are but one heart and one soul. Divine guidance will never fail the Church; in matters of faith and morals it is assured through her infallible teaching authority. Yet, there are many other things in the government of the Church, left to the prudence of ecclesiastical authorities. Human limitations and the corruption of the human heart can do much harm. Ecclesiastical authorities need the prayers of all the faithful that they may always allow themselves to be guided by the light of the Holy Spirit so as to see and to do what is best for the glory of God and the salvation of souls.

Then we pray for all the faithful that they may be strong and steadfast in the profession of their faith; lastly, for all those apostolic men and women, tillers of the soil, who by their labors for the conversion of pagans, heretics, and sinners, stand in the forefront of the Church Militant. Theirs is an arduous task and often heroic faith and fortitude are needed. They deserve our prayers in a very particular manner so that their labors may be blessed and soon there may be but one flock and one shepherd.

2. MEMENTO FOR THE LIVING

After the prayer for the whole Church follows the memento for the living. In ancient times the names of those who were to be especially remembered at the Holy Sacrifice were read aloud at this place; at the

The priest pauses for the memento of the living,
those for whom Holy Mass is offered

present time the priest recalls them in silence. After this the faithful who are present are remembered, and the manner in which this is done is extraordinarily appealing.

Remember, O Lord, Thy servants and handmaids, N. and N., and all who stand about the altar, whose faith has been tried and whose devotion is known to Thee.

The faithful assisting at Mass are spoken of as standing about the altar. This very term takes us back to those early times, when the sacred mysteries were celebrated in the privacy of a Christian home or in the catacombs. The place was small and the faithful close to the celebrating priest, actually standing about the altar. In the catacombs those silent graves of the martyrs along the narrow passage ways spoke an eloquent language. The faithful knew what they had to expect for the profession of their faith; but they had accepted it and the following of their crucified King and Leader with all the devotion of their hearts. Their very presence in this place was evidence of their loyalty. Indeed, their faith needed no further recommendation; it had been tried and their devotion to Christ was known.

Even though not standing about the altar, the faithful must be close to priest and altar also in our days as "a holy priesthood, a chosen race, a holy nation." (I Peter 2:5) True, in many cases Christian fervor leaves much to be desired, but on the whole, the faithful have proved their faith and loyalty to Christ also in our days. They have built churches and schools to worship God and to preserve the faith of the young.

There are millions who have not conformed to the unchristian principles of a materialistic world and in many cases they have suffered discrimination, persecution, the loss of property and life because of their religion, Their faith, too, has been tried and their devotion to Christ is known.

For whom we offer up to Thee, or, who offer up to Thee, this sacrifice of praise for themselves and all their own, to obtain the redemption of their souls, their hoped-for salvation and safety, and render their vows to Thee, the eternal God, living and true.

The redemption of their souls had real meaning for those early Christians. They beheld all around them, and, if they were converts, had experienced in their own lives, the emptiness and moral wretchedness of the pagan world. There was no light of faith to show men the purpose of their lives, no guidance in the aberrations of pagan superstition, no encouragement to resist enslavement by the evil lusts of human passions, no hope for a blessed eternity. All this the Christians had found in the Church, and for this redemption they offered up the sacrifice of praise and thanksgiving. But they also remained fully aware of the weakness of human nature; they had seen others falter and fail; they realized the need of help and they found it, strength and safety, in this Sacrifice.

Conditions in our days have much in common with those prevailing in the early times of Christianity. In fact, the means employed in many cases to make the faithful give up their faith are more cunning and cruel, more inhuman and diabolical than ever before.

So much the more is it necessary for the faithful to gather around the altar and to draw courage from this Sacrifice by which the powers of hell were defeated, and to persevere "unto perfect patience and long-suffering, joyfully rendering thanks to the Father, who has made us worthy to share in the lot of the saints in light." (Colossians 1:10) Here they will renew their faith, strengthen their hope, enkindle their love to live up to their baptismal promises and thus to render their vows to the eternal God, living and true.

3. IN UNION WITH THE CHURCH TRIUMPHANT

Startling as it may sound at first hearing, it is a truth following from Catholic doctrine that the blessed in heaven are one with us in offering the Holy Sacrifice. This prayer is proof of it; the law of prayer is the law of faith. Their merits and prayers add to our hope for an abundant share in the blessings of Holy Mass.

This we do in communion with and honoring the memory, especially of the glorious ever virgin Mary, the Mother of our God and Lord Jesus Christ, and also of Thy blessed apostles and martyrs, Peter and Paul... and all Thy saints.

The saints in heaven are members of Christ's mystical body in a more perfect manner than we. What Christ does as their Head, they do with Him. Jesus, though risen from the dead and dying no more, renews His sacrifice in a mystical manner, offering His sufferings and death; so do the saints offer again and again the labors and sufferings of their lives. And as

God is honored by the re-enactment of Christ's sacrifice, so He is honored by the repeated offering of the
saints' labors and sufferings joined to the Eucharistic
Sacrifice.

The saints were members of the Church Militant
and remained united with the faithful on earth in the
unity of the mystical body of Christ. They became
saints through the Church and they are forever grateful for what they have received. More than ever are
they desirous of working for the ends of the Church,
the glory of God, and the salvation of souls. Their
glorified state, far from rendering them incapable of
such work, increases the efficacy of their prayers and
holy desires. Must we not expect them to be present
at the celebration of Holy Mass in some mysterious
though eminently real manner?

*By their merits and prayers grant that we may in
all things be shielded by Thy protection and help.
Through the same Christ our Lord. Amen.*

The greater the merits of the saints are, the more
powerful is their intercession. Therefore, the Blessed
Virgin and Mother of Jesus is always put in the first
place; then the apostles are mentioned, the faithful
companions of Jesus and heralds of His Gospel; lastly,
some of the early martyrs as representatives of all the
saints, whose life and death exercised such an inspiring
influence upon the faithful.

Now the saints have received their reward, but
their merits and prayers are ever present to God. And
the saints themselves can again and again give expression to their desire that whatever they have done on

earth may continue to bring forth fruit for the glory of God and the good of souls.

The particular favor we wish to secure through the merits and prayers of the saints is defense and protection. Christian life is a warfare against satan and the evil spirits who roam through the world, seeking the ruin of souls. At all times and in all places, in our occupations, in prayer and at work, at home and in church, in shop and office, these evil spirits watch for opportunities to ruin souls. It is, indeed, a war on many fronts. The saints have fought the fight, they have experienced the dangers of the Christian warfare, they understand our needs and they offer their merits and prayers in our behalf, that we too may gain the crown of victory in life everlasting.

God is wonderful in His love. He has given us His divine Son to be our Savior, He has given us the saints in order that, assisted by their merits and prayers and inspired by their example, we may make ourselves worthy one day to be members of the Church Triumphant, companions of the saints in glory.

4. PEACE AND SALVATION

In the Old Testament the priest would lay his hands upon the victim in a sin offering, to signify that his sins and the sins of the people passed over upon the animal. In like manner does the priest now extend his hands over host and chalice to signify that Jesus, the Lamb of God, "was wounded for our iniquities; He was bruised for our sins; the chastisement of our

peace was upon Him, and by His bruises we are healed."
(Isaias 53:5) We, therefore, have every reason to pray
for the fruits of our Savior's sacrifice, namely, peace,
deliverance from eternal damnation, and a place in
the number of God's elect in heaven.

*And so we beseech Thee, O Lord, graciously to
accept this oblation from us, Thy servants, and from
Thy whole family.*

The Holy Sacrifice is eminently divine service,
acknowledging our state of servitude in reference to
God. Both, priest and people, are servants of God, but
also members of God's family. Servants we are, not in
virtue of a freely accepted contract, but in virtue of
our very nature; members of God's family we are
through the "Spirit of adoption, by virtue of which we
cry, Abba Father." (Romans 8:16) By rendering service lovingly and loyally we prove ourselves worthy
of membership in God's family.

*Dispose our days in Thy peace, bid us be delivered
from eternal damnation and numbered in the flock
of Thy elect. Through Christ our Lord. Amen.*

This petition for peace was inserted into the prayer
by Pope Gregory the Great because of the troubled conditions of his times. But the petition is practical for all
times. There will always be need of prayer for peace,
because there will always be sin. Sinners have no peace,
and sin makes the nations miserable. Hence, this petition is really a prayer for avoidance of sin and repression of evil in private and public life. What a boon it
would be for mankind if all human affairs were reg-

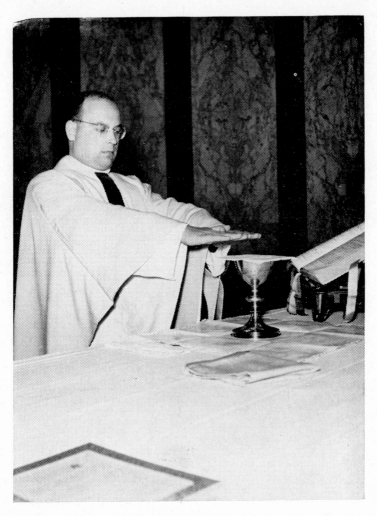

*His hands over the Chalice the priest
prays for peace in our days*

ulated according to God's holy will—peace throughout the world.

Damnation is the eternal loss of peace; hell the
place of eternal despair, of weeping and gnashing of
teeth, the place where the worm does not die and the
fire is not extinguished. Yet, damnation remains a
dreadful possibility for us as long as we live and must
fill us with salutary fear. There is no better place to
pray for deliverance from eternal damnation and no
stronger hope for a favorable answer than the re-enactment of our Savior's sacrifice. "For God has not destined
us unto wrath, but to gain salvation through our Lord
Jesus Christ, who died for us." (I Thessalonians 5:19)

Deliverance from eternal damnation implies eternal salvation. Those who are saved are the chosen ones,
the flock of Christ; He is their Good Shepherd and
they are His sheep. He knows His sheep and they know
Him. As the shepherd separates the sheep from the
goats, so will Jesus at the Last Judgment separate the
reprobate from the elect, and then pronounce sentence.
Where will our place be on that day? We do not know,
but we hope, as we must hope as Christians, that we
will find a place in the flock of God's elect. If, as long
as we live, we listen to the voice of the Good Shepherd,
if we do not desert His flock and remain faithful and
obedient children of His holy Church, He will protect
us and no one shall be able to pluck us from His hands.

5. CONSECRATION

We are now transported in spirit to the Supper
Room in Jerusalem, where Jesus is assembled with His

apostles, on that ever memorable evening of which St. John writes, "Before the feast of the Passover, Jesus, knowing that His hour had come to pass out of this world to the Father, having loved His own who were in the world, He loved them to the end." (John 13:1) The end of our Savior's life was at hand. The cross had loomed before His eyes ever since He had entered this world; now He is to face it in its stark and dread reality. But the New Testament, the Testament of love, needed as yet the sacrament of love, the memorial of His love to the end of time, and there was no hour more fitting to give it to the world. "Therefore, He our God and Lord, though He was about to offer Himself once by His death upon the altar of the cross, wished to leave to the Church, His beloved Spouse, a visible sacrifice, such as the nature of man calls for. By means of it the bloody sacrifice, which was to be offered once upon the cross, should be represented, its memory kept alive to the end of time, and its saving power applied unto the remission of those sins which are daily committed by us." (Council of Trent and Mediator Dei) In an intensely dramatic scene there is now re-enacted before us what took place in the Supper Room on that sacred evening. The priest acts as Christ acted, speaks the words which Christ spoke. Jesus acts through the priest.

Who the day before He suffered took bread into His holy and venerable hands and, with eyes lifted up to heaven, to Thee, O God, His almighty Father, gave thanks to Thee, blessed and broke and gave to His disciples, saying: Take you all and eat of it, FOR THIS IS MY BODY.

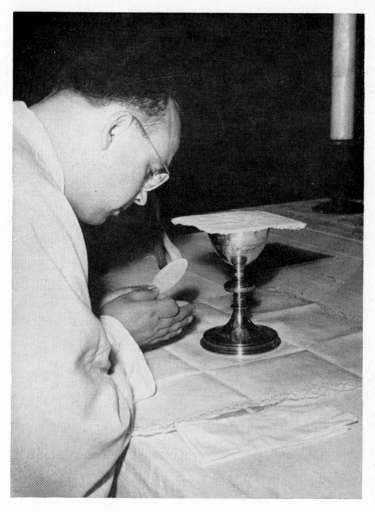

*"This Is My Body:" the priest utters the Words over
the bread which thereby is transubstantiated
into the Body of Christ*

A tremendous mystery has been enacted. A little bell is rung, all is hushed in silence; the priest kneels down in adoration, then lifts up the host for the adoration of the people. All eyes are fixed upon it, and hearts and lips repeat the cry of St. Thomas, "My Lord and my God." What has happened? With the Israelites in the desert, beholding for the first time the miraculous manna, we ask, "Manhu, what is it?" Outwardly the host appears the same as before, but faith tells us that it is no longer bread. The substance of the bread has disappeared; it has been changed into the substance of the body of Christ; the appearance of bread alone remains.

> Hidden God, devoutly I adore Thee
> Truly present underneath these veils;
> All my heart subdues itself before Thee,
> Since it all before Thee faints and fails.

In like manner, after they had supped, taking also this glorious chalice into His holy and venerable hands, and giving thanks to Thee, blessed and gave to His disciples, saying: Take and drink you all of this, FOR THIS IS THE CHALICE OF MY BLOOD, OF THE NEW AND EVERLASTING TESTAMENT, THE MYSTERY OF FAITH, WHICH SHALL BE SHED FOR YOU AND FOR ALL UNTO THE REMISSION OF SINS. As often as you will do these things, do them in remembrance of Me.

Again the little bell is rung, the priest kneels down in adoration and then lifts up the chalice for the adoration of the people. The mystery of the host has been repeated in the wine. The liquid in the chalice looks and tasts like wine, but faith tells us that it is no longer wine. The appearance of wine alone has remained; its substance has been changed into the substance of the blood of Christ.

> From whose love-pierced, sacred side
> Flowed Thy true blood's saving tide:
> Be a foretaste, sweet to me,
> In my death's great agony.

The chalice upon the altar is now indeed a glorious chalice, not because of material or workmanship, but because it contains our Savior's blood, the same blood that was contained in the chalice consecrated by our Lord Himself at the Last Supper, the same blood that was shed in His sacred Passion. Truly, the mystery of faith! And now Jesus, by bidding the apostles to do what they had seen Him doing in remembrance of Him, makes them the first priests of the New Testament, and thus provides for the mystical re-enactment of His Sacrifice and His perpetual presence on earth to the end of time. He wants those whom He loved to the end to be forever mindful of His love, and to find in this memorial of His love the inspiration and strength for His following on the way of the cross.

Let holy Mass be the sun of our lives, the first thought in the morning, the last in the evening, so that all may be enveloped in the golden rays of eucharistic love. Before the altar of sacrifice we shall learn to live and to love, to love unto death.

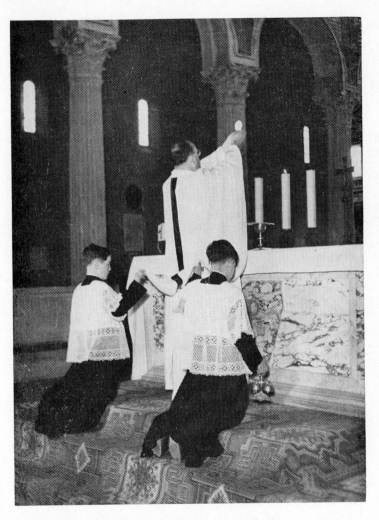

The priest holds the Sacred Host
that the faithful may adore It

The priest holds up the Chalice that the faithful
may look upon it and adore the Precious Blood

V

The Canon after the Consecration

AGAIN the priest prays that God will accept our offering—that God will be pleased with our sacrifice, as He was once pleased with the sacrifices of the Old Testament. Then the gifts offered were the fruits of the field, animals, food and drink, bread and wine. Now the gifts offered by Christ and His Church are His own Flesh and Blood. Just as before the Consecration, the priest now pauses to pray and to name those who need our prayers. This time he prays for the dead, for the members of the Church Suffering, that they may have repose and light and peace. Just as before the Consecration, the priest now names some of God's Saints; martyrs, virgins, and holy women of the early Church. Into their company we pray God to admit us—not considering our merits, but rather pardoning our offenses.

1. COMMEMORATION AND FULFILLMENT

THE overwhelming grandeur and all-embracing saving power of the Holy Sacrifice of the Mass is the theme of this part of the Canon. Holy Mass, because of its essential identity with the sacrifice of the cross, is the fulfillment of all typical sacrifices of the Old Testament, bloody and unbloody ones; as the sacrifice of our salvation, it brings deliverance to the poor souls and salvation to the faithful persevering to the end. It is the grandest act of Jesus Christ, the Son of God, our Savior and Mediator, through whom and with whom and in whom all honor and glory is given to God.

It is in obedience to Christ's command, "Do this in remembrance of me," that we offer up Holy Mass. United with Jesus we have a share in its essential act, the Consecration. However, in order to bring more fully into the consciousness of the faithful that Holy Mass is also *their* sacrifice, there follows now an explicit offering of the divine Victim on our part. It is contained in the three prayers following the Consecration. The first of these oblation prayers speaks of Holy Mass as a commemoration and fulfillment.

Wherefore, O Lord, we Thy servants, but also Thy holy people, call to mind the blessed Passion, Resurrection from the dead, and the glorious Ascension into heaven of the same Jesus Christ, Thy Son, our Lord.

The same idea of Holy Mass being offered in mem-

ory of the Passion, the Resurrection, and the Ascension
of our Lord was expressed in the oblation prayer after
the washing of the hands. It follows from the fact that
Holy Mass is the unbloody re-enactment of the Savior's
bloody sacrifice, of the body delivered for us, of the
blood shed for us; thus the memory of the Passion
stands in the foreground. However, since, "Christ having risen from the dead, dies now no more, death shall
have no longer dominion over him," (Romans 6:19)
the memory of His Resurrection and Ascension is inseparable from it.

Jesus Christ now is Priest and Victim in His glorified state, and Holy Mass is and remains the fulfillment
of all sacrifices of the Old Testament which prefigured
it. The Council of Trent states authoritatively, "This
is the oblation, which was prefigured by the diverse
types of sacrifices during the period of nature as well
as during the period of the Law, in as much as it com-
prises, as their consummation and perfection, all good
things which are signified by them." And in the Secret
of the seventh Sunday after Pentecost, holy Church
prays, "O God, who hast given fulfillment to the variety
of the sacrifices offered under the Law in the perfection
of the one sacrifice, accept this sacrifice from Thy
devoted servants."

*We offer to Thy exalted Majesty from among Thy
gifts and presents the pure Victim, the holy Victim,
the immaculate Victim, the holy bread of life everlasting and the chalice of eternal salvation.*

Not all animals could be used for the Old Testament sacrifices, but only the so-called clean animals,

which had been designated by God as such. Chosen for sacrifice they became holy unto God and were further sanctified by a special blessing. The immaculateness of the victim required that it be free from any kind of defect or deformity. In the case of irrational animals the presence of these requirements could do nothing beyond giving them a mere legal perfection. But these requirements typified the moral perfection of the divine Victim. This divine Victim is chosen from all eternity, sanctified by the hypostatic union with the second Person of the Most Blessed Trinity, conceived by the Holy Spirit, born of the Immaculate Virgin and Spouse of the Holy Spirit. Jesus is the Holy One, the Saint of saints, holy with the holiness of God Himself; in Him, therefore, all the victims of the Old Testament find their glorious fulfillment.

The principal types of the unbloody sacrifices were the sacrifice of Melchisedech and the loaves of proposition. The sacrifice of Melchisedech will be spoken of more fully in the next section. As to the loaves of proposition, the law prescribed that twelve loaves of bread were to be offered weekly in thanksgiving for and remembrance of the material sustenance of the people, particularly by means of the manna during their wanderings through the desert. Jesus, the divine Victim, makes Himeslf in Holy Mass the true manna, the bread of life for the sustenance of His people on their pilgrimage to the heavenly land of promise. "My flesh is food indeed, and my blood is drink indeed. ...This is the bread that has come down from heaven; not as your fathers ate manna and died. He who eats this bread shall live forever." (John 6:56) But no longer are twelve loaves needed. There is but one bread. Even though there be millions of consecrated hosts, they are one and the same bread, because their substance is the substance of the one body of Jesus Christ.

This prayer suggests a sublime lesson. We offered ourselves to be victims together with Christ, and therefore we must be pure and holy and immaculate. Pure through freedom from sin, holy through sanctifying grace, immaculate through the perfection of life. If human weakness is not equal to the task, let us remember that we have at our disposal the bread of life everlasting and, therefore, of never-failing strength.

2. ABEL, ABRAHAM, MELCHISEDECH

Deign to look upon this oblation with favor and grace and to accept it as Thou didst accept the gifts of Thy servant, just Abel, the sacrifice of Abraham our father, and the holy sacrifice, the clean oblation, which Thy high priest Melchisedech offered to Thee.

This is a startling petition. Jesus Christ, our divine High Priest and Victim is infinitely more perfect and pleasing to the Father than were those holy men and their sacrifices. Moreover, the Council of Trent states, "This is the clean oblation, which can be defiled by no unworthiness or malice of those who offer it." Why then this petition? The answer is that *we* have cooperated with the divine High Priest and Victim by our prayers and actions, and have joined to the offering of the divine Victim our own selves. But the gift of ourselves as well as our cooperation in the sacrifice are far from being perfect; they are not even as perfect as they could have been with greater effort on our part. Hence, there is good reason for praying that in spite of our imperfections and deficiencies, God will accept our sacrifice and service as He accepted the sacrifices of those holy men.

The book of Genesis records that Cain and Abel offered sacrifice to God, Cain of the fruits of the earth, Abel of the firstlings of the flocks. God accepted the sacrifice of Abel with favor and rejected the sacrifice of Cain. This rejection of his sacrifice aroused the anger and envy of Cain, which eventually led him to murder his brother. St. John gives us the reason for Cain's manner of acting. "And wherefore did he kill him? Because his own works were wicked, but his brother's just." (I John 3:12) Hence, we must conclude that Abel's sacrifice was acceptable to God because he was a just man and offered his sacrifice with sentiments of sincere piety and grateful love. So our offering will be acceptable to God if ours is a truly Christian life, and if we offer to God the firstlings, the best we have and can give.

It was at an advanced age that *Abraham* became the father of Isaac and received the divine assurance that in Isaac all the nations of the earth would be blessed. Yet, when Isaac had grown into boyhood, God demanded of Abraham that he offer up this his son as a holocaust. Humanly speaking this command must have shattered the hopes of Abraham and broken his heart. Yet, he set out at once to do what he had been commanded, firmly believing that God who had given him this son could also raise him up from the dead. His faith was not disappointed. In the same moment in which he raised his hand to administer the fatal blow, his hand was stayed by an angel. God did not demand the life of Isaac, He was pleased with the faith and obedience of Abraham, and solemnly repeated and ratified the promises He had made to Abraham. Our offering at the altar will be pleasing to God if it is accompanied by a life of faith and obedience, of full surrender to His will. God's will must be done at all times, no matter what may be the consequences. But, if God strikes He can also heal, if He humbles He can also exalt, if He kills He can also raise to life. He will always deal with us according to infinite wisdom and love.

Mystery surrounds the person of *Melchisedech*. All that holy Scripture records of him is that he offered bread and wine to the Most High God, when Abraham had rescued Lot and his family from the hands of the marauders. The absence of any further information on his life is to focus our attention on his priesthood. St. Paul points out the significance of Melchisedech when he writes, "First, as his name shows, he is king of justice, and then he is also king of Salem, that is, king of peace. Without father, without mother, without genealogy, having neither beginning of days nor end of life, but likened to the Son of God, he continues a priest forever." (Hebrews 7:2f) These few facts also give the reason why his sacrifice was pleasing to God: his justice, love of peace, and unworldliness; his priesthood is typical of the priesthood of Christ, who is priest forever according to the order of Melchisedech. Hence, in order to cooperate with our divine High Priest at

Holy Mass in a manner pleasing and acceptable to God we must be, like Melchisedech, just and lovers of peace and, though in the world, keep out of our hearts the spirit of the world.

Thus understood, this prayer not only becomes intelligible, but also directs our attention to the fundamental virtues of the Christian life.

3. ANGEL AND ALTAR

The third and last oblation prayer after the Consecration speaks of an angel taking our oblation to an altar in heaven, and of the richness of the blessings bestowed upon us through our partaking of the altar. It is a prayer of profoundest theological and mystical depth, a grand homage to the all-embracing mediatorship of the divine High Priest.

Suppliantly we beseech Thee, almighty God, command this oblation to be carried by the hands of Thy holy angel...

Who is this angel? According to various interpretations this angel may be the guardian angel of the celebrating priest, or of the particular church or place in which Holy Mass is celebrated, or the word may stand for angels in general. However, we may also see in this angel Jesus Christ Himself, and this view is more satisfactory. Holy Scripture repeatedly speaks of Jesus as an angel, that is, a messenger sent by God. Especially clear are the prophets Isaias and Malachy.

According to Isaias the promised Messias is the angel of the great counsel, which counsel is the decree of our redemption. The prophet Malachy speaks of two angels: one that will go before the Messias to prepare His way, and that clearly is St. John the Baptist; the other one is the angel of the testament, the Lord, who comes to His Temple to bring to perfection the covenant of God with men. Holy Church, too, speaks of Jesus as the angel of the great counsel in the Litany of the holy Name of Jesus. All this is sufficient reason to think of Jesus as the angel mentioned in this prayer since in Holy Mass Jesus continues to carry out the great counsel of our salvation.

Upon Thy altar on high, before Thy divine Majesty.

In the Apocalypse St. John speaks of a golden altar in heaven standing before the throne of God. In the ordination of subdeacons holy Church refers to this vision of St. John to impress upon the candidates the excellence and sublimity of the service of the altar. The rite says, "The altar of holy Church is Christ, as John testifies, who says in the Apocalypse, that he saw standing before the throne of God a golden altar, in whom and through whom (speaking of the altar as a person) the gifts of the faithful are sanctified and offered to the Father." Holy Church, then, looks upon the altar on which Mass is celebrated and the heavenly altar as one and the same. Both symbolize Christ. Just as clear and definite is the statement we find in the second nocturn of the feast of the dedication of the archbasilica of the Most Holy Redeemer, "The altar, anointed with chrism, should express the figure of our Lord Jesus

Christ, who is our Altar, Victim, and Priest." Nothing could express more profoundly and emphatically Christ's all-embracing mediatorship. He is our one and all; all our prayers and good works are offered to the Father through Him.

If then, Jesus is the angel and the altar, this prayer offers no more difficulty. Jesus, the angel of the great counsel, is commanded, that is, sent by the Father to carry out the great counsel of our salvation. The Eucharistic Sacrifice is part of this decree. So Jesus takes His own sacrifice and that of the faithful united with Him into the eternal Holy of holies and presents it to His heavenly Father, thus, in the words of St. Paul "always making intercession for us."

May we all, who through this partaking of the altar shall receive the sacred body and blood of Thy Son, be filled with all heavenly blessing and grace. Through the same Christ our Lord. Amen.

Since the altar symbolizes Christ, partaking of the altar can mean only a more intimate union with Jesus, through Holy Communion and a more abundant share in the blessings of Holy Mass. One with Him in the unity of life and love, we also share in the merits of His Passion, in His love of God and souls, in His obedience and zeal, in His meekness, humility, and patience. We need never be afraid of asking too much. "He who has not spared even His own Son, but has delivered Him for us all, how can He fail to grant us all things with Him?" (Romans 8:32) So it comes to pass that we are changed more and more into Him, that He lives in us and we in Him. "It is no longer I that live, but Christ lives in me. And the life that I now live in the flesh, I live in the faith of the Son of God, who loved me and gave Himself up for me." (Galatians 2:20) We are filled with all heavenly blessing and grace.

4. REFRESHMENT, LIGHT, PEACE

In the Apostles' Creed we profess that Christ after His death descended into hell, that is, the limbo of the fathers, the place where the just of the Old Testament were detained until heaven would be opened by the Savior. It is to these souls that the soul of Christ descended to bring them the glad tidings of their imminent entrance into heaven. Similarly does holy Church, after the oblation of Christ's unbloody Sacrifice, descend so to say into purgatory in the beautiful and touching memento for the dead, praying that the fruits of the Holy Sacrifice be applied to those suffering souls and that they be admitted into heaven's glory.

Remember also, O Lord, Thy servants and hand-maids, N. and N., who have gone before us with the sign of faith and repose in the sleep of peace.

"He who believes and is baptized shall be saved." (Mark 16:16) The souls of purgatory believed and were baptized, if not with the baptism of water then with the baptism of desire and, therefore, they were saved. True, they have sinned; but they also repented and, at least in the last decisive moment, they raised aloft the sign of faith. Believing in Christ they died and so they now repose in the sleep of peace.

For the believing Christian death is a falling asleep in the Lord. The very name which we give to our burial places: cemeteries, means place of sleep, of rest. As the sleeper rises again, refreshed, to start a new day, so the dead will rise at the trumpet call of the angel on the day of judgment to begin their eternal day. Until then they are said to sleep in peace. They are at peace, because they possess the blissful certainty that they are safe and secure for eternity; no longer are they troubled by the lust of the eyes and the flesh, and the pride of life. Satan and the world cannot tempt them anymore. Their sufferings do not disturb their peace, because they see in them the means provided by the mercy of God to cleanse and prepare them for the blessed vision of God. Nevertheless they suffer severely and appeal to us for help.

Grant, we beseech Thee, O Lord, to them and to all who rest in Christ the place of refreshment, light, and peace.

Refreshment is the cool shade of the evening after the heat and burden of the day. Work has come to an end for the holy souls, but the cool shade is withheld from them, because they did not do the full share of the work assigned to them or they did not do it with the perfection God had expected. Refreshment is the quenching of hunger and thirst. Surely, the souls in purgatory do not suffer material hunger and thirst, but their whole being cries out for God, for that heavenly vision of God that inebriates the saints with the torrents

The priest prays for the dead that are gone
before us with the sign of Faith

of delight. But as yet they are unworthy. On earth they disregarded the hunger and thirst of God for their undivided love and preferred the delights of the world. However, the fountains of refreshment flow from the altar; we can direct their course to those holy souls. Let us do it in this prayer.

God is light and dwells in heavenly light, compared to the brightness of which purgatory is darkness. Those holy souls long to plunge into that ocean of light and be transformed into light. But, while on earth they closed their eyes in many ways to the light of faith and divine inspirations to follow their own desires; therefore, they are now left in darkness. However, the light of our Savior's mercy shines from the altar, and we can pray that it may soon kindle in those souls the perpetual light of the beatific vision.

Even though the souls in purgatory enjoy a holy peace, as stated in the first part of this prayer, theirs is not as yet the full and perfect peace of the blessed. They cannot be fully at peace until they rest in God. But they must wait. While they were on earth, God offered them the intimacy of His friendship. He dwelt in their hearts; He dwelt in the Blessed Eucharist, but they were cold and indifferent and prefered the company of creatures. Therefore, God withholds from them now the delights of His vision. Yet, the love of Jesus burns brightly upon the altar; He will not be angry forever. We can speed the day of the poor souls' reconciliation with their Father, the day of their entrance into the joy of their Lord.

There is no other means by which we could give more relief to the souls in purgatory than the Holy

Sacrifice of the Mass. Should not the love of Jesus and of those holy souls prompt us to make use of it? These holy souls are grateful, and they will remember us as long as we stand in need of help. Moreover, charity toward the dead will teach us some very important lessons. They are: to bear our share of the heat and burden of the day, to appreciate the light of faith and divine inspirations, to remember the presence of God and to seek the company of Jesus in the Blessed Sacrament, to make better use of the means of grace and of the opportunities to atone for our sins. Life is short and every moment brings us closer to its end. As we implore relief for the poor souls we make ourselves ever more worthy of the place of refreshment, light, and peace.

5. HEAVEN OUR GOAL

What we implore for the poor souls is also our desire and hope, "Thanks to the Father, who has made us worthy to share the lot of the saints in light." (Colossians 1:12) Humbly and trustfully we pray for it now.

And to us sinners also, Thy servants, who hope in the multitude of Thy mercies...

We are sinners and admit it. The malice of our sin is aggravated by the fact that we are the servants of God, bound to render service to Him by our very nature. Trusted and admitted into the household of God we have shown ourselves unworthy of this divine trust and love.

*The priest strikes his breast with the hand
as a sign of sorrow and penitence*

But our hope lies not in our merit but in the mercy of God, and His mercy is above all His works. Jesus loved us and therefore delivered Himself for us unto death. Host and chalice upon the altar are the memorial of His mercy. Every act of the incarnate Word of God during His earthly life was an act of mercy. Count them: all the steps He made, journeying up and down the country seeking the lost sheep, preaching, healing, doing good to all. Count the drops of blood He shed in His agony, in His scourging and crowning with thorns, in His crucifixion. Count the multitude of His mercies in His eucharistic life: every Holy Mass, from that first one in the Supper Room down the centuries to the one at which we assist, all the Communions received by the faithful, all the Viaticums carried to the sick and dying, all those little hosts in chapels and churches throughout the world; they all speak of the mercy of Him whose delight is to be with the children of men. Count all the absolutions given by Jesus Himself during His earthly life, all those given through the ministrations of His priests, those words of love and power that brought hope and joy into millions of sin-laden, sorrowful hearts; they are all in the multitude of His mercies. Then lift up your eyes to the saints in heaven. Whether they shine in the white splendor of baptismal innocence or in the purple glow of repentance, they all sing the mercies of God. That they were able to do what they did they owe to the mercy of God, and the reward which they received for their works exceeds all expectation, all proportion. These His mercies are our hope.

Vouchsafe to grant some part and fellowship with Thy holy apostles and martyrs...and all Thy saints.

We beg for some part in the inheritance of the saints. St. John in the Apocalypse endeavors to give us some idea of the enchanting beauty of the heavenly Jerusalem, but its glory is beyond human language. The Lamb of God is its light; there flows the river of life, clear and crystal from the throne of God; there grows the tree of life; there death shall be no more, nor mourning, nor crying, nor sorrow.

And dwelling in that heavenly city we behold the great multitude from all tongues and tribes and nations, clothed in white garments and palms in their hands, and their hymns of joy and jubilation resound through the heavens. What will be our delight when we shall behold Jesus in the glory of His eternal majesty, the marks of the wounds sparkling like wonderful rubies in His hands and feet! What meeting will it be when we shall stand in the presence of our heavenly Mother, our hope, our sweetness, and our life! And then there are all those saints of the Old and the New Testament; there we behold the glorious choir of the apostles, the armies of martyrs in the blood-red lustre of their love, the confessors and virgins and all the uncounted numbers of the redeemed that have reached their goal. Among them are our dear ones, members of our family, relatives, friends, benefactors. And all this will be not a vision from afar, but present and everlasting reality.

God's merciful love has created heaven. Jesus the eternal High Priest and Victim opened it for us after

sin had closed it. He did it by His blood, the blood
which is now upon the altar. His desire is that we
should be eternally happy with Him. Therefore, though
conscious of our unworthiness, we pray with unlimited
trust in His goodness and mercy:

*Admit us, we beseech Thee, into their company,
not weighing our merit, but mercifully granting forgiveness.*

6. CHRIST OUR MEDIATOR

The Canon closes with a grand homage to Christ,
our divine Mediator. All grace and all heavenly blessings have come to us through Him. All honor and
glory which ever have been or will be rendered by
men to God are due to Him.

*Through whom, O Lord, Thou dost always create,
sanctify, vivify, bless, and bestow upon us all these
good things.*

The consecrated host and wine upon the altar are
spoken of as good things. Good they are in the most
eminent sense of the word, since they contain and represent all that is good: the Body and Blood of our
Savior Jesus Christ, beneath the appearances of bread
and wine. They were created, not at the Consecration,
but at the beginning of time, for "All things were
made through Him." (John 1:3) Even though the
human nature of Christ was conceived in a miraculous
manner through the overshadowing of the Blessed Vir-

gin by the Holy Spirit, the elements out of which the body of Christ was formed were taken from the body and the blood of His holy Mother and thus they ultimately go back to the beginning of time, when all things were created by the Word of God.

The substance of the body and the blood of Jesus Christ, as part of His human nature, have been sanctified by the second Person of the Most Blessed Trinity in the hypostatic union. And it was the same Jesus Christ, who through the priest spoke the words of the Consecration and changed the substance of bread and wine into the substance of His own most sacred Body and Blood.

Beneath the appearances of bread and wine is present the living, glorified Christ, such as He is in heaven. To give us life he has made Himself the living and life-giving Bread.

The blessing contained in this most Holy Sacrifice and Sacrament is the fullness of the graces merited by Christ through His Passion and Death. So this Blessed Sacrament is for us the food that strengthens us for a life of holiness and prepares us for life everlasting.

All these wonderful gifts have been bestowed upon us; we have been made rich in Jesus Christ. Ours is, in all truth, the Body and Blood of Jesus Christ. Ours is His Sacrifice and Sacrament, the cause and pledge of our salvation and of all that we need for reaching our heavenly destiny.

Through Him and with Him and in Him is rendered to Thee, God the Father almighty, in the unity of the Holy Spirit, all honor and glory.

While saying these words the priest traces the sign of the cross with the host three times over the chalice and two times between the chalice and himself and in the end, raising host and chalice a little, performs the so-called little elevation.

Whatever honor and glory were ever given to God in the past or will be given to Him in the future is due to Jesus. He made it possible through His cross. His grace gives value and efficacy to the good men perform. He is the angel standing before the heavenly golden altar, offering the prayers and good works of men to God. No work will be accepted by the Father unless it is presented through Him.

Our divine Mediator is not like a human benefactor who bestows some benefit upon a friend and then lets that friend shift for himself. Jesus stays with us and works with us. He becomes our brother, identifies Himself with the least one of His brethren, inspires by His example, strengthens by His grace, rejoices when He can present us to the Father as His own.

Not only through Him and with Him but also in Him do we honor and glorify God. We are thus introduced into the innermost depths of our union with the divine Mediator. He abides in us and we in Him. He is the vine and we are the branches, He is the wine and we are the drop of water poured into it. We share in His life and all His perfections. Our purity shines in the immaculateness of His life, our patience is immersed in the silence of the Lamb of God, our obedience partakes of the conformity of will of Him who became obedient unto death. In Him the holiness of all saints receives its beauty, value, and perfection.

As we cast a reviewing glance at the prayers of the Canon, one idea stands out prominently, and that is the Christocentric character of Catholic worship. This is of eminently practical significance. Christ is our One and All. There are many devotions fostered or permitted by the Church, but their aim is always to bring us closer to Christ. True devotion to Mary leads to Jesus, and of the Holy Spirit our Lord Himself says that this Holy Spirit will glorify Him. The way to peace on earth and to salvation and eternal life is honor and glory given to God through and with and in Jesus Christ, our divine Mediator.

VI

From the Pater Noster
to Holy Communion

UP to this point the Mass has consisted of a lengthy preparatory section—of prayers to God and instructions from God—followed by the actual sacrifice, the offering to God the Father of the Gift of His own Son's Body and Blood. Now, in exchange for the sacred Gift we have offered, we receive something from God. And what we receive in return is the Body and Blood of Jesus Christ in the Sacrament of the Holy Eucharist.

1. OUR FATHER

THE *Our Father* introduces the Communion service of the Mass. The significance of this part of the Mass may be said to be perfectly summarized by St. Peter when he writes, "For indeed his divine power has granted us all things pertaining to life and piety through the knowledge of him, who has called us through His glory and power, through which he has granted us the very great and precious promises, so that through them you may become partakers of the divine nature, having escaped from the corruption of that lust which is in the world." (II Peter 1:4) Here we gather and rejoice in the fruits of the Holy Sacrifice. The sonorous per omnia saecula saeculorum breaks the solemn silence of the Canon. Forever and ever Jesus is our Savior, forever and ever all honor and glory shall be rendered to the Father through Him. The Our Father consists of an address and seven petitions. The first three of these petitions have for their object the glorification of the Father; the last four implore divine assistance for our material and spiritual needs.

Enlightened by the doctrines of salvation and formed by divine institution we make bold to say: Our Father, who art in heaven. Hallowed by thy name. Thy kingdom come. Thy will be done on earth as it is in heaven.

We were enlightened by the doctrines of salvation in the first part of the Mass, particularly in the Epistle and Gospel; we were formed, transformed into children of God by the divine institution of the whole economy of salvation, particularly through the sacraments of baptism and penance. Holy, grateful love now wells up in our hearts as we turn to the almighty God and Giver of our salvation, addressing Him as our Father. It is truth, not fiction that our Creator and Lord is also the Father of all those who were born again of the water and the Holy Spirit. But then, all of us who have been thus transformed are members of the family of God, children of God, brothers and sisters among ourselves, and heirs of heaven. Heaven is the goal of our hopes and desires, our eternal homeland. While on earth our task is to know and reverence, to love and serve God, thus glorifying, hallowing His name, to counteract the godless spirit of the world that blasphemes the holy name of God and refuses to render Him the honor and service which are His due. Loving God we shall be eager to do what He desires; but His desire is that all men should be saved and come to the knowledge of the truth. We shall, therefore, pray for the coming of His kingdom, His visible kingdom on earth is the Catholic Church; through baptism men become its members. Through living faith Christ's kingdom is established in our hearts and thus we are prepared for the heavenly kingdom of glory. Glorious vistas open up for the child of God! God's will must be the law in the kingdom of God; only thus can it accomplish its purpose. The will of God is infinitely wise, just and holy, loving and merciful. It must be done on earth as it is in heaven. It if cannot be done on earth with the same degree of perfection because of the weakness of human nature, then it can be done in the same spirit and that is gratefully, lovingly, with unlimited trust in divine Providence.

Give us this day our daily bread.

Having prayed for the interests of our heavenly Father we now think of our own and they are many. We depend upon God for our daily sustenance. Surely, we must eat our bread in the sweat of our face; we must work for it. But it is God, who gives us health and strength to work; He gives fertility to the soil, growth to the grain, and so it is to Him that we address ourselves asking for our daily bread. But what a humble and trustful petition this is. We do not ask for wealth or abundance, but only for those things that are necessary for life, and even these, not for weeks or months ahead, but just for this day, leaving the care for our future to His fatherly love.

Forgive us our trespasses (debts) as we forgive those who trespass against us (our debtors).

As we depend upon God in the needs of the body so we depend upon Him in the needs of the soul. We have failed to render to God the service which is due to Him, we have sinned and stand in need of His forgiving mercy. God is willing to forgive us, if we forgive those who have failed against us and are our debtors. This is just and fair, generous and merciful on the part of God, when we compare the immense debt which we owe to God with the trifles our fellowmen owe to us. Let us beware of making this petition a mockery and a provocation of God's justice by an unforgiving spirit.

Lead us not into temptation.

Surely, God cannot lead us into temptation if we understand by temptation an incitement to sin. But God can allow that we be tempted by the devil and by evil men. He can send us tribulations which may test our obedience and patience. Our prayer should be that God will deprive us of our faculties, of life itself, if He foresees that in a given temptation we will come to fall. If such be our habitual disposition, then a fall into mortal sin becomes a practical impossibility.

But deliver us from evil.

Natural evils are not evils in themselves; they may be the greatest blessings. There is but one real evil in the world and that is sin; and evil are the fruits of sin. Mortal sin causes the loss of sanctifying grace and all merits, brings on temporal punishment and in the end hell, the evil of all evils. Hell is the negation of all we have prayed for in the Our Father. It is the eternal separation of the child from the Father, the loss of heaven, eternal hatred and despair, for there the worm of conscience does not die and the fire is not extinguished.

The Our Father is the most beautiful prayer, taught by Jesus Himself, the eternal Son of God and our Savior. Let us reflect on it, use its petitions as ejaculatory prayers to direct us in our work, to console us in our trials, to strengthen us in temptation, to keep us always close to our Father. Thus we shall taste the sweetness of being the children of God, the honor and privilege of being allowed to call upon the almighty God as our Father. Amen.—So be it.

2. FREE AND SECURE

The prayer following the Our Father is a fuller development of the last petition: deliver us from evil. We wish to be delivered from all evils, past, present, and future, and henceforth to live in peace, free from sin, and secure against any further disturbances of peace.

Deliver us we beseech Thee, O Lord, from all evils, past, present, and future.

Past evils do not exist any more; but what has happened may happen again. We have sinned and it is possible that we sin again. Moreover, sins of the past may have left their sad effects with us, as also a disease, an accident, a crime may have consequences that last as long as life. The effects of sins committed are a weakened spiritual condition, liability to punishment, temporal or eternal. In these effects past evils are still with us and we surely wish to be delivered from them.

Present evils, of which we think here, are the innumerable occasions and incitements to sin arising from evil concupiscence, from the provocations of our fellowmen and the many tribulations of life. We are also fully aware of the activity of the evil spirits, prowling about the world and seeking the ruin of souls. All these things are evils in as much as they may lead us into sin, and our prayer is that we may escape from their ruinous influence.

The future lies dark before us; the signs of the times are anything but reassuring. The powers of hell are working with feverish haste and determination to make satan the lord of the world. Shall we be able to withstand their wicked designs? Shall war with all its horrors, loss of health and home and fortune, persecution for the sake of faith fall to our lot? Shall we have the courage to bear such tribulations? With the grace of God we will, and we pray for it in this place.

And by the intercession of the blessed and glorious Mary, ever Virgin, Mother of God, and of Thy holy apostles Peter and Paul, Andrew, and of all the saints, graciously grant peace in our days, so that assisted by Thy mercy we may ever be free from sin and secure against all disturbances.

Peace is a precious possession; peace of heart and peace among nations and the various classes of society. The popes have exhorted the faithful again and again to pray for peace, that wars may come to an end, that the rights and dignity of the human person be respected, that men may live in harmony with their God-given destiny. But, if we pray for peace, we must also do the things that lead to peace. Loving submission to God's all-wise and holy will in all conditions of life is the surest way to peace of heart, nay the only way; it is a wonderful contribution to peace in the world. As to our fellowmen, charity leads to peace more ef-

fectively than any other device. Charity respects the
rights of others; therefore, does the Apostle say, "Owe
no man anything except to love one another." (Romans
13:8) And over and above being just, "Charity is patient, is kind, ...bears with all things,...endures all
things." (I Corinthians 13:4ff)

Secure against disturbances of peace is the man
who is free from sin and firmly anchored in hope and
love. He will not be spared the temptations and tribulations of life; this would be against the very idea of the
Christian life as a following of Christ Crucified, and
is not the object of this petition. But it is possible, even
in the midst of the severest trials, that we are at peace
in the innermost depths of the soul and rejoice as the
Apostle did rejoice in the midst of all his tribulations.
Security based on unshakable faith and trust is the
object of this prayer and it will be supported by the
saints, whose intercession we implore. As their divine
Master, so they all entered into their glory through
many tribulations. It remains for us to increase our
faith and trust in divine providence. Against the will
of God nothing can happen, and to those who love God
all things work together unto good, so that amid the
changing conditions of this life our heart be ever set
where true joys abide.

3. BREAKING, MINGLING, CONSECRATING

The closing of the prayer which we have just now
considered is striking, both in its words and the cere-

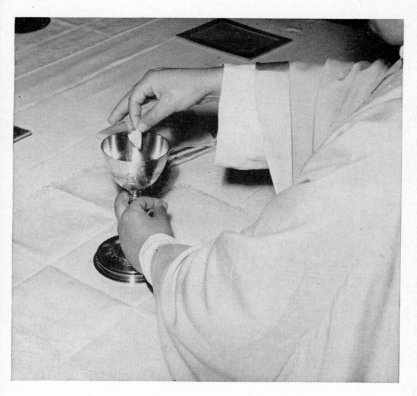

*The priest breaks the Sacred Host in half,
breaks off a small piece from the portion in
his left hand and drops it into the chalice*

monies. Holding the host over the chalice the priest breaks it into two halves: the part in his right hand he places on the paten; from the other half he breaks off a small particle. With the latter he traces the sign of the cross three times over the chalice and finally drops it into the sacred Blood. The words which accompany these ceremonies are:

Through the same Jesus Christ, Thy Son, our Lord, who lives and reigns with Thee in the unity of the Holy Spirit forever and ever. Amen.
May the peace of the Lord be always with you.

The answer of the server is: and also with you. *May this commingling and consecration of the body and the blood of our Lord Jesus Christ impart to us, who will receive it, life everlasting.*

The breaking of the host is performed in imitation of our Lord who did the same at the Last Supper, and serves the practical purpose of reducing the large host to a convenient size for the Communion of the priest. But, as most of the ceremonies of Holy Mass are profoundly symbolical, we must expect that this breaking of the host over the chalice illustrates an important truth. It symbolizes that the sacred Blood contained in the chalice was made to flow from the body of our Savior during His Passion; it is the Blood that cleansed us from our sins and brought us peace. The dropping of the particle of the host into the chalice then reminds us of the fact that at the Resurrection Body and Blood were reunited. This reunion of Body and Blood in the glorified body of the Savior was its final consecration to be forever the temple of God and tabernacle of the

Most High; in like manner is this commingling of the sacramental species their final dedication to be the bread of life that imparts to us life everlasting. But life everlasting is also everlasting peace.

4. AGNUS DEI

The three invocations of Jesus as the Lamb of God form a fitting connection between the Our Father and Holy Communion. We may see in them a reference to the paschal lamb, the manna, and the Lamb triumphant in heaven.

Lamb of God, who takest away the sins of the world, have mercy on us.

We are familiar with the story of the Israelites in Egypt and their eventual liberation through Moses. In the night of their departure, as the last plague struck the Egyptians, the Israelites were commanded to slaughter a lamb and to paint its blood on the doorposts of their houses as a sign of protection. Then they were to eat the lamb in haste, ready at a moment's notice to depart. This lamb was called paschal lamb from a phrase, which means passing, because the angel of God, as he slew the firstborn sons of the Egyptians, passed by the houses of the Israelites sparing their sons.

The paschal lamb is a type of Jesus, the true paschal lamb. He was slain upon the cross; His blood is our protection. His death delivered us from the slavery of satan and inaugurated our departure for our heavenly homeland. Holy Mass is the unbloody re-enactment of the slaying of the true paschal lamb and we ought to be ever mindful of this fact. The Council of Trent states, "Having celebrated the ancient pasch, which the multitude of the children of Israel offered up in memory of their departure from Egypt, He instituted the new pasch, in which He Himself wished to be offered up by the Church through the priests under visible signs, in memory of His departure from this world to the Father, when by the shedding of His blood He redeemed and delivered us from the power of darkness and translated us into His kingdom."

Lamb of God, who takest away the sins of the world, have mercy on us.

Many were the dangers and hardships of the Israelites during their wandering through the desert. But God protected His people and in innumerable ways proved to them His loving care and providence. He caused Pharaoh and his army to be drowned in the Red Sea, He went before them in a pillar of cloud, He gave them water from a rock for their thirst and sent them quails to satisfy their desire for meat; above all, He fed them with the miraculous manna until they reached the promised land.

All this is typical of the chosen people of the New Testament. Their way to the promised land of heaven leads through the desert of this world, and many are the hardships and temptations to which we are exposed. But God is our protector and helper. As the greatest gift bestowed upon the Israelites was the manna, so is the true manna the greatest gift granted to the

Christian people. And this manna is the flesh and blood of the Lamb of God, "This is the bread that has come down from heaven; not as your fathers ate the manna and died. He who eats this bread shall live forever." (John 6:59) We receive this true manna in Holy Communion and it will sustain our spiritual life until we reach the heavenly homeland.

Lamb of God, who takest away the sins of the world, grant us peace.

After forty years of wandering through the desert the Israelites arrived in the land, which God had promised to Abraham and his descendants. The paschal lamb and the manna had prepared and sustained them for it. All their hopes and expectations were now fulfilled.

Heaven is the Christian's land of promise, the goal of his hopes and desires. Once he has reached it, he will fully realize that he owes it all to the true paschal lamb, the true manna, to Jesus, who died for him and then gave Himself to him as the bread of life. So St. John in the Apocalypse sees the Lamb of God upon a throne and the multitude of the saints adoring Him and giving thanks, "Worthy is the Lamb who was slain to receive power and divinity and wisdom and strength and honor and glory and blessing." (Apocalypse 5:12) Heaven's joys are beyond thought and imagination in their all-surpassing bliss, and they are the gift of the Lamb of God, "They shall neither hunger nor thirst any more, neither shall the sun strike them nor any heat. For the Lamb who is in the midst of the throne will shepherd them and guide them to the fountains of the waters of life, and God will wipe away all tears from their eyes. ...And death shall be no more; neither shall there be mourning, nor crying, nor pain any more, for the former things have passed away." (Apocalypse 7:16; 21:4) That is peace in its ultimate bliss and perfection. May the Lamb of God grant it to us.

The Agnus Dei suggests a very important and inspiring lesson. Life is a pilgrimage; we are constantly moving closer to its end. Hence, let us not attach our hearts to persons, places, or possessions, which we must leave behind sooner or later. Life is a pilgrimage through desert country, infested by hostile powers; let us, then, not expect the peace and comfort of home, but rather hardship and struggle. Let us keep our gaze steadily fixed on our heavenly homeland. There eternal liberty and peace shall be ours, after the short years of this passing life.

5. PEACE AND UNITY

Peace was the object of the last petition of the Agnus Dei, and in many other places does the Church pray for peace. Peace is the most favorable condition for the Church to carry out her mission. And there ought to be an anticipation of heavenly peace in the Church, because it is the kingdom of peace, ruled by the Prince of peace. So we continue to pray for it.

Lord Jesus Christ, who hast said to Thy apostles: Peace I leave with you, My peace I give you.

The peace of Christ! Jesus spoke those words at the

Last Supper, about two hours before the beginning of
His Passion—the terrible agony in the garden of Geth-
semane. He was surrounded by the shadows of death,
but His heart was at peace. It was the peace of the beatific vision; His soul was flooded with the delights of
heaven even in the midst of agony and suffering. His
was the peace of perfect and absolute conformity with
the will of the Father; He had accomplished the task
which the Father had entrusted to Him. It was the
peace of certain victory and the knowledge of the
blessings that would come to the world through His
sacred Passion.

The peace of the beatific vision is not granted to
us in this life, but the vision of faith may be strong
and penetrating, discovering the hand of a loving Providence in all the conditions of life, in all the sufferings
of the Church. Nothing happens by chance; all things
were known to God and taken up into His plan of the
world. "These things I have spoken to you that in me
you may have peace." (John 16:33)

*Look not upon my sins, but upon the faith of Thy
Church.*

Sin is the greatest disturber of peace. All heresies
and schisms, all strife and struggle within the Church
are due to sin; to pride, envy, lust. What a diseased
limb is for the health of the body, the sins of individual
members of the Church are for the mystical body of
Christ. In one way or other they disturb peace and
unity and interfere with the work of the Church. We
most emphatically do not want to obstruct the work
of the Church.

As the sins of the faithful exercise a baneful influence in the Church, so the living faith and the holy lives of other members exercise an invigorating, sanctifying influence. As St. John Chrysostom says, "He who is meek and humble, merciful and just, does not enclose such virtuous deeds within himself, but he will send them forth as glorious fountains for the benefit of others. And he who is pure of heart and peace-loving and suffers persecution for the sake of truth contributes by his life in like manner to the welfare of all." And if God would have spared Sodom and Gomorrha for the sake of five just men, we surely have reason to hope that He will bless us and the work of the Church for the sake of so many saints. This is the reason why we implore our divine Master not to look upon our sins but upon the faith of His Church—His holy Church. But this very petition contains a powerful appeal that we contribute to the peace of the Church, not only by the words of prayer, but also by the deeds of a Christian life.

Vouchsafe to grant her peace and unity according to Thy will. Who livest and reignest, God, forever and ever. Amen.

The unity of the Church in her faith, sacraments, and government is a mark of the true Church and will never fail her. But among some members of the Church the unity of love and action may be lacking. Even in the early Christian communities quarrels and contentions were to be found as we learn from the Epistles of St. Paul. Who will say that such things have disappeared in our modern Church-life? Jesus Himself prayed for unity among the members of the Church in His last, high-priestly prayer, "Yet not for these only do I pray, but for all those who through their word are to believe in me, that all may be one, even as Thou, Father, in me and I in Thee; that they also may be one in us, that the world may believe that Thou hast sent me." (John 17:20) Peace and unity among the members of the Church were of utmost concern to St. Paul. It is such mutual love and helpfulness of unity that is in his mind when he writes, "The cup of blessing that we bless, is it not the sharing of the blood of Christ? And the bread that we break, is it not the partaking of the body of the Lord? Because the bread is one, we, though many, are one body, all of us who partake of the one bread." (I Corinthians 10:16) As many grains have entered into the making of bread, many grapes into the making of wine, so the multitude of the faithful have been united in the unity of the mystical body of Christ. There is but one such mystical body as there is but one Christ, and there is but one bread to give life to its members and to keep them in living union with the head and the other members, and that is Holy Communion, the one and same body and blood of Christ.

A fuller realization of this oneness in Christ would to the same extent do away with the divisive force of racial and national prejudice and the pursuance of special interests to the detriment of the whole Church. It would be a mighty contribution to bring to its full realization the motto of Pius XI of glorious memory, "The peace of Christ in the kingdom of Christ."

6. UNION INSEPARABLE

The immediate preparation for Holy Communion is made in the following two prayers. The first one states in its three petitions the principal fruits of Holy Communion as the object of our desire: to be delivered from all evils and iniquities, always to cling to the commandments of God, never to be separated from Him. The solid basis for our hope to have these petitions granted is the work done by the three divine Persons in behalf of our salvation.

Lord Jesus Christ, Son of the living God, who by the will of the Father and the cooperation of the Holy Spirit hast by Thy death given life to the world.

Father, Son, and Holy Spirit were active in our salvation. The Father, "so loved the world that He gave His only begotten Son, that those who believe in Him may not perish, but may have life everlasting." (John 3:16) This loving will of the Father is carried out by the Son, "Behold, I come to do Thy will, O God." (Hebrews 10:7) It was a dreadful price the Son paid for our salvation in His agony and Passion, but the thought of the will of the Father strengthens Him, "My Father, if this cup cannot pass away unless I drink it, Thy will be done." (Matthew 26:42) The Holy Spirit cooperates. It is through Him that our Savior is conceived by the Blessed Virgin Mary; Jesus Himself gives testimony that He has been anointed for His mission and sent by the Holy Spirit. St. Paul tells us that Jesus offered Himself to the Father as an immaculate Victim

through the love of the Holy Spirit. And after Christ
has accomplished His mission, it is the Holy Spirit
who brings it to its ultimate perfection. He, so to speak,
takes over the Church for the work of salvation on
Pentecost Day. Could we be given more convincing
proofs of God's will to save us?

*Deliver me through this Thy most sacred body
and blood from all my iniquities and all evils.*

Freedom from mortal sin is the first prerequisite
for a worthy reception of Holy Communion. Holy
Communion is a sacrament of the living; it is the food
of the soul, and food in order to be beneficial demands
a living organism. But even though there is no mortal
sin, there may be venial sins to obstruct the free opera-
tion of grace. Moreover, many potential iniquities and
evils are left in us through concupiscence. The effect
of Holy Communion is to cleanse us from venial sin
and to strengthen us against these potential iniquities,
the inclination to vanity and pride, to sensuality and
intemperance, to uncharitableness and injustice. This
very petition is an implicit act of sorrow for past sins
and a definite detestation and rejection of any future
offense of God, and thus opens the soul for an abundant communication of grace.

*Make me always cleave to Thy commandments
and suffer me not to be separated from Thee, who with
the same God, the Father and the Holy Spirit livest
and reignest, God, forever and ever. Amen.*

Cleaving to the commandments of God is to love
and observe them; their observance is the proof of our

love and love keeps us united with Jesus. He Himself
has said so, "He who has my commandments and keeps
them, he it is who loves me. ...If anyone love me, he
will keep my word, and my Father will love him and
we will come and make our abode with him. He who
does not love me, does not keep my words." (John
14:21, 23ff) The observance of the commandments
will preserve us from all evils and iniquities. If, because of our weakness and fickleness, we must figure
with a relapse into past sins, then at least this expression of our sincere desire to cleave to His commandments will lessen their frequency and malice.

Separation from Christ would be our ruin, "If anyone does not abide in me, he shall be cast outside as
the branch and wither. And they shall gather them up
and cast them into the fire, and they shall burn." (John
15:16) This is a prayer for perseverance in the love
of God until death. But love is humble, distrusting self
and putting all hope in God. At the Last Supper Peter
protested his loyalty to Jesus. He would never be scandalized in his Master, he would never desert Him, he
would go with Him into death; yet, he denied Jesus.
The history of the Church records many examples of
men, priests, and ordinary faithful, who followed Peter
in his denial, nay even Judas in his betrayal of Jesus,
and that in spite of most fervent protestations of loyalty
to Christ and His Church in their earlier life. Our own
experience should teach us a lesson not to trust in our
own strength and make us humble, and such humility
adds to the value of this prayer.

Separation from Jesus through mortal sin does not
come all at once. Many infidelities and small transgres-

sions have preceded, many lights and inspirations disregarded, many venial sins committed, until at last the
weakened condition of the soul yielded to a grievous
temptation, and mortal sin extinguished the life of
grace. If we want the end, we must want the means.
The sacramental grace of Holy Communion will assist
us to take care of our duties, to listen to those many
inspirations of grace, to make use of the innumerable
opportunities to strengthen our will and to increase
our love of God, to form strong habits of virtue, and
thus we shall be preserved from that terrible calamity
of mortal sin—separation from Jesus, our Life.

7. PROTECTION AND HEALING

Should it be possible that the sacrifice of our salvation and the sacrament of life ever become the occasion for condemnation and eternal death? Alas, it is
a dreadful possibility, because Holy Communion may
be received unworthily. That we may be preserved
from such a misfortune is the object of the following
prayer.

*Let not the partaking of Thy body, O Lord Jesus
Christ, which I, though unworthy, make bold to receive,
turn to my judgment and condemnation.*

God is holy and whomsoever approaches God must
be holy. Even material things dedicated to God or
used for His service are sacred and must be treated
with the utmost reverence. Therefore, church and altar,

the sacred vessels and vestments, must be blessed or consecrated. Sacred ceremonies profoundly significant in their symbolism are employed in the celebration of Holy Mass. All this is to impress the faithful with the holiness of the divine mysteries.

What then must we say of him who receives Holy Communion in the state of mortal sin? To do this is an abomination in the sight of God; no material defilement of vessels or vestments is comparable to it. When King Nabuchodonosor desecrated the sacred vessels from the Temple of Jerusalem at a profane banquet, mysterious fingers appeared and wrote upon the wall of the banquet hall the doom of the king and his kingom: Mane, Thekel, Phares—Numbered, Weighed, Divided. Infinitely greater is the sacrilege of an unworthy Communion. No wonder this sin was so severely punished by God in the early times of Christianity, as we learn from St. Paul's first Epistle to the Corinthians. Even if in our days extraordinary punishment for this sin is rare, its malice remains the same and punishment is sure to come, if not in this life, then in the next. For, "He who eats this bread or drinks the cup of the Lord unworthily will be guilty of the body and the blood of the Lord. But let a man prove himself and so let him eat of the bread and drink of the cup; for he who eats and drinks unworthily, without distinguishing the body, eats and drinks judgment to himself." (I Corinthians 11:27ff)

But according to Thy goodness may it be unto me protection for mind and body and as the taking of a remedy. Who livest and reignest with God the

*Father in the unity of the Holy Spirit, God, forever
and ever. Amen.*

One of the effects of Holy Communion is that it
spiritualizes our life. Spiritual ideals and heavenly desires gradually take possession of the mind, and to the
same extent worldly ideals and desires lose their appeal. Under the influence of Holy Communion worthily
received there develops in the soul a certain sensitive-
ness to whatever is unholy and dangerous. The soul,
having experienced the warmth of divine love, feels
the icy draughts of sin even at a distance. The love of
Jesus never sleeps and gives immediate notice of the
approach of the tempter. Here is our protection. And
should God allow that persecution, torture and death
should become the lot of His faithful followers, Holy
Communion will also then be their strength and victory, as it has been and is in the case of innumerable
martyrs and confessors of the faith.

And there is healing power in Holy Communion.
Human nature is morally sick in consequence of original and personal sin. Bodily sickness implies that the
organism is not functioning properly: the heart, the
lungs, the digestive system. Sickly persons become easily fatigued, irritable, dejected, and often are afflicted
with abnormal cravings for things which are injurious
to health and recovery. In a similar manner the moral
nature of man has been affected by original and personal sin. This is the reason why men are inclined to
evil, find the practice of virtue difficult, and frequently
come to fall. St. Pius X in his encyclical on frequent
Communion emphatically states that Holy Communion

is the remedy for this moral weakness of men, and
that for this reason it should be received frequently,
if possible even daily. True, there will be no perfect
healing in this life, but there can and will be continuous
improvement in our condition, until the infirmities of
this life give way to the health and vigor of heavenly
life. Holy Communion brings us an increase of the
divine life of grace, and an increase of this divine life
means also an increase of holy ambitions, spiritual
strength and efficiency, joy and peace in the Lord,
"He who eats my flesh and drinks my blood, abides in
me and I in him. ...As I live because of the Father,
he who eats me, he also shall live because of me. ...He
who eats this bread shall live forever." (John 6:57ff)
Could there be any stronger motives to receive Holy
Communion frequently, daily? The efforts we make
in this regard are a reliable norm by which to judge
our attitude toward the attainment of Christian perfection.

8.   BEFORE HOLY COMMUNION

Let us first recall the object of our Savior's sacrifice.
Jesus died for our salvation, that is, to atone for our
sins, to reconcile and unite us again with the Father.
In Holy Mass He re-enacted in an unbloody manner
His bloody sacrifice. We joined Him in doing this, offering ourselves with Him and through Him, so that
we too might contribute our share to this atonement,
reconciliation, and union. Now, in Holy Communion

we receive the tangible pledge that God has accepted our offering and received us into the union of His life and love. The reception of Holy Communion is an act of tremendous significance. It is the greatest gift which God could give us—He cannot give more than Himself; it means an incomprehensible exaltation for us— we are raised to a participation in the divine life; it brings inspiration and invincible strength for the pursuit of Christian perfection. The thought of this marvelous grandeur of Holy Communion arouses desire for it. However, we cannot forget what we are of ourselves and what we have done in the past. The remembrance of our sinfulness cannot but keep us humble; on the other hand, God's goodness inspires confidence, and so we pray for healing from our weakness and spiritual infirmity, for perseverance in the love of God, so that the ultimate object of all that Jesus has done for us may be attained in our being preserved unto life everlasting. These are the thoughts expressed in the short but profoundly meaningful prayers immediately preceding the reception of Holy Communion.

After the priest has received Holy Communion under both species, the faithful receive it under the species of bread only. Profound knowledge of the human heart and consummate skill in arousing holy emotions characterize the final touch which holy Church adds to her preparation for Holy Communion.

The necessity of utmost purity of heart is impressed upon the faithful by the liturgical absolution which, turning to the people, the priest pronounces, "May the almighty God have mercy on you, forgive your sins, and lead you to life everlasting. May the

almighty and merciful God grant you pardon, absolution, and remission of your sins. Amen." Then, holding
up a sacred host before the people, the priest says,
"Behold the Lamb of God, behold Him, who takes
away the sins of the world. O Lord, I am not worthy
that Thou shouldst enter under my roof, but only say
the word and my soul shall be healed." Unlimited trust
in the anointing power of our Savior's death, humble
sorrow for sins committed, loving desires for spiritual
health and holiness of life fuse in this beautiful touching prayer, soul-stirring in its threefold repetition.

9. O LORD, I AM NOT WORTHY

It was after the sermon on the Mount, when
Jesus had returned to Capharnaum, that a Roman centurion approached Him. Although a pagan, he had
great faith in Jesus of whose miracles he had heard.
A servant of this man was sick and it shows the kind
and sympathetic nature of the centurion that, upon
hearing of the approach of Jesus, he at once made up
his mind to seek help with this miracle-working prophet.
Jesus immediately showed Himself ready to go to the
house of the centurion in order to heal the servant. This
was more than the centurion had expected; he considered himself unworthy of such an honor and said to
Jesus, "Lord, I am not worthy that Thou shouldst enter
under my roof; only say the word and my servant shall
be healed." Jesus was pleased with the humble faith
of this pagan and said to the people surrounding Him,

6. — *Holy Mass and Life.*

"Amen, I say to you, I have not found so great a faith in Israel." Then He spoke the word that healed the centurion's servant. Holy Church has taken these words into the liturgy of the Mass and uses them in preparation for Holy Communion. They are to arouse in the faithful the faith and humility of this centurion.

O Lord, I am not worthy that Thou shouldst enter under my roof.

Surely, this is not to be an unworthy Communion, strictly so-called; we have the moral certainty that we are in the state of sanctifying grace. Yet, we are not worthy. Our Blessed Mother in her exalted purity and holiness is not worthy; the Cherubim and Seraphim are not worthy; the greatest saints have pronounced these words, and that with a profounder realization of their unworthiness than we do. No created being is worthy, deserving, entitled to such an intimate union with our Lord and Savior as is granted us in Holy Communion. The sense of unworthiness is deepened by the fact that we do not even possess that degree of worthiness which we could and should have acquired. Who can say that he has never sinned, that he has made all possible atonement for the sins committed, that he followed all the inspirations of grace, complied with the duties of his state of life? We could be saints and are very mediocre in our spiritual life; we could be millionaires in spiritual treasures, yet have wasted our chances; we could be heroes and are cowards. Even though all is forgiven by our kind and merciful Lord, the very thought of indifference and ingratitude in the past is extremely uncomfortable on this occasion, when

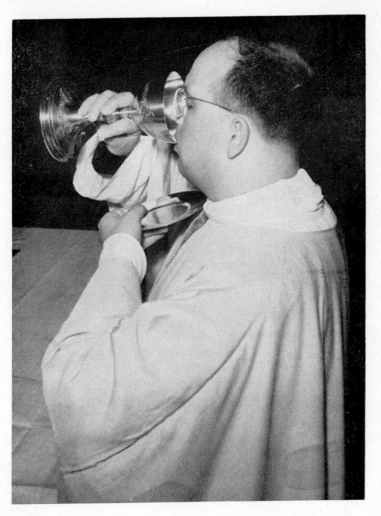

The priest receives Holy Communion, the
Body and the Blood of Jesus Christ

we are face to face with the all-exceeding love of our Savior.

But only say the word and my soul shall be healed.

The very purpose of our Savior's coming into this world is to bring us forgiveness and grace. Jesus is the Lamb of God that takes away the sins of the world; He is the physician of souls to bring health to the sick. His forgiving mercy is unlimited; so must be our confidence in Him. With humble faith and trust we beseech Him that He would say to us the word of power and love that will heal us. We beg Him to say the word that He spoke to the blind man of Jericho so that we may see the light, showing us the way to holiness and heaven; the word that He spoke to the deaf when He restored their hearing, that we may listen to the call of grace and the guidance of holy Church; the word He spoke to the paralytic so that we may freely move on the road of Christian perfection; the word of love which He addressed to all who labor and are burdened, so that we may find rest for our souls.

We shall have reason to say this prayer as long as we live. Perfect spiritual health is not the lot of man in this life; we hope for it in the life to come. But there is possible daily improvement and progress in virtue. Our charity can grow in intensity, our patience in endurance, our suffering in love, our manners in humility, our efforts in generosity. It is for such growth in our spiritual health that we pray, and we know that sublime heights of sanctity are within the reach of the Christian even in this life. But the final answer to this prayer shall be given when we enter the land of eternal youth, and when He to whom we address this prayer, "will refashion the body of our lowliness, conforming it to the body of His glory." (Philippians 3:21)

10. THE BODY OF OUR LORD JESUS CHRIST

Jesus, the Word of God through Whom all things were made, the Giver of all life because He is the life of the world, has made Himself the bread of life in Holy Communion, in order to let us share in His life and to sustain in us the life of grace until it passes over into the everlasting life of glory. An increase of this divine life, a steady growth and perseverance in it to the end of our lives is the object of the prayer, which the priest says as he himself receives Holy Communion and as he distributes it to the faithful.

May the body of our Lord Jesus Christ preserve my (your) soul unto life everlasting.

With eyes enlightened by faith we look upon the sacred host; it is not bread, but the Body of Jesus. In the synagogue of Capharnaum Jesus stated clearly and definitely, "The bread which I will give you is my flesh for the life of the world." (John 6:52) At the Last Supper Jesus gave to the apostles what appeared to be bread with the words, "This is my body; do this in remembrance of me." The celebration of Holy Mass was the fulfillment of the command of Jesus. So we believe that the host which we received in Holy Communion is the Body of Jesus, the Body conceived by the Holy Spirit, born of the Virgin Mary, the Body that hung on the cross, rose from the dead, and gloriously ascended into heaven, where It is seated at the right hand of the Father.

He who is present beneath these appearances of bread is our Lord because He is God. He proved His divinity by the countless miracles He wrought. And although He is now in heaven, He continues to act as the Lord of nature in the wonders of the Eucharist. There are the appearances of bread without the substance of bread. Christ is present beneath these appearances; whole and undivided in every particle of the host, whole in all the hosts throughout the world.

The name of God, made man, is Jesus; Jesus means Savior. The angel directs St. Joseph, "Thou shalt call His name Jesus; for He shall save his people from their sins." (Matthew 1:21) So does the angel speak to the shepherds, "There has been born to you today in the town of David a Savior, who is Christ the Lord." (Luke 2:11) He came to save us from the slavery of satan, from sin and death. There is no other name by which we could be saved.

Jesus is our Savior because He is the Christ, the Anointed One. In the Old Testament prophets, priests, and kings were anointed. Jesus unites their offices in His Person. He is the divine Teacher that taught men the way of salvation; as He was about to leave this world He commissioned the apostles and through them the Church to teach all nations and to make all men His disciples. Jesus acts as the divine High Priest in His bloody sacrifice on the cross and as "Priest forever according to the order of Melchisedech" in the Eucharistic Sacrifice. Through His blood we were redeemed and became His property by a new title.

He is now our King, and the redeemed are the members of His kingdom. However, as He informs Pilate, His kingdom is not of this world, not a political but a spiritual kingdom. He rules over minds and hearts, placing before His followers His law and His example, that all might pattern their lives after His own.

Holy Communion brings to us the Body and the Blood of the glorified, immortal Christ; therefore, it sustains within us the divine life and is the pledge and guaranty of the eternal life of glory. "Thus by partaking of His flesh we are illumined by the light of eternal truth, and are transfigured and transformed by its glory; and in His blood the ocean of eternal life and divine love floods our hearts. By the divine power inhabiting the Lord's flesh we are transformed in soul into the image of His divine glory, and in body into the image of His own glorified body... But this sacrament is at the same time a pledge and guaranty that the seed will some day flower into full beauty, that the Logos (Jesus) will irradiate and transform us with the plenitude of His light, and that He will completely flood us through and refresh us with the torrent of His love and His life, so that in knowledge and in love our lives will appear as the full expression and outpouring of the divine life." (Scheeben-Vollert) Indeed, if the touch of the hem of Christ's garment healed the sick woman in the Gospel, if by the application of the relics of the saints, countless miracles have been performed, what must we not expect from the living and life-giving union with the living, glorified, immortal Christ in Holy Communion, "He who eats this bread shall live forever." (John 6:59)

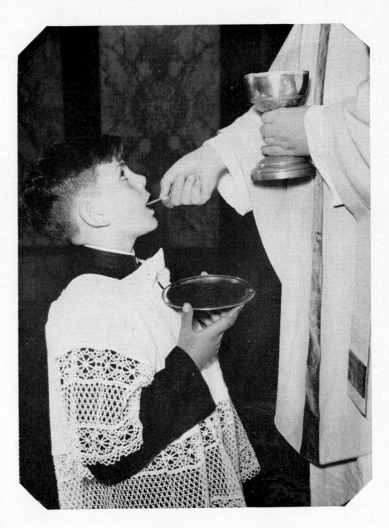

The priest gives Holy Communion to the people

VII

The Closing Parts

THE REMAINDER of Mass is rather brief, once Communion has been distributed. After all, we have done the work of the Mass. We have worshipped God—first by offering Him the perfect Gift of His Son, then by receiving from Him the Gift of that Son in Holy Communion. So the concluding prayers of Mass are simple and not too long. When they are over our thoughts will be properly directed to God. We will be able to meditate and consider what we have accomplished at Mass.

1. MAY IT CLEAVE TO MY SOUL

THE PRAYERS after Holy Communion contain substantially the same petitions as those mentioned before, that is, healing from our spiritual infirmities, elimination of all that is evil, an increase of the divine life, perseverance to the end. What else could they be? "What have I in heaven and what do I desire upon earth? Thou art the God of my heart and my portion forever." As the priest purifies the chalice and then his fingers, he prays:

What we have received with the mouth, may we keep with a pure mind, and may the temporal gift be for us an everlasting remedy.

May Thy body, O Lord, which I have received, and the blood which I have drunk cleave to my soul; and grant that no stain of sin may remain in me after the pure and holy mysteries have refreshed me. Who livest and reignest forever and ever. Amen.

Holy Communion is a temporal gift, meant only for this life, as a remedy to prepare us for the life to come. If it is to produce this effect, it must be received with a pure mind, a mind sincerely intent upon the avoidance of sin and progress in Christian perfection; it must become a vital force in our lives; it must cleave to our souls in our memory, mind, will, emotions.

The memory of Holy Mass ought to stay with me throughout the day. There are events in the life of every man, which imprint themselves indelibly upon his memory; usually they are events associated with some great sorrow or joy. There can be no event comparable in sorrow and in joy to what has taken place upon the altar. Holy Mass is the re-enactment of Christ's bloody sacrifice on the cross, an event so sorrowful that even nature manifested its grief and horror—the sun was darkened, the earth trembled, and the rocks were split asunder. There was present on the altar and received in Holy Communion the same Body that hung upon the cross, the same Blood that was shed from the Savior's wounds. But out of this death life has sprung, and out of this sorrow joy has blossomed forth, for by it we have received forgiveness of our sins, have been made the children of God and heirs of heaven. Could we ever forget it? Yet, we think of a thousand things, our work, our troubles, our joys, our friends and relatives, but fail to remember that one event that should occupy the first place in our memory, and thus do not experience the refreshing power of these sacred mysteries.

If these sacred mysteries are remembered the mind will show their effect in judging things according to the standards of Christ. He came down to this earth, suffered, and died, and perpetuates His sacrifice in Holy Mass for us and our salvation. St. Paul reminds us of the fact that we have been bought at a great price, and St. Peter writes, "You were redeemed...not with perishable things, with silver or gold, but with the precious blood of Christ." (I Peter 1:18) What must be the value of the soul that Jesus does not consider His own blood too great a price to pay for its

salvation! What do I think of the value of my soul?
What do I do in order to guard it against sin, to save,
and sanctify it? In the light of the Body and the Blood
of Jesus Christ what must I think of those worldly
pursuits, riches and pleasures, which endanger the salvation of my soul? What of my neglect of prayer, my
selfishness, my sins?

These sacred mysteries are the standing proof of
Jesus' words that He loved us to the end. He gave us
all that He could give, Himself, in life and in death
and in His heavenly glory. Does not such love call for
loving surrender and generous loyal following, no matter what might be the cost? Yet, as the author of the
Imitation of Christ says, "Jesus has now many who love
His heavenly kingdom, but few who carry His cross.
Many desire His consolations, but few are eager for
tribulations. He finds many companions for His banquet, but few for His fasting. All wish to rejoice with
Him, few only are willing to suffer something for Him.
Many follow Jesus as far as the breaking of the bread,
few only as far as the drinking of the cup of the Passion." Why? Because these sacred mysteries do not
cleave to the will, and therefore cannot exercise their
motivating energy.

Emotions are part of the human make-up, though
they are present in varying degrees of intensity in different persons. Whatever they may be, the sacred mysteries of the Mass must cleave to them. The primary
cause that arouses them and the ultimate object to
which they tend must be the Body and the Blood of the
Lord. If there is any sorrow, let it be because God is
offended, His love ungratefully rejected, His cause

neglected. If there is any fear, let it be because we are not as yet definitely saved and are in the dreadful possibility of losing our souls, of being eternally separated from Him who is our life. If there is any hope, it must be grounded upon our Savior's cross, in which there is salvation, life, and resurrection. If there is any true and lasting joy to brighten our lives, it must flow from these sacred mysteries at which we have assisted, the pledge of life everlasting and anticipation of the heavenly banquet. The day on which we have assisted at Mass and received Holy Communion is truly a day which the Lord has made; let us rejoice and be glad.

These prayers after Holy Communion, short though they are, are inexhaustible in their richness and power. Where they are said in the proper way, no stain of sin can remain in the soul. True, the very repetition of this prayer day after day suggests that it will be perfectly answered only in the next life. As long as we live here below we shall pay tribute to human weakness. We cannot prevent dust from settling on objects, but we can prevent it from accumulating; we cannot escape all the poisonous germs in the poisoned atmosphere of the world, but we can take medicine to counteract the effect of the poison .If, upon our return from Holy Mass and Holy Communion, we could begin our day's work all pure and free from any stain of sin, and if during the day the Body and the Blood of our Savior would cleave to our soul, to memory, mind, will, and emotions, we would proceed with giant strides on the road of Christian perfection. "For this, the highest and most worthy sacrament, is the health of body and soul, the cure of every spiritual weakness; in it my defects are remedied, my passions restrained, and temptations overcome or allayed. In it greater grace is infused, growing virtue is nourished, faith confirmed, hope strengthened, and charity fanned into flame." (*Imitation of Christ*—Bruce)

2. THE FINAL OBLATION

The liturgical Communion service is brought to a close by the Communion and Postcommunion prayers. The Mass proper is finished: Ite missa est—Go, the Mass is over. In former centuries, when the celebration of Mass lasted much longer than it does at present, the faithful were dismissed at this place. In the course of time three very appropriate features were added, that is, the final oblation, the blessing, and the last Gospel. Standing in the middle of the altar, with his head inclined and his hand touching the altar, the priest prays:

May the homage of my service be pleasing to Thee, O Holy Trinity, and do Thou grant that the sacrifice, which I, unworthy though I am, have offered in Thy sight, may be acceptable to Thee and through Thy mercy a propitiation for me and for all, for whom I have offered it up. Through Christ our Lord. Amen.

This final oblation is a summary repetition of the primary object of the Holy Sacrifice, a ratification of the gifts we have offered, a rectification of any faults or disorders that may have occurred in the performance of the sacred mysteries. The celebration of Holy Mass is an act of homage offered to the Blessed Trinity. The sacred place in which this was done, vessels and vestments of distinguished form and material, the beauty and sublimity of the prayers and ceremonies, all added to the solemnity of this act of homage. The fact that Jesus Christ, our divine High Priest and Victim, acted as our Mediator gave it infinite value. But the honor and privilege, which we enjoyed in cooperating with the divine High Priest, also imposed definite duties upon us.

It was the Father's well-beloved Son who acted in these mysteries. The Father so loved the world, that He delivered His eternal Son into death that we might live. Any culpable irreverence or negligence we may have become guilty of during the sacred action is an offense to the most loving Father, an act of ingratitude. The eternal Son was present beneath the sacred species, and our way of handling these assumes a most intimate, a personal touch; indifference, carelessness, must be particularly painful to Him. But above all Jesus expected from us similarity of sentiments. As He delivered Himself for us because He loved us, so we, too, are to love Him and give ourselves to Him and to His service. But, if our thoughts and desires were occupied with worldly things, if we remained attached to our own will, if there was unwillingness to accept our full share of the cross, we filled His sacred Heart with sorrow. The Holy Spirit watched the sacred action with personal interest. It was through Him that Jesus was conceived and anointed in preparation for His mission, and in the love of the Holy Spirit Jesus offered Himself to the Father as an immaculate victim. The Holy

Spirit is divinely eager to complete the work of Jesus by applying to our souls the grace merited by Christ. But, if our cooperation in this mystery of love was cold and lifeless, if we showed little appreciation of the gifts of grace, if the oblation of ourselves was superficial and half-hearted, we obstructed the work of the Holy Spirit and offended Him.

The petition that our oblation may be pleasing to the Holy Trinity is an implicit act of sorrow and reparation for our faults and deficiencies; according to its intensity, it will make our oblation pleasing to God and acceptable by a sort of retroaction. This so much the more as Jesus is the propitiation for our sins. Our disobedience is swallowed up in His obedience unto death; our ingratitude is covered by the filial gratitude of Jesus, who gave thanks at all times, but particularly by making Himself our thanksgiving in the blessed Eucharist. If there is any injustice in our work, it is rectified by the justice of Jesus, who returned to His heavenly Father all that He had received from Him and fully accomplished the work for which He had been sent into the world. Our pride and impatience are taken away by the humility and meekness of the Lamb of God, who went to the slaughter without opening His mouth. So we could continue with all our faults and failings. They are displeasing to God, it is true. But Jesus the divine Victim is ours. Ours are His Person and His holiness, ours His piety and conformity with the will of the Father, ours is His sacrifice. In Him all is as it ought to be, just as the heavenly Father wished it to be. But if all this is ours, we have a right to make use of it, that is, to offer it up in atonement

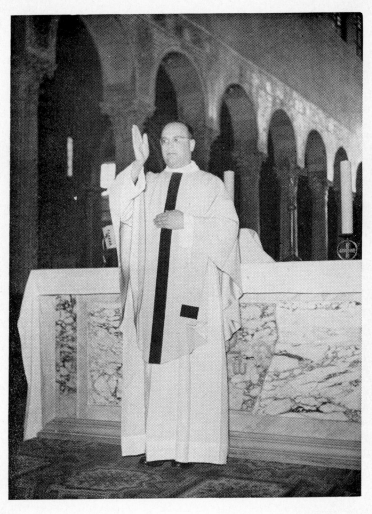

The priest blesses the people in the name of the
Blessed Trinity and by the commission of the Church

for our sins and imperfections. This is precisely what we do in this prayer. Therefore, we also have the certainty that all our faults will be forgiven, that our sacrifice will be accepted as a propitiation for our sins.

Reflections of this kind should arouse within ourselves a more vivid realization of the atoning power of the holy Sacrifice with regard to our daily sins and failings. God is infinite in His goodness and mercy. No length of time can exhaust it, no number of relapses will wear it out, no human infirmity is incurable to the healing power of His love. In spite of our sin we can be the carefree and joyful children of God, because we know that, "If anyone sins, we have an advocate with the Father, Jesus Christ the just; and he is a propitiation for our sins, not for ours only but also for those of the whole world." (I John 2:1)

3. GOD BLESS YOU

The Mass is finished. The faithful are about to return to their homes to take up their daily round of duties. There begins for them now the Mass of life, in which they are to carry out the lessons learned at the Holy Sacrifice. The inspiration and power of the Holy Sacrifice will be with them; that they may faithfully cooperate holy Church blesses them:

May the almighty God bless you, the Father, the Son, and the Holy Spirit.

The blessing of the almighty God is sufficient for all our needs, powerful enough to overcome all obstacles to our salvation; it is infinite, inexhaustible, has no limitations as to time or place. From the blessing of the Father we may expect a more profound realization of the fact He is our Creator and Lord whom we must serve; our Father in whose wost loving providence we must trust; our last end to which all other ends must be subordinated. The blessing of the Son must impress upon us the value of the human soul, for which He paid the ransom of His blood. To save it is the foremost business of our lives; but we can save it only by following Him as our King. As King and Savior He is also our Judge, who will assign to us our place in eternity. The blessing of the Holy Spirit will open our eyes to the greatness of the treasures of His grace and gifts by which He changes our souls into temples of God. He forms in us the image of Christ and will bring it to perfection in the beatific vision, "Beloved, now we are the children of God, and it has not yet appeared what we shall be. We know that, when he appears, we shall be like to him, for we shall see him just as he is. And everyone who has this hope in him makes himself holy, just as he also is holy." (I John 3:2ff)

4. THE LAST GOSPEL

Mysteries of incomprehensible wisdom, power, and love have been enacted upon the altar. The central figure of these mysteries was our divine High Priest

The priest faces the people, gives them the ancient form of salutation, "The Lord be with you"

and Victim, Jesus Christ. Holy Church wishes that we should never lose sight of Him. Therefore, she places at the end of the Mass the beginning of the Gospel of St. John, which in a grand way summarizes the majesty of His Person and work.

Jesus is the eternal Word of God, that was with God in the beginning because It has no beginning. In the Word was reflected the infinite imitability of the divine nature and the Father, choosing out of this infinite number of possible worlds, created the existing universe; thus all things were created through the Word. In Him was life, ever active in urging men to open their eyes and see the light which He had kindled in the glory of the universe, for "the heavens announce the glory of God, and the firmament proclaims the works of His hands." But the light shone in darkness; men did not see it because their works were evil. Then, there was a man sent by God, by the name of John, to be a witness to the Word. John preached penance, a change of mind and heart, that would turn the people away from their evil ways. This light now shone in their midst; it was the Lamb of God, that takes away the sins of the world. But even now, as the incarnate Word of God came into His own, His own did not receive Him. They kept their eyes closed to the light and refused to accept the gifts which He offered. Great, beyond all thought and expectation, were His gifts. To all those who believed in Him He gave the life and glory of children of God. The eternal Son of God became man that men might become the children of God. And so the Word of God was made flesh and dwelt among us and we have seen His glory, the glory of the

Only-begotten of the Father, full of grace and truth.

We have seen the glory of the incarnate Word of God in our midst. Holy Mass is the memorial of all His wonderful works, of His Incarnation, His teachings and miracles, His Passion, Resurrection, and Ascension. There remains nothing but to admire, adore, and give thanks—Deo gratias! May we not assume that Jesus in heaven retains some marks of His eucharistic priesthood in the same manner as He retains the marks of His bloody sacrifice? Thus we shall be able eternally to adore the mysteries of the altar—adoremus in aeternum sanctissimum sacramentum. For all eternity we shall give thanks for all the inspiration and power we drew from His sacrifice, the joy and consolation of Holy Communion, for all those hours of peace and happiness we spent in His eucharistic presence.

> Contemplating, Lord, Thy hidden presence,
> Grant me what I thirst for and implore,
> In the revelation of Thy essence
> To behold Thy glory evermore.

Conclusion

TO LIVE the Mass has become a familiar saying in our days of liturgical revival, and it must be admitted that it is most appropriate. Holy Mass, as the unbloody re-enactment of our Savior's bloody sacrifice, not only brings us salvation in the objective order, but in its celebration also conveys and exemplifies the fundamental principles of Christian living, by the following of which we actually attain salvation and holiness. Following the interpretation of the Mass given in this book these principles may be reduced to the following rules of life:

1. Keep sin out of your life and strive after the utmost purity of conscience. It would be contradiction, inconsistency, and insincerity to assist at the sacrifice of atonement, to profess sorrow for our sins, and to ask forgiveness as we do, especially at the beginning of the Mass in the prayers at the foot of the altar, without making sincere efforts to avoid sin.

2. The Christian's life program must be: Glory to God in the highest. Whatsoever does not or cannot serve this purpose must be absolutely excluded.

3. Know your religion. Religious instruction as given in sermons and in many Catholic books and

magazines supply such knowledge. Some such books and magazines should be found in every Catholic home. But endeavor to read also the Sacred Scriptures, especially the Gospel.

4. Let your daily "Offertory" be your good intention by which you dedicate to the glory of God your daily work and your daily crosses. They are part of the atonement which God expects of you. By humbly accepting them, even rejoicing in them, you can atone for the folly of sin by the folly of the cross.

5. Let your ideal be to be changed into Christ. Your natural self must die and make room for Christ, that He may form your heart according to His own. The pain and agony which you experience in this transformation are your "Consecration."

6. Abide in Jesus that Jesus may abide in you. Live in the blessed consciousness of that union with Him, which He sustains and strengthens by His grace and particularly Holy Communion.

7. See Jesus in your fellowmen and love them with supernatural love. God is their Father and all are His children, brothers and sisters of Christ, and heirs of the heavenly kingdom. Whatever you do to them you do to Christ. Holy Communion, the bread of life for all, is one and the same in all who receive it, since there is but one Christ; therefore also, all must be one in Him.

The above are but the main principles derived from Mass for the conduct of our lives. But a prayerful consideration of the various parts of the Mass will suggest the most practical and often surprising applications to life. The more the significance of the Mass is understood, and the more its power is used for the realization of the ideal of Christian living, the more holiness there will be among the faithful. Living the Mass is the strongest protection against the spirit of the world; it is the most effective apostolate for the conversion of non-Catholics. It is not by words only that men shall be converted to Christ and His Church, but next to the grace of God it will be done through the example of Catholics who live their faith, and they live their faith most perfectly, if they live the Mass.

> Thou, who Mary didst forgive
> And who badst the robber live,
> Hope to me dost also give.
> Here Thy grace and virtue send,
> Grant salvation in the end
> And in heaven felicity.

Publications of the Society of St. Paul may be ordered from:

ST. PAUL BOOK CENTERS

2187 Victory Blvd.
Staten Island 14, N. Y.

St. Paul's Monastery
Canfield, Ohio

Old Lake Shore Road
Derby, N. Y.

3442 McDougall Ave.
Detroit 7, Michigan

DAUGHTERS OF ST. PAUL

196 Washington Street
Boston, Mass.

78 Fort Place
Staten Island 1, N. Y.

827 Fifth Avenue
San Diego 1, California

141 West Rayen Ave.
Youngstown, Ohio

325 Murray Street
Alexandria, La.

207 Broadway
San Antonio, Texas

TABLE OF CONTENTS

PART I—NATIONALISM

1. The Roots of Nationalism   9
2. The Awakening of Nationalism and Liberty   16
3. Nationalism and Tradition   29
4. Nationalism and Revolution   38
5. Nationalism and *Realpolitik*   54
6. Nationalist Conflicts and Pan-Movements   65
7. Racialism and Totalitarianism   73
8. World-wide Nationalism   81

PART II—READINGS

1. MACHIAVELLI: *Liberate Italy from the Barbarians*   93
2. MICHELET: *Unity of the Fatherland*   97
3. HERDER: *Germans and Slavs*   103
4. HEGEL: *The State*   110
5. GUIZOT: *Historical Studies*   113
6. *Proclamation of Greek Independence*   116
7. MAZZINI: *The Unity of Italy*   118
8. ACTON: *Nationality*   121
9. NAPOLEON: *On National Unity*   126
10. LIST: *Nationality and Economy*   129
11. RENAN: *The Meaning of Nationality*   135
12. O'SULLIVAN: *Manifest Destiny*   140
13. SCHURZ: *Liberal Patriotism*   144
14. HYDE: *On the Revival of Gaelic*   146
15. GRIFFITH: *Nationality and Economy*   149
16. DANILEVSKY: *Pan-Slavism*   151
17. HAVLICEK: *The Dangers of Pan-Slavism*   155
18. DOSTOEVSKY: *Russian Messianism*   160
19. WAGNER: *The Jewish Danger*   164
20. WAGNER: *German Art*   166
21. MUSSOLINI: *The Doctrine of Fascism*   170
22. NEHRU: *Socialism and Nationalism*   175

23. SUN YAT-SEN: *Message to Soviet Russia*   179
24. MAO TSE-TUNG: *A National Popular Culture*   181
25. *The Uganda Flag*   183

ality. Thus the people of the United States do not claim common descent to form a nationality, and the people of Switzerland speak three or four languages and yet form one well-defined nationality. Although objective factors are of great importance for the formation of nationalities, the most essential element is a living and active corporate will. It is this will which we call nationalism, a state of mind inspiring the large majority of a people and claiming to inspire all its members. It asserts that the nation-state is the ideal and the only legitimate form of political organization and that the nationality is the source of all cultural creative energy and of economic well-being.

The Modernity of Nationalism. Even before the age of nationalism, we find individuals who profess sentiments akin to nationalism. But these sentiments are confined to individuals. The masses never feel their own life—culturally, politically, or economically—to depend upon the fate of the national body. Danger from the outside may arouse a passing feeling of national cohesion, as it happened in Greece during the Persian Wars or in France in the Hundred Years War. But as a rule, wars before the French Revolution did not arouse deep national emotions. In the Peloponnesian War Greeks bitterly fought Greeks. In religious and dynastic wars of early modern times, Germans fought against Germans, and Italians against Italians, without any realization of the "fratricidal" nature of the act. Even as late as the eighteenth century, soldiers and civilians in Europe entered the service of "foreign" rulers and served them often with a loyalty and faithfulness which proved the absence of any national sentiment.

Nor was nationality regarded as a source of cultural life until very recently. Education and learning, the formation of man's mind and character, were throughout most of history not determined by any national limits. Religion was regarded in many ages as the fountainhead of all cultural and spiritual life. During and after the Renaissance, education in Europe everywhere was rooted in the common tradition of classical civilization. The ideals of knighthood in Medieval Europe or the model of the French court in the seventeenth and eighteenth centuries spread beyond all national boundaries. Only in

Part I

NATIONALISM

THE ROOTS OF NATIONALISM

What is Nationalism? Nationalism is a state of mind, in which the supreme loyalty of the individual is felt to be due the nation-state. A deep attachment to one's native soil, to local traditions and to established territorial authority has existed in varying strength throughout history. But it was not until the end of the eighteenth century that nationalism in the modern sense of the word became a generally recognized sentiment increasingly molding all public and private life. Only very recently has it been demanded that each nationality should form a state, its own state, and that the state should include the whole nationality. Formerly, man's loyalty was due not to the nation-state, but to differing other forms of social authority, political organization and ideological cohesion such as the tribe or clan, the city-state or the feudal lord, the dynastic state, the church or religious group. Throughout many centuries the political ideal was not the nation-state but the, at least, theoretically world-wide empire comprising various nationalities and ethnic groups on the basis of a common civilization and for the assurance of a common peace.

Nationalities are the products of the living forces of history, and therefore fluctuating and never rigid. They are groups of the utmost complexity and defy exact definition. Most of them possess certain objective factors distinguishing them from other nationalities like common descent, language, territory, political entity, customs and traditions, or religion. But it is clear that none of these factors is essential to the existence or definition of nation-

9

nineteenth century Europe and America and in twentieth
century Asia and Africa have the people identified themselves with the nation, civilization with national civilization, their life and survival with the life and survival of
the nationality. From this time on nationalism has dominated the impulses and attitudes of the masses, and at the
same time served as the justification for the authority of
the state and the legitimation of its use of force, both
against its own citizens and against other states.

Ancient Hebrews and Greeks. In spite of its modernity some fundamental traits of nationalism were developed long ago. The roots of nationalism spring from
the same soil as Western civilization, from the ancient
Hebrews and the ancient Greeks. Both peoples had a
clearly defined consciousness of being different from all
other peoples. the Hebrews from the Gentiles, the Greeks
from the Barbarians. The bearer of group consciousness
was with them not king or priesthood but the people as
a whole, every Hebrew or every Greek. With the other
peoples of antiquity, only rulers and empires left their
traces on history. With the Hebrews and the Greeks it
was the national character and the spiritual creative
energy of the people which endured. It is because their
cultural continuity proved stronger than racial, political,
or geographic continuity, that they live on today. The
idea of the nation-state was unknown to them but they
had the strong consciousness of a cultural mission.

Three essential traits of modern nationalism originated
with the Hebrews: the idea of the chosen people, the
emphasis on a common stock of memory of the past and
of hopes for the future, and finally national messianism.
At the beginning of Hebrew history stands the Covenant
concluded between God and His people. From the time
of the prophets on, the Hebrews envisaged the whole of
history as a unified process, as a continuity from one
source to one goal, with a special distinctive role for the
Hebrews at its center. In the kingdom of God the drama
of universal history was to find its atoning conclusion and
the idea of the Covenant its fulfillment. Messianism became a philosophy of history justifying the ways of God
to suffering man. Not only oppressed nationalities took
refuge in the hope of a messianic mission; at other times

it became a symbol of national pride and an often dangerous call to greatness and overreaching power; it expressed
also the struggle of heretical sects and oppressed classes
for the realization of their dreams and aspirations, and
as the secular idea of historical progress it still retains
today some of its religious fervor.

The Greeks shared with the Hebrews the feeling of cultural and spiritual superiority over all other peoples and
expressed this feeling in the most trenchant terms. In
addition the Greeks developed the concept of supreme
loyalty to the political community, in their case the city-
state or *polis*. Every citizen had to identify himself completely with the life of the *polis*, to become thoroughly
politicized. Sparta in ancient Greece and Plato in his
Republic postulated the absolute precedence of the state
over the individual and idealized a closed and authoritarian state. But at the end of the fourth century B.C.,
Alexander's dream of a world empire, un-Greek in its
origin, helped to transform the sharp division between
Greeks and Barbarians into a new and universal attitude,
surpassing all ethnic frontiers and distinctions. Under the
influence of Alexander's aspiration, the Greek Stoic
philosophers taught mankind to consider that their fatherland was the whole inhabited earth, the *cosmopolis*, and
that man was a citizen not of a nation but of mankind.

The Universalism of the Roman Empire.   This Stoic
philosophy influenced Roman thought in the last two
centuries B.C. at the very time when the city-state grew
into an empire organizing the then known part of the
earth on the basis of a common law and a common civilization. The universalism of the empire which was rooted
in Hellenistic civilization but devoid of the exclusiveness
of the Greek state, prepared the soil for the spread of
universal Christianity, which was rooted in Judaism but
devoid of the ethnic exclusiveness of Israel. Later the
Roman Empire—with its center transferred to Constantinople—and the Christian church fused into one body.
Under their combined influence the political and cultural
thought of the Middle Ages was characterized by the
conviction that mankind was one and had to form one
community. Down to modern times religion, with its
unifying regulation of thought, social life, and attitudes,

entirely dominated the private and public life of all Christian, as well as of all Mohammedan countries. The greatest poet of the Christian Middle Ages, Dante, gave to the idea of universalism and of the continuation of the unifying mission of the Roman Empire as majestic and as enduring an expression as any idea and hope could ever pride itself on having received. No thought of the political unity of Italy, or of the rejection of the Germans as bearers of the imperial dignity, ever entered his mind.

Renaissance and Reformation. In the fourteenth century it became clear that the unification by the imperial power for which Dante had hoped could not be realized. At the same time the Papacy, the other center of universal hopes, found itself in Avignon in captivity. Thus the search for new sources of authority and integration began. The two great spiritual revolutions known as Renaissance and Reformation form the transition from the Middle Ages to modern times in Western Christendom. The ancient classics and the Old Testament were then read in a new light and with a new understanding. In both of them the seeds for a rising national consciousness were found. Words and associations taken from the patriotic devotion of the classical Greeks for the *polis* and of the republican Romans for the *patria* were revived. The new emphasis on ancient history aroused in the Italian intellectuals a consciousness of their supposed identity with the ancient Romans. Medieval writers had written in the service of the Church and for the glory of God. Renaissance humanists were employed by princes and cities and wrote for their glory. But the Renaissance was too passing a phenomenon and too much restricted to the small literate circles to develop any nationalism. The Reformation put an end to the brief secular interlude of the Renaissance. Christianity and religious disputes became again the center of all life and activity. The European peoples of the sixteenth and seventeenth centuries did not fight for national values but for dogmatic truth. People were expelled or punished not for ethnic or linguistic differences but for religious heresy or apostasy.

A lonely voice for nationalism was raised in Italy of the Renaissance by Niccolò Machiavelli (1469-1527). A Florentine like Dante, he had, however, no use for universalism or religion, the two great forces dominating Dante's life. In the last chapter of his famous book *The Prince* (*See Reading No. 1.*), he appealed for a strong man to liberate Italy from the Barbarians. But Machiavelli's was a lonely voice crying in the wilderness. No Italian was interested in, or even understood, the cause of Italy. Nevertheless, Machiavelli was important in the preparation of nationalism. In his *Prince* he visualized the new secular state independent of any religious or moral sanction, where the power of the state became an end in itself, and all means to this end appeared justified. He anticipated future developments when he wrote: "Where it is an absolute question of the welfare of our country, we must admit of no considerations of justice or injustice, of mercy or cruelty, of praise or ignominy, but putting all else aside must adopt whatever course will save its existence and preserve its liberty."

There is as little direct connection between Reformation and nationalism as there is between Renaissance and nationalism. Protestantism was originally as universal a religious movement as Catholicism. But the fact of its existence destroyed the religious universalism of the Christian Middle Ages. Its appeal to individual conscience facilitated the multiplication of sects and creeds. Its emphasis on reading the Bible and on the sermon as a center of the divine service strengthened the vernacular languages. Translation of the Bible into the vernacular languages lent them a new dignity and frequently became the starting point for the development of national languages and literatures. Thus literature was made accessible to the people at the very time that the invention of printing made the production of books easier and cheaper.

Whereas the Reformation promoted the religious and linguistic pluralism of modern times, the new concept of the state and of princely power developed during the Renaissance created the new centralized dynastic states which at least in Western Europe became the form out of which later the nation-state would arise. The absolute monarchs destroyed the various feudal and local allegiances and thereby made the integration of all loyalties in one center possible. The growing economic interdependence demanded larger territorial units than the manors, cities, and principalities of the preceding period could supply. Only these larger units allowed the necessary scope to the dynamic spirit of the rising middle-class and their capitalistic enterprise. But these new centralized states, as the Tudors created them in England and Louis XIII in France, were not yet nation-states. With them, the king was the state. Only in seventeenth century England, and then in France during the Revolution of 1789, did the state cease to be the king's state; it became the people's state, a national state, a fatherland. The nation, no longer the king, felt itself responsible for the country's destiny. From then on nation and state became identified in Western Europe, as civilization became identified with national civilization.

From the beginning of the Roman Empire to the end of the Middle Ages men had commonly stressed the general and the universal and seen imperial unity as the desirable goal. Against the universalism of the past the new nationalism glorified the peculiar and the parochial, national differences and national individualities. These tendencies have become more pronounced as nationalism has developed in the later nineteenth and in the twentieth century. In the seventeenth and eighteenth centuries, in the early stage of nationalism in the West, the common standards of Western civilization, the survival of the Christian and Stoic traditions, the regard for the universally human, the faith in reason, one and the same everywhere, and in common sense,—all these were too strong to allow nationalism to develop its full tendencies and to disrupt the society of man. Thus it could happen that nationalism in its beginning in the West appeared compatible with cosmopolitan convictions and with the general love of mankind.

THE AWAKENING OF
NATIONALISM AND LIBERTY

The First Modern Nation. The first full manifestation of modern nationalism occurred in seventeenth century England. That century for the first time saw England as the leading nation of the European community; she exercised this leadership in the very fields which characterized the modern age and which sharply distinguished it from preceding epochs, in the scientific spirit, in political thought and activity, in commercial enterprise. Inspired by an immense confidence in the new possibilities opening up, the English people felt upon their shoulders the mission of history. They, the common people of England, were the chosen people at a great turning point from which a new true Reformation was to start. For the first time the authoritarian tradition on which the Church and the State had rested was challenged by the seventeenth century English Revolutions in the name of the liberty of man.

Under Puritan influence the three main ideas of Hebrew nationalism were revived: the chosen people, the Covenant, and the Messianic expectancy. The English nation regarded itself as the new Israel. Thus English nationalism arose out of a religious matrix and has preserved this original character throughout. It has never known the bitter conflict between nationalism and religion found elsewhere. At the same time English nationalism became identified, to a degree unknown anywhere else, with the concept of individual liberty. This new feeling for liberty found its greatest expression in the writings of John Milton (1608-1674). With him nationalism was not a struggle for collective independence from an "alien yoke"; it was the affirmation of individual freedom from authority, the self-assertion of personality in face of its own government or church, "the deliverance of man from the yoke of slavery and superstition." Liberty to Milton was religious, political, and personal. His plea for the freedom of unlicensed printing in the *Areopagitica* culminated in the outcry: "Give me the liberty to know, to utter, and to argue freely according to conscience, above all liberties."

In the words of its leader, Oliver Cromwell (1599-1658), the Puritan Revolution raised for the first time two great causes into the clear light of history. "Liberty of conscience, and liberty of the subject—two as glorious things to be contended for, as any God hath given us," he proclaimed in his speech before Parliament on September 4, 1654. The "free Church" demanded a "free State." Yet the time was not ripe. The Puritan Revolution was still filled with all the emotional fervor and the factual intolerance of the age of religion. It was apparently defeated by the Restoration, but its main aspirations were revived and confirmed, thirty years after Cromwell's death, in the Glorious Revolution: the supremacy of law over the king, the preponderance of Parliament in lawmaking, the impartiality of justice, the security of individual rights, the freedom of thought and press, and religious tolerance. The Glorious Revolution lifted the new liberties above the welter of fanatical religious and party strife: it made them the common foundation of the whole nation and anchored them as "true and ancient rights of the people of this realm" in its historical tradition. The Puritan Revolution degenerated into a parliamentary and military dictatorship; the Glorious Revolution made the new and growing order of liberty and tolerance so firmly rooted in national life and character that no serious attempt has ever been made to undermine them. The Glorious Revolution created the climate of reconciliation, of discussion and compromise in which alone democracy can permeate national life.

Nationalism and Liberty. Nationalism as an active force in history was confined in the eighteenth century to the shores of the North Atlantic. It expressed the spirit of the age in its emphasis upon the individual and his rights and in its participation in the humanitarian character of the Age of Enlightenment. The rise of English nationalism in the seventeenth century coincided with the rise of the English trading middle-class. Both found their foremost expression in the political philosophy of John Locke (1632-1704). In characteristic fashion, his first *Treatise on Government* started with a sentence which summed up his humanitarian and his national point of view: "Slavery is so vile and miserable an estate of man, and so directly opposite to the generous temper and courage of our nation, that it is hardly to be conceived that an Englishman, much less a gentleman, should plead for it." Locke's philosophy also performed a great service to the new middle-classes by its emphasis upon property and the new justification for property, based not upon conquest but upon man's labor and toil. Yet, Locke served more than his class by the two fundamental principles which he upheld, namely, that the individual, his liberty, dignity, and happiness, remain the basic elements of all national life, and that the government of a nation is a moral trust dependent upon the free consent of the governed. While in France, and generally throughout Europe, the authoritarian absolutism of King and Church emerged victorious from the struggles of the seventeenth century, England was the one country where the hold of absolutism had been broken. There alone a freely and vigorously expressed public opinion grew up and secured its influence upon the conduct of national affairs, though this conduct remained for the time being in the hands of an oligarchy. Yet, in England a national spirit permeated all institutions and created a living tie between the governing class and the people. It was under the influence of liberal English nationalism, that the French *philosophes* fought in the eighteenth century against the authoritarianism, the intolerance, and the censorship of their church and state.

English influence upon France, strengthened by Voltaire's visit to England in 1726 to 1729 and his reports on English life and liberty, was significant not only for France. In the eighteenth century France had been for two hundred years the intellectual leader of Europe. French had become the universal language of the educated circles everywhere. The English ideas of personal liberty and national organization became known abroad through the intermediary of French thinkers, and were absorbed and transformed into the general consciousness of eighteenth century Western mankind through the genius of French rational thought and the clarity of the French language. Thereby the national and historical liberties of Englishmen gained universal importance. They became a model for the awakening liberal thought of the age. They exercised little immediate influence on French political, social, and religious realities before 1789, but they were a potent factor in the birth of American nationalism in 1775.

Nationalism in British North America. The political and intellectual life of the thirteen colonies in North America was based upon the foundation of the Puritan and Glorious Revolutions. The English traditions of constitutional liberties and common law could grow more freely in the wide and open spaces of the yet unexplored continent than in the old country. In the colonies there were no survivals of the feudal past impeding the new development. The Puritans in New England preserved the feeling of being the new Israel, their self-identification with the ancient Hebrews, at a time when this feeling had already disappeared in England. Providence seemed to open up immense possibilities before the new country; eighteenth century European glorification of primitive and unspoiled nature added to the significance of America's virgin territory; the new rational interpretation given to English liberty by the French *philosophes* helped to broaden the historical liberties of the old country into universal liberties in the new world. The Americans reared in the freedom of Englishmen felt the strength for the birth of a higher form of freedom. Their struggle for the interpretation of the English Constitution, fundamentally a civil war within the British Empire between Tories and Whigs, not only secured a freer Constitution for the whole empire. It gave also birth to a new nation, born in liberty by the will of the people, originating not in the dim past of history or the feudal and religious tradition of the Middle Ages, but in the bright light of the Age of Enlightenment.

The new nation was clearly not based upon common descent or upon a common religion and it was not separated by its own language or its literary or legal traditions from the nation from which it wished to differentiate itself. It was born in a common effort, in a fight for political rights, for individual liberty and tolerance,—English rights and traditions but now raised into inalienable rights of every man, universalized as a hope and message for the whole of mankind. The diversity and tolerance of religion which existed in eighteenth century America to a degree unheard of at that period, was matched by the diversity and tolerance of the racial strains mingling in the "melting pot." What held the new nation together was an idea, the idea of liberty under law as expressed in the Constitution. The American Constitution entered into force at the beginning of 1789, the year of the French Revolution. In spite of its imperfections, the Constitution has withstood the test of time better than any other constitution on earth. It has lasted because the idea for which it stands is so intimately welded with the existence of the American nation that without the idea there would have been no nation. For the first time a nation had arisen on the basis of "these truths held to be self-evident, that all men are created equal, that they are endowed by their Creator with certain inalienable rights, that among these are life, liberty and the pursuit of happiness"—truths which the nation could not give up without destroying its own foundation. These "truths" deeply influenced the beginning phase of the French Revolution which enthroned French nationalism in place of French royalty as the decisive factor in French history. But into the new French nationalism a new element entered, the myth of the collective personality as envisioned by the fertile and unstable mind of Rousseau.

Jean Jacques Rousseau. Under the influence of English ideas the Enlightenment or Age of Reason had proclaimed the liberty of the free personality. Rousseau (1712-1778) shared this belief in the freedom of man. But he sensed that this individualism was not enough; with the old dynastic and religious authority in the state breaking down he saw the necessity of establishing the collective personality of the nation as the new center and justification of society and social order. The sovereignty of the state had found its visible embodiment in the prince whose will was the state. *Regis voluntas suprema lex.* How could the new sovereign, the people, express a unified will? How could the people become one as the prince was one? To that end the whole people must be united in the closest possible feeling of affinity, of common destiny and common responsibility. Rousseau, who was born in the Swiss city republic of Geneva, looked longingly back to the ancient Greek city-states, to the exclusive and all-inclusive devotion of their citizens to the *polis*. In France Rousseau, who lived there as an unhappy exile, saw the evils of arbitrary government by a prince and a court. He wished to replace it by a rational government where man would will the social order out of his own free will and obey laws because he prescribed them for himself. To this end Rousseau wrote the *Social Contract* (1762); in it he created an ideal community out of the patriotic virtues of the ancient city-states, Geneva's Calvinist tradition of being a saintly nation, and the proud feeling of independence of the rural Swiss republics. Rousseau was convinced that the true political community could be based only on the virtue of its citizens and their ardent love of the fatherland. Public education had to implant these feelings in the hearts of all children.

Rousseau was also the first great writer who did not share the belief that the aristocratic and rationalist civilization of his century represented the highest program so far achieved in man's development. He was dismayed by the egoistic life of pleasure of French society in his day, its lack of interest in public life, and its disregard of responsibility for social welfare. He called for a new sense of community mindedness, for a reformation not of the mind but of the heart, for nobler sentiments and emotions, for a simpler and more dedicated life. He thought that he found purer virtue, so sadly missed among the upper educated classes, among the common men, especially the peasants; they were still living near the source of all goodness, nature, unspoiled by the artificiality of civilization. For Rousseau it was no longer the aristocracy of birth and brain which stood in the center of the nation and gave it strength and direction, but the people themselves. Their active participation as equal citizens, held together by a feeling of brotherhood and mutual devotion, appeared to Rousseau the only moral and rational foundation of the state. At the same time he believed that the love of the national community, that an emotional and almost religious patriotism, would form the life-blood of the development of the human personality. In his Utopia—and Rousseau's *Social Contract* is as much a Utopia as Plato's *Republic*—Rousseau placed the sovereignty in a virtuous and united people, expressing their will in the "general will" which—in the Utopia—was a product of all the individual wills and yet could be different from any of the single wills, because it was the expression not of anything accidental or arbitrary, but of the reasonable and the good, of that virtuous patriotism that should animate each member.

Rousseau had a tremendous influence upon succeeding generations. His faith in the healing forces of nature, in the purity of the unspoilt human heart, his respect for the common people, his insistence on individual liberty, and his call to national patriotism, shaped much of the thinking of the Western world between 1770 and 1850. To the generation at the end of the eighteenth century the young republic across the Atlantic Ocean seemed like a realization of Rousseau's ideals, a national community without court and aristocracy, without state church and dominant priesthood, with people living the simple virtuous life of nature and innocence. There none of the vested interests and refinements of civilization seemed to hinder the growth of the spontaneous goodness of man. English liberty and Anglo-American moral enthusiasm seemed to have accomplished great things in the unfavorable climate of Britain and in the remoteness of the forests of the new world. How much greater things could France accomplish, a country favored by nature and civilization and highly renowned even under a despotic rule, if she would enjoy the blessings of reason and liberty!

The French Revolution. Such a regeneration of France under a reign of rational liberty was the primary purpose of the Revolution of 1789. The political and cultural leadership which France had exercised in the Western world under the absolute monarchy of the seventeenth century was manifestly in decline. The glory of the French arms was dimmed, great parts of the French Empire were lost, French public finances were at the brink of bankruptcy, the economic and intellectual life of the nation was shackled by outworn traditional institutions and laws. A feeling of deep uneasiness permeated the whole social body of France.

Originally, the French Revolution was inspired by the English model of constitutional liberty and limited government, but in France the authoritarian and absolutist tradition had done little to prepare the people for self-government and for the limitation of the powers of the sovereign. The absolute sovereignty of the king was replaced, as the Revolution progressed, by the absolute sovereignty of the people. In the spirit of Rousseau many Frenchmen called for a common patriotic enthusiasm and for an aroused national will. They looked for guidance to the alleged civic virtues of Sparta and of republican Rome, to their stern patriotism and their combative spirit. The nationalism that developed among the English-speaking peoples in the century between the Glorious Revolution and the outbreak of the French Revolution respected the privacy of the individual: the nation-state was regarded as a protective shell for the free interplay of individual forces. The nationalism of the French Revolution stressed that the duty and dignity of the citizen lay in political activity and his fulfillment in complete union with his nation-state.

The year 1789 witnessed the birth of the French nation in a sudden burst of enthusiasm. At the beginning of the year the centrifugal forces were still very strong in France. The division into provinces and cities with their own traditional laws, local economy, and systems of weights and measures, and into classes and castes with their own well-defined privileges, rights, and duties, set up unsurmountable barriers across all aspects of national life. In June, 1789, the traditional "Estates General" were reconvened for the first time since 1614; but the interval had been too long, the conditions of social life had in the meantime changed too much. The Estates were transformed under the pressure of the Third Estate into a National Assembly, a body no longer representing the separated estates, but the united nation. In August a further and tremendous step toward the birth of a French nation was taken: all geographic and class barriers fell, and the various classes and castes renounced all the infinite variety of their privileges and historical rights. National unity was for the first time achieved. In the same month, the Declaration of the Rights of Man and Citizen established the base of the new order, a nation of free individuals protected by law. In making the autonomous individual the starting point and the justifying end of all society, the Declaration was a consummation of the Age of Enlightenment, of the Glorious Revolution and of 1775-6. It protected the dignity, privacy, and happiness of the individual against the growing pressure by government and collectivity. Throughout the nineteenth century, faith in the Declaration succeeded in preventing the new nationalism from degenerating into an authoritarian and totalitarian creed. The danger of such a degeneration, however, was already present in the passion for national unity and for rational efficiency which underlay the French Revolution and which carried its nationalism far beyond that of England and the United States to an excessive centralization and a pseudo-religious creed.

The passions generated by this new nationalism threatened to break the dikes set up by eighteenth century respect for the individual and his sphere of liberty. The coming of the new nationalism coincided with the transition from rural to urban economy, with the growing social dynamism and mobilization of capitalism, with the quicker pace of life spurred on by mechanized industrialization and popular education. The traditionally organized and integrated villages and guilds gave way to the unorganized city masses increased by migration from the countryside. Masses and mass psychology created new problems. Lacking the stability of the traditional society, the masses were more easily swayed by utopian hopes and stirred by unreasonable fears. With the new mobility of the age, élites formed in more rapid succession and grew more skillful in manipulating the hopes and fears of the masses. For the élites and for the masses, nationalism became the foremost medium for organization and self-expression. (Later socialism began to compete with nationalism, until in Stalinism and Hitlerism the two dynamic and revolutionary mass appeals fused.) From the time of the French Revolution, social and economic questions played an increasingly important part, wherever nationalism penetrated. Thus between 1789 and 1795 the new nationalism led to two contradictory climaxes: the recognition of individual dignity in the Declaration, and the outburst of collective passions hostile to individual rights. Janus-like, the new age faced two ways.

The New Nationalism in Action. For historical reasons two ancient papal enclaves, Venaissin and Avignon, had survived within France. They invoked now the new principle of national self-determination for their union with France. The popular will was ascertained in a plebiscite. This method was followed in innumerable cases in the age of nationalism, but already as the French Revolution progressed, it was abused in the name of national interest. "Longings" for unity were manipulated, the popular will was falsified. Yet, in its beginning in France the feeling of national union and fraternity was spontaneous. It genuinely expressed itself in the *fête de la féderation* celebrated for the first time on July 14, 1790, the anniversary of the capture of the Bastille prison by the Parisian people. (*See Reading No. 2.*) In all the communities of France an altar of the fatherland was erected with the inscription: "The citizen is born, lives and dies for the fatherland." Before it the population assembled with patriotic songs, took an oath to uphold national unity and to obey and protect the supreme law giver, the sovereign people.

But this national unity did not last long. Political and religious divisions split the nation. The regenerated nation demanded its own regenerated church; it was distrustful of the traditional universal ties of the faith. Hitherto, all the fundamental acts of human life—birth, marriage, and death—had been the province of the church and received from it meaning and legitimacy. In 1792 the registration of all acts of family and personal status before the authorities of the new nation-state was made compulsory. In its first enthusiasm, the new patriotism went even further. Calendar days, new born children, and city streets received names expressing the new civic religion.

Many of the adherents of the traditional religious faith were forced into a conflict of conscience between the old religious and the new national dogmas and authorities. Until then education had been left largely in the hands of the church. The new nationalism also brought a fundamental change thereto.

The French Revolution established the first comprehensive system of national education to raise new generations of virtuous and patriotic citizens. Education was for the first time regarded as a duty and chief interest of the nation. Only a common education, it was felt, could realize the unity of the fatherland and the union of its citizens. The emphasis shifted from the classics and the humanities to patriotic songs and history, and at least in theory to manual training and gymnastic exercises. Their new pride in the nation wished to make its capital the artistic center of the world. In 1793 the former royal palace of the Louvre was transformed into the first national museum. The arts, above all music, were no longer to serve only individual enjoyment or religious sentiment. They were to arouse national passions. The famous patriotic song, the *Marseillaise,* stirred the people when arranged for massed brass instruments. National festivals were planned as mighty spectacles in which the people themselves participated and played a leading role. Festivals and schools advanced also the spread of French as the only language used throughout the nation, where formerly among Bretons and Flemish, Basques and Alsatians, Catalans and Provenceaux, native idioms had almost exclusively been used.

Before the Revolution higher education in France stressed Latin more than French, classical authors more than French writers. The new nationalism changed that. None expressed the new feeling better than Maximilien Robespierre (1758-1794) in his *Report to the National Convention* on national festivals on the 18th Floréal, 1794: "Yes, this delightful land which we inhabit and which nature caresses with love is made to be the domain of liberty and happiness. This sensitive and proud people is truly born for glory and virtue. Oh, my fatherland, if fate had caused me to be born in a foreign and distant country, I would have addressed heaven continuously for thy prosperity; I would have been moved to tears by the recital of thy combats and thy virtues; my attentive soul would have followed with a restless ardor all the movements of thy glorious revolution; I would have envied the fate of thy citizens; I would have envied that of thy representatives! I am French, I am one of thy representatives! . . . Oh, sublime people! Accept the sacrifices of my whole being. Happy is the man who is born in your midst; happier is he who can die for your happiness."

The New Nationalism and War. The French Revolution, which at first proclaimed a message of universal peace, drove France and Europe into a war more prolonged and more devastating than any since the wars of religion. In the turmoil ancient states disappeared, new loyalties were born, national passions were aroused for the first time, from Ireland to Serbia and Russia, from Spain and Italy to Norway. The wars of the French Republic appealed to a degree unknown before to the national devotion and unity of the people. On September 25, 1792, Georges Jacques Danton (1759-1794) demanded that "France must be an indivisible whole: she must have unity of representation. The citizens of Marseilles wish to clasp hands with the citizens of Dunkerque. I, therefore, ask the death penalty against whomsoever wishes to destroy the unity of France, and I propose that the National Convention decree unity of representation and execution as the foundations of the government to be established. Not without trembling will the Austrians learn of this holy harmony; then, I swear to you, our enemies will perish." This passion seemed to bear fruit: the newly organized republican armies defeated the enemy. Not the monarchy but the nation triumphed on the battlefields. The victory converted France from the loyal monarchism of 1789 to the republican nationalism of 1793, from the peaceful spirit of eighteenth century Enlightenment to the aggressive dynamism of modern nationalism.

The initial victories were soon followed by reverses made even more dangerous by internal insurrections. They aroused in the leading French minority the bitter determination to concentrate all forces in order to fight out the war and to liquidate without mercy all domestic opposition and disunity. The Terror saved the Republic but it did not strengthen in the nascent French nationalism the spirit of compromise and agreement and the respect for liberty under law. Robespierre regarded only the "sincere and virtuous patriots" as true citizens; the others had to be forced into becoming true children of the fatherland. Threatened by the despotism of kings, Jean Paul Marat (1743-1793) exclaimed that France had to organize the despotism of liberty. Only a dictatorship of virtuous men, devoted exclusively to the interest of the whole nation and reflecting the true general will, seemed able to serve the fatherland. Any opposition to its leadership appeared treason to the nation. Everything had to be sacrificed to the fatherland. The whole nation was to be mobilized, the war had to be nationalized in all its aspects. "When the fatherland is in danger," Danton proclaimed on September 2, 1792, "no one can refuse his service without being declared infamous and a traitor to the fatherland. Pronounce the death penalty for every citizen who refuses to march, or who directly or indirectly opposes the measures taken for public safety."

In the eighteenth century, wars had been fought with limited contingents and limited efforts. For the first time in 1793 the National Convention requisitioned everybody and everything in the service of the nation, at least in theory. Men and industry were mobilized, writers and artists were engaged to kindle the people's enthusiasm. All these efforts bore fruit. The invading armies were repelled. The young French nation was saved, but it was saved by the army, and even after the hour of danger had passed, the army remained preeminent in national thought to a degree unknown in the English speaking nations. The new French nation-state emerged covered with greater military glory than ever in the days of her mightiest kings. *"O terre des guerriers! O France! O ma patrie!"* a republican poet addressed the fatherland in 1797. The popularity of the army helped the ascent of General Napoleon Buonaparte (1769-1823) to power.

Napoleon. Napoleon appealed to the new French nationalism, but he himself was not a nationalist. He put the finishing touch to the centralized nation-state. with its

unified system of law, bureaucracy, and education, but
he did it in the spirit of the eighteenth century enlightened despots. He was ready to use national aspirations as
far as they seemed to fit into his system, without having
any sincere desire to satisfy them. He gave vague encouragement to nationalist desires in Italy and Poland
but he subordinated them to the momentary interest of
his empire and dynasty. Napoleon's ambition was not
the nation-state, not even the expanded nation-state, but
the renewal of Charlemagne's or Caesar's empire. His
instrument was not the people aroused to a new sense of
patriotism but the power of the state, a mechanism forged
by the princes of the Renaissance and improved by the
absolute monarchs. Napoleon was defeated not only by
his overbearing ambition but also by the new force which
his wars aroused abroad and which he did not understand—the nationalism of the European peoples, especially that of the Germans. What these peoples—
Germans, Italians, Spaniards, Russians,—did not learn
from the French Revolution—the spirit of 1789 hardly
touched them—they learned from Napoleon: nationalism,
not as a vehicle of individual liberty but as adoration of
collective power.

— 3 —

NATIONALISM AND TRADITION

In the modern West, nationalism which arose in the
eighteenth century, the Age of Enlightenment, was predominantly a political movement to limit governmental
power and to secure civic rights. Its purpose was to create
a liberal and rational civil society representing the middle-
class and the philosophy of John Locke. When nation-

alism, after the Napoleonic wars, penetrated to other lands—Central and Eastern Europe or to Spain and Ireland—it came to lands which were in political ideas and social structure less advanced than the modern West. There was only a weak middle-class: the nation was split between a feudal aristocracy and a rural proletariat. Thus nationalism became there first a cultural movement, the dream and hope of scholars and poets. This rising nationalism, as the whole modern social and intellectual development outside Western Europe, was influenced by the West. Yet this very dependence on the West hurt the pride of the native educated class, as soon as it began to develop its own nationalism, and led it to oppose the "alien" example and its liberal and rational outlook. Thus the new nationalism looked for its justification and differentiation from the West to the heritage of its past. It often extolled ancient traditions in contrast to the Western Age of Enlightenment. While English and American nationalism was, in its origin, connected with the concepts of individual liberty and represented nations firmly constituted in their political life, the new nationalism, not rooted in a similar political and social reality, lacked self-assurance. Its inferiority complex was often compensated by over-emphasis. German, Russian, or Indian nationalism appeared as something deeper than Western nationalism, richer in problems and potentialities. The quest for its meaning, the musing about a national "soul" or "mission," the discussion of its relationship to the West, all these became characteristic of the new nationalism.

Johann Gottfried Herder. Nationalism in the West was based on the concept of a society which was the product of political factors; German nationalism substituted for the legal and rational concept of "citizenship" which the Germans call *Staatsbürgerschaft*—the infinitely vaguer concept of "folk"—in German *Volk*—which lent itself more easily to the embroideries of imagination and the excitations of emotion. The folk's roots supposedly reached into the soil of the remote past; it did not grow in the bright light of rational political ends but in the long unconscious development of the people, the very people whom Rousseau had proclaimed the true embodiment of the goodness of nature. Rousseau's German disciple, Herder (1744-1803). developed the theory of the folk-soul or the folk-spirit (*Volksgeist*) and its roots in the long chain of national tradition from hoary primitive times on.

Herder viewed nature and history as organic growths, as self-revelations of the Divine—innumerable manifestations of life, an endless creative process in which attention should be centered not on the general and common but on the individual and unique. Herder was the first to insist that human civilization lives not in its universal but in its national and peculiar manifestations. The creative forces of the universal individualized themselves primarily not in the single human being but in the collective personalities of human communities. Men were above all members of their national communities; only as such could they be really creative, through the medium of their folk language and their folk traditions. Folk songs, and folk-lore, entirely neglected until then, were regarded by Herder as the great manifestations of the unspoilt creative spirit.

Herder was not a nationalist in the modern sense of the word. He did not demand the creation of a nation-state nor the unification of nations. To him nationality was not a political or biological but a spiritual and moral concept. Politically he remained an enlightened humanitarian and pacifist. Though born in the lands of the king of Prussia, he hated Prussian militarism and gladly accepted Russian rule. In 1769 he wrote that "The states of the king of Prussia will not be happy until they are divided up," and he characterized their inhabitants as "too much ignorant Germans and too much subjects." He was in no way partial to the Germans. Each nationality was to him a manifestation of the Divine, and, therefore, something sacred which should not be destroyed but cultivated. He equally respected all national languages. Each man, Herder thought, could be himself only by thinking and creating in his own mother-tongue. He was the first to claim that the rights of nationality were above all the rights of language, he claimed these rights also, and above all, for the languages which were at that time only spoken by illiterate peasants and deemed to be without future or dignity.

Herder was deeply convinced that true nationalism would promote the cause of peace. Princes and states may think of war, politics and power; nations and father-lands, Herder wrote, could think only of peaceful human coexistence. "They would never wash their hands in blood, and even if forced to shed blood they would do it as if it were their own blood." He was convinced that the essential conditions for a good and civilized folk life were better fulfilled by the peaceful Slav peasant peoples than by the Germans, a proud warrior nation. (*See Reading No. 3.*) Herder predicted for the Slavs a glorious future, and his sympathy for the Slav peoples, languages, and folkways was a powerful stimulant for the awakening of national consciousness among young Slav intellectuals at the beginning of the nineteenth century. Herder's emphasis on cultural national individuality and its rights and his high evaluation of popular traditions and folkways deeply influenced nationalist thought in Central and Eastern Europe.

Wars of National Liberation. In the eighteenth century, intellectual life in Germany, Italy, and Russia, as throughout Europe, was under the influence of the French Enlightenment. Its rational and universal ideas were generally accepted and French was the common language of European intellectual society. The nationalism of the French Revolution and the Napoleonic wars changed all that. French victories and domination aroused not only the desire for the creation of other modern nation-states after the French model, they turned the attention also to French ideas. This new nationalism did not penetrate to the people; it remained confined to the intellectuals, and even among them only to part of them. Many saw in Napoleon not the hated conqueror but the great personality and reformer and praised him in speeches and poems. But, as a result of the protracted wars and of the emphasis on French nationalism, national sentiment gathered strength until it reached its first peak in the Russian "Great Patriotic War" of 1812, which immensely enhanced Russian self-esteem by the victory over Napo-

leon, and in the German "War of Liberation" of 1813
which led to the Battle of the Nations at Leipzig in
October 1813 and to the entrance of Prussian and
Austrian troops into Paris in the following year.

In Italy and Germany Napoleon indirectly supported
the rise of nationalism by abolishing many of the
medieval relics and by laying the foundations for modern
government. In Italy the first kingdom of Italy was his
creation, and the French Marshal, Joachim Murat (1767-
1815), whom Napoleon installed in 1808 as king of
Naples, made himself in 1814 when Napoleon's star
waned the champion of Italian unity. But popular support
for the national cause was slight. Patriotism remained
for the time being confined to poets and writers of whom
the best known were Vittorio Alfieri (1749-1803), who
in his *Il Misogallo* furiously attacked the French for
daring to lead other peoples in civilization and liberty
while the palm of leadership belonged by history and
nature to the Italians, and Ugo Foscolo (1778-1827),
who in his ode *De' Sepolcri* summoned the mighty dead
of Italy's past from their tombs to fight again the battle
of their country. On the return of the Austrians in 1814,
Foscolo as a convinced patriot went into exile, first into
Switzerland and then to England, the same road which
twenty years later his younger fellow patriot, Mazzini,
was to take.

A similar turn from liberal cosmopolitanism and friendship for France to a nationalism opposed to France and
looking back to its traditions was exemplified in Russia
by the writer and historian, Nicolai Karamzin (1765-
1826). As a young man he was an enthusiastic Franco-
phile; later, he wrote a History of the Russian State, a
work that gained wide popularity and aroused great pride
in Russia's past and ancient institutions, which Karamzin
glorified. "The existence of each individual," he wrote,
"is intimately bound up with the fatherland; the noble
sentiment which ties us to it forms part of the love of
ourselves. Universal history embellishes the world before
our mind; that of Russia beautifies the fatherland, the
center of all our existence and of our affections." Karamzin wished, writing in 1812, that the Russians of his
time would be as convinced as their ancestors were "that

the Orthodox Russian is the most perfect citizen on earth and Holy Russia the first state." In the struggle against Napoleon, who saw himself as the heir of Charlemagne and Caesar, the Russians regarded their emperor as the rightful heir of the Roman emperors of Constantinople, of the Chistian Roman Empire of which Holy Russia was the truly Christian heir. To the popular Russian imagination Napoleon represented in 1812 the anti-Christ leading the hosts of the heretic West against Moscow, the citadel of the true faith.

German Romanticism. The connection between nationalism and tradition received its strongest expression in German romanticism. Romanticism as an esthetic revolution was a European movement, a resort to imagination which produced a poetry richer in emotional depth and more potent in magic evocation than eighteenth-century poetry had been. But German romanticism, poor in creative genius, wished to be more than poetry, it was an interpretation of history and society, of the totality of human life, which mobilized the fascination of the past to fight against the principles of 1789. Starting as extreme individualists the German romanticists developed the opposite longing for a true, harmonious community, an organic folk-community, which would immerse the individual in the unbroken chain of tradition. Such an ideal folk-community seemed to the romanticists to have existed in the Germanic Middle Ages. They edited and praised the medieval sagas and poetry, folk songs, and fairy tales. Medieval castles appealed to their imagination as a reminder of past national glory and beauty. Even nature became an attribute of nationality—German forests and German rivers, especially the Rhine, which impressed Friedrich Schlegel (1772-1829) as "the all too faithful image of our fatherland, our history and our character."

To the optimistic idealization of the future, so characteristic of the Age of Enlightenment, the romanticists opposed a similar idealization of the national past. Adam Müller (1779-1829), the political philosopher of German romanticism, admired Edmund Burke and claimed that the eighteenth century British politician belonged more to the Germans than to the British who, according to

Müller, never fully understood him. But the German romanticists had none of Burke's practical wisdom, nor his respect for individual liberty and constitutional rights. To them the nation-state or folk-state was not a societal organization based upon human law with the purpose of assuring man's liberty, security, and happiness, but an organic personality, God's creation like the individual himself, only infinitely greater and more powerful and the fountainhead of all individual life. Though the great German philosopher, George Wilhelm Friedrich Hegel (1770-1831), was not a romanticist but a rationalist, his concept of the state resembled that of the romanticists. For him the State was the Divine Idea as it exists on earth. (*See Reading No. 4.*)

Early German Nationalism. Romanticism influenced the character of the incipient German nationalism during the anti-Napoleonic wars. The greatest German minds of the preceding period were opposed to nationalism. The philosopher, Immanuel Kant (1724-1804), was a representative of the liberal, individualist, and cosmopolitan Enlightenment. The two greatest German poets, Johann Wolfgang von Goethe (1749-1832) and Friedrich Schiller (1759-1805), turned not to the folk-community of the Middle Ages but to the individualism of Greek antiquity as a source of regeneration. Goethe throughout his life and even during the wars against Napoleon expressed his deep admiration for the French and French civilization. "There is as little for us in the somber old-German epoch as we could get out of Serbian folk-songs or other primitive folk poetry," the old Goethe told his secretary, Eckermann. "One reads it, of course, and for a while is interested, but only to cast it aside. Mankind is already too much shadowed by its own passions and dooms to need still more darkening by contemplating the gloom of primitive and bararic times. Mankind needs clarity and serenity, needs to turn to those epochs of art and literature in which superior human beings achieved a finished culture and then, serene within themselves, were able to pour out the blessings of that culture upon others."

Goethe saw in Napoleon a great human phenomenon embodying beyond all ethnic or national frontiers the

spirit of historical development. His contemporary, the
German philosopher Johann Gottlieb Fichte (1762-
1814), like most German nationalists saw in the Prussian
state the citadel of culture and ordered liberty. When
Prussia was defeated by Napoleon in 1806, Fichte's
Addresses to the German Nation, which he delivered in
Berlin in the winter of 1807-1808, called the Germans
not only to national regeneration but to cultural world
leadership. Through their language, mind, and history
the Germans alone were destined for it. Among the
civilized peoples of Europe, the Germans alone, Fichte
maintained, spoke an original language, not like the
French, English, Spaniards, or Italians, who, in spite of
their at least partly Germanic origin, had stultified their
intellectual life by the use of an adopted or derived
language. Fichte was convinced that among the modern
nations the Germans alone were capable of the highest
perfection. Therefore, they had to resist Napoleon, as
their ancestors had resisted Roman domination. Should
the Germans succumb to the French, it would mean the
end of all the best hopes of mankind and of culture.

A similar attitude was taken by Ernst Moritz Arndt
(1769-1860), who also maintained that the Germans
excelled over all other nations by having preserved their
racial purity and by speaking the purest language. Herder
had believed in the equal rights of all national tongues.
The new German nationalists, however, proclaimed the
superiority of their language as against the Latin and Slav
languages. At the same time Arndt centered upon language as the factor constituting a nation; all German
speaking people had to be united in a common fatherland. Arndt was one of the most powerful agitators for
the national uprising of the Germans against the French;
of similar importance was Friedrich Ludwig Jahn (1778-
1852) or "Father Jahn" as he was commonly called.
He was the author of *Deutsches Volkstum* (*German
Folkdom,* 1810), in which he glorified the originality of
the German folk, a divine creative force. Jahn had a
great influence upon three movements which have remained characteristic for nationalism in Central and
Eastern Europe and have even spread later to Asia:
military free-corps of patriotic volunteers; gymnastic

associations for the training of patriotic fighters; and student unions imbued with nationalistic enthusiasm. All three groups were filled with revolutionary activism; responding to appeals overcharged with emotionalism and stressing the disciplined dedication to national service, they identified it with a strangely conceived "freedom" which had little in common with the Western concepts of individual liberty.

The war of 1813 against Napoleon was fought by the armies of Russia, Prussia, and Austria. No German political entity existed then. The only "German" forces which participated in the war was the free-corps, commanded by Adolf Freiherr von Lützow, a band of patriotic volunteers in black uniforms. Many of them were members of the gymnastic organization, the *Turnerschaft,* which Jahn had founded in 1810 in Berlin. These gymnastic organizations, later imitated by other peoples—among the Czechs and other Slavs they were called *Sokols* or Falcons—did not serve primarily the purpose of physical education or the ideals of fair play, of sportsmanship, or of the good loser. They were a preparation for a nationalist end and served it by the spirit of disciplined unity and militant preparedness. They were a potential army trained for the ardently desired day of the battle against the enemy. The same spirit animated the student fraternities or *Burschenschaften,* of which the first was founded at the University of Jena in 1815. They accepted black-red-gold as the colors of German unity. All these youth movements were to prepare national unification and independence. Jahn never tired of calling upon the Germans to protect their minds, their habits, and their character against all alien influences. He was convinced that the hero who by fanaticism and fury would unite the nation and make it powerful would be venerated by the people as a saviour and would be forgiven for all his sins. For nothing could be allowed to stand in the way of the one ultimate goal—the formation of the nation-state.

NATIONALISM AND REVOLUTION

Post-Napoleonic Disillusionment. The defeat of Napoleon in 1814 and 1815 did not realize the desires and ambitions of the nationalistic youth. In France, deprived of her imperial glory, many nationalists smarted under the reduction of her territory to the frontiers of 1790 and saw in Napoleon's defeat at Waterloo a national humiliation. The Congress of Vienna gave a limited satisfaction to the national demands of the Germans and the Poles but none to those of the Italians. After all Germany had formed until 1806 the Holy Roman Empire of the German Nation, and Poland had known an independent national statehood until 1795. No similar Italian state had ever been in existence. The various German states were organized in 1815 into a loose confederation, called the German *Bund*, and a major part of Poland was constituted as an autonomous kingdom with its own national rights within the domains of the Russian Empire. The former Austrian Netherlands (Belgium) were joined with Holland into the Kingdom of the Netherlands; Norway, until then a part of Denmark, was joined with Sweden but under its own national constitution. On the whole, however, the territorial arrangement of 1815 took little cognizance of the new nationalist aspirations. After a quarter of a century of incessant wars and changes the peacemakers at Vienna stressed above all peace and order. The Holy Alliance of the Princes, under the leadership of the Emperors of Russia and Austria and the King of Prussia, the principal victors over Napoleon, was to assure in a spirit of Christian morality and brotherly solidarity the tranquillity of Europe.

The peoples on the whole were not dissatisfied with the conservative order after the years of violent turmoil. But the youth and the intellectuals, stirred by the expectations aroused by the new principles of the French Revolution, by the daring of Napoleon and by the emotional fervor of romanticism, resented the unheroic stillness of the Restoration period which the Congress of Vienna inaugurated and of which the Holy Alliance and its champion, the Austrian Chancellor, Prince Metternich, became the hated symbol. In their common hostility against the Holy Alliance of the Princes the patriots, as they called themselves after the example set at the beginning of the French Revolution, of all nations felt their close affinity. Their nationalism stressed the collaboration of the peoples against the monarchs and the desire for liberal constitutions to limit the absolutism of the rulers; a Holy Alliance of the Peoples was proclaimed against the Holy Alliance of the Princes. The patriots of one people showed their active sympathy whenever and wherever patriots of other peoples revolted against the order established at the Congress of Vienna. At a time when in Europe outside Britain a free public opinion and a constitutional political life hardly existed, the patriots formed secret societies and believed in plottings and uprisings to achieve their aims.

The great advance of historical scholarship in the first half of the nineteenth century powerfully contributed to the new nationalism of the educated classes. Everywhere the documents of the past were collected and edited; the people began to take a new interest in their own history and drew from it a new pride. In Germany the great patriot, Baron Heinrich Friedrich Karl vom und zum Stein (1757-1831), promoted the publication of the *Monumenta Germaniae historica,* the medieval sources of German history. Each of the published volumes carried the inscription *Sanctus amor patriae dat animum* (The sacred love of the fatherland animates us). Similar publications were undertaken in other nations. (*See Reading No. 5.*) Among the nationalities which had lost their political statehood, historians like František Palacký (1798-1876) among the Czechs gave a new luster and a new meaning to almost extinct memories. This fascination by the past was most helpful to the first successful national uprising, that of the Greeks in 1821. (*See Reading No. 6.*) It was followed all over Europe with great sympathy, for were the Greeks not the descendants of Homer and Praxiteles, of Aeschylus and Socrates, of Plato and Demosthenes, and would not an independent Greece mean the rebirth of all the ancient glories? The immense hopes aroused by the Greek war of independence are an example of that strange alliance of historicism and nationalism which believes not only in the legendary continuity of blood but even in the equally mystical survival of the national genius over many centuries.

    Mazzini.   The revolutionary agitations reached an initial climax in July 1830, when the Bourbon monarchy was overthrown in Paris and Louis Philippe ascended the French throne as the citizen-king. The French example inspired short-lived revolutionary uprisings in Italy, Germany, and Poland. They failed miserably because they were nowhere supported by the people. Only in Belgium did the revolution succeed. On August 25, 1830, in Brussels, the Belgian capital, students attended a performance of the then popular opera, *La Muette de Portici,* by Auber, which glorifies an uprising of the Neapolitan people in 1647 against Spanish rule. The students were stirred by the duet *"Amor sacré de la patrie"* (O sacred love of the fatherland) into a manifestation which after several developments led to the recognition of Belgian independence by the European powers on October 14, 1831. On the whole, the revolution of 1830 was successful in Western Europe; it liberalized there the constitutions of France, Belgium, and Britain; it brought the middle-classes into power and carried on the historical development which had started in 1688 and 1789. But in Central and Eastern Europe the old order remained unshaken in 1830. The uprisings were quickly suppressed. From Italy, Poland, and Germany a stream of refugees poured into Switzerland and England. Among them was the Italian, Giuseppe Mazzini (1805-1872).

    Mazzini's thought was typical of the nationalism of that period. He became the indefatigable apostle of nationalist thought and action, carried on by a youth educated in the right spirit. Faced by the inertia of the people and the pusillanimity of the middle-classes, Mazzini called for the energetic leadership of Young Italy. "The secret of raising the masses," he wrote, "lies in the hands of those who show themselves ready to fight and conquer at their head." He called upon the youth and the people to sacrifice everything to the attainment of a united, centralized, strong nation. He was even convinced that true art could flourish only in such a nation. He forgot that art did bloom in exemplary greatness in Italy in the late Middle Ages and in the Renaissance, when there was no Italian country, and that this art had inspired mankind when it did not seek to arouse a nation. Like so many nationalists Mazzini in the fire of his apostolate misread history. And he equally misread it when he extolled the Italian revolution which he wished to lead far beyond the French revolution, which he regarded as negative. The French Revolution had established liberty and destroyed the old world; on its ruins a new faith had to arise to fill the void left by the French Revolution. Mazzini was convinced that only the Italians could bring a positive message for the new age and establish that unity which Rome had already twice brought to mankind, in the age of the Caesars and in the age of the Popes. A third and greater Rome, the Rome of the People, would bring leadership and unity to Europe to a higher degree than Rome of Antiquity or of the Middle Ages ever could. "Today a third mission is dawning for our Italy," Mazzini wrote in 1858, "as much vaster than the missions of old as the Italian People, the free and united country, will be greater and more powerful than Caesar or Popes." (*See Reading No. 7.*)

Young Europe. In 1831 Mazzini founded a movement, *Giovine Italia* (Young Italy). As an emigré in Switzerland he inspired similar movements among the German and Polish emigrés and tried to constitute them into an association of Young Europe. These secret revolutionary organizations did not amount to much as actual fomenters of revolution. But Mazzini had coined a new word and concept which reverberated throughout the nationalist movements of the nineteenth century as far as Young Turkey and Young China. Mazzini believed in the fundamental comradeship of all the young nationalist movements. The years between 1830 and 1848 were a period of stirring hope and generous optimism. Mazzini had an unshakeable faith—in the tradition of Rousseau

and Herder—in the goodness of the people while governments and states appeared to him as corrupt. This faith
was shared by the French historian, Jules Michelet (1798-
1874), whose book *Le Peuple,* written in 1846, expressed
the feeling of heroic patriotism and messianic fervor of
the period. Like Mazzini, Michelet believed that the
People incarnated nationality and that the diverse nationalities, once they would be freed from the despotism of
government, would form a peaceful European union.
Michelet was a friend and supporter of the Polish poet,
Adam Mickiewicz (1798-1855), who then lived in Paris
as an emigré. This great poet, after the failure of the
uprising of 1831, in which he had not participated, became one of the leaders of Polish nationalism. Through
their messianic fervor he and his fellow-emigré poets
upheld Polish confidence in the midst of defeat and
despair. Polish martyrdom received a meaning by this
messianic interpretation. Poland was proclaimed the
Christ among the nations; innocently crucified, it would
rise again and its liberation would become the liberation
of all mankind from oppression and war.

Mickiewicz, Mazzini, and Michelet, like the Young
Europeans in general, were nationalists and democrats.
They realized that the wakening of the nationalities demanded the active participation of the people. In the
industrialized countries of Western Europe the call to the
working classes was then frequently couched in nationalist terms, appealing to their patriotic pride and resum-
ing the slogans of the Parisians of 1792-3. In Central
and Eastern Europe the problem confronting the patriots
was that of the emancipation of the peasants. The Polish
national cause had been largely defeated by the apathy
of the rural masses and their distrust of the nobility. The
Polish democrats, among whom the historian Joachim
Lelewel (1786-1861) was the most prominent, pressed
for a greater consideration to be given to popular education and to the equality of all classes. But Lelewel, who
at the University of Vilna had been the teacher of
Mickiewicz, like so many of his fellow countrymen spent
the last thirty years of his life in exile, unable to influence the developments at home. More successful was
the Danish parson and poet, Nikolai Frederick Severin

Grundtvig (1783-1872), a fervent patriot who established folk high schools among the Danish peasants where the national poetry and history formed an essential part of the instruction.

Similarly, the peasant problem was solved in the nineteenth century in Ireland, politically by the emancipation of the Catholic voters throughout Great Britain and Ireland in 1829, socially and economically through the land reforms of successive British governments, beginning with Gladstone's Irish Land Act of 1870. But the Irish aspirations went farther. Under the leadership of Daniel O'Connell (1775-1847) an agitation was started for the repeal of the union of 1800 between Britain and Ireland and the reestablishment of an Irish Parliament. A more radical note was sounded by Young Ireland, which in 1842 founded the Dublin weekly *Nation*. Young Ireland went beyond the Catholic framework of O'Connell's agitation. It appealed to all the inhabitants of Ireland, Catholics and Protestants, Celts, Normans and Saxons. At the same time, however, it exalted the great past of ancient Ireland, which in the early Middle Ages had been the center from which education and Christanity radiated over parts of Europe. Young Ireland's greatest poet, Thomas Osborne Davis (1814-1845), was a Protestant who in his poems glorified among others King Dathi, the last pagan monarch of Ireland who had extended his conquests to the continent of Europe and invaded the Roman Empire.

The revolutionary unrest of the period spread also to Spanish America. Under the influence of the American and French revolutions, the Creole population, Americans of Spanish descent who felt treated as second-rate subjects compared with the Spaniards sent from the old country to fill all important positions, rose to the leadership of Simon Bolívar (1783-1830), a Venezuelan, and José de San Martin (1778-1850), an Argentinian, and fought to gain national independence for the Spanish colonies. By 1823 the Spanish rule was terminated. But the development was different from that in Anglo-America. Spain had offered to its American subjects as little training in self-government and democracy as to its own subjects at home. The Ibero-Americans could as little overcome this political and social backwardness in the nineteenth century as the Spaniards could. Like Spain herself Spanish-America could not apply the principles of democracy and federalism which Anglo-America introduced, both in the United States and Canada. In most Spanish-American republics anarchy and dictatorship alternated. Military leaders, known as *caudillos*, frequently seized and held power. Only the former Portuguese colony of Brazil knew under the monarchy of Pedro II (1840-1889) a more orderly continuous development. The Indian native populations remained in most cases outside the new nations. Only in the twentieth century were efforts made, by far the most important one in Mexico, to integrate them into the nation, to revive their ancient folk culture, to study their history and traditions, and to bring about a synthesis of the American and Spanish civilizations.

National Movements in Central-Eastern Europe. In 1815 Central-Eastern Europe was ruled by the three monarchs united in the Holy Alliance and by the Ottoman (Turkish) Sultans. Great Russians, Germans, and Turks, these were the three dominant nationalities all over the vast territory inhabited by many and varied ethnic groups. These groups had nothing in common except the lack of national statehood; they represented different racial, linguistic, and religious divisions. The most numerous linguistic group were the Slavs among whom the Great Russians were the only independent nation. The Russians were Greek Orthodox as were the Serbs and Bulgars who lived in the Balkan peninsula under Turkish domination. The Roman Catholic Poles who had formed a mighty commonwealth in the eighteenth century, including many non-Polish peoples—Lithuanians, Ukrainians, and Byelorussians—were by 1815 part of the lands ruled by the Emperor of Russia, the King of Prussia, and the Emperor of Austria. The latter monarch ruled also over the Roman Catholic Czechs in Bohemia and Moravia and the Slovaks in northwestern Hungary, and over the equally Roman Catholic Croats and Slovenes who lived in the southern part of his Empire, near and akin to the Serbs. The Slav Ukrainians and the Byelorussians, most of them Greek Orthodox, others Greek

Catholics, were in their majority subject peoples of the Great Russians. As a result of their geographic situation the Ukrainians formed in modern times a battleground for Russian and Polish imperial conflicts, though the Ukrainians are a numerous people, second among the Slavs only to the Great Russians themselves.

Though the Slavs formed the majority of the populations between Germany and Italy, they intermingled with other nationalities living there, making the ethnic map of Central-Eastern Europe even more checkered. Along the Baltic Sea we find the Lutheran Finns, Estonians and Latvians and the Roman Catholic Lithuanians. Throughout the expanse of the Russian Empire various nationalities, mostly of Finnish or Tartar descent, were living, which in the course of Russian imperial expansion had been absorbed but not assimilated. In the Hungarian plain along the middle Danube the Roman Catholic Magyars had settled, and to the north of the lower Danube the Greek Orthodox Romanians had preserved a Latin dialect from the time that the ancient Romans had there established their Dacian province. In the southern part of the Balkans and in Asia Minor Greeks were settled; their religion and culture played a dominant role among the Slavs and Romanians in the Balkan peninsula who were politically ruled by the Sultan in Constantinople but spiritually and socially by the Greek Patriarch of Constantinople. In addition there were the Albanians in the western Balkans, partly Mohammedans, partly Greek Orthodox and partly Roman Catholic, and finally the orthodox Armenians in Asia Minor.

The century between 1815 and 1918 witnessed the struggle for national independence on the part of all these nationalities. By 1918 the Russian, Austrian, Prussian, and Ottoman dynasties had lost their power. But everywhere throughout this territory, except in the case of the Baltic peoples, the creation of independent and satisfied nation-states after the Western model encountered almost insuperable difficulties. In most cases it was impossible to draw clear-cut ethnic frontiers. Yet it was not only the intermingling of racial, linguistic, and religious groups which presented obstacles to solutions acceptable to all the elements involved. Even more dangerous to peace than the conflicting "natural" rights of the nationalities were their "historical rights." Each nationality claimed the frontiers as they existed at the time of its greatest historical expansion, frontiers which disregarded the ethnic and historical development of intervening centuries. Many territories had formed at different times part of different national spheres and were now claimed by each of the nationalities. Thus nationalism did not lead as Mazzini and Young Europe had expected to a fraternal association of neighboring peoples and to international peace. The awakening of the peoples released collective passions which became in the century after 1848 the most potent factor in arousing hatreds and fomenting wars. Democratic federalism in multi-ethnic empires would have offered a solution; it demanded, however, a preference for orderly development by compromise similar to that pursued in the English speaking world. But on the European continent such an approach was successfully applied only in Switzerland, where, after a brief civil war in the Fall of 1847, democratic federalism provided the framework for the peaceful development in liberty of populations speaking German, French, and Italian, and having highly diversified traditions and religious backgrounds. Outside Switzerland, German, French, and Italian speaking populations fought bitter wars against each other in the last one hundred years and sacrificed liberty to the demands of nationality. The nineteenth century English liberal Catholic, Lord Acton, foresaw the danger of this development. (*See Reading No. 8.*) Nowhere was this danger felt more acutely than in Central-Eastern Europe after the success there of the nationalist revolutions.

This success was prepared by the cultural efforts of scholars and poets. Under the influence of Herder they concentrated on writing literature in the vernacular languages and in exploring the folk traditions. Until the beginning of the nineteenth century the educated classes had used French, German, and Latin as their language. Now the young generation set out to write grammars and compile dictionaries of their native tongues, to translate foreign works, to collect folksongs, to explore national antiquities, to do research in historical chronicles and archives. All that was not done for its own sake but *ad majorem nationis gloriam,* to enhance the glory of one's own nation, and to establish its equality, if not its superiority in relation to its neighbors and to the more advanced nations. Among the Slovaks Jan Kollár (1794-1852), a Lutheran minister and poet, lamented in his sonnet cycle, *Slavy dcera* (The Daughter of Slava, 1824), the decline of Slav power, called for the unity of all Slav peoples and prophesied their future greatness, peopling the immense territory from the Elbe River to the Pacific Ocean, from the Arctic Sea to the Mediterranean. Among the Czechs Palacký recalled the Hussite wars of the fourteenth century when the Czechs had been the first fighters for the Reformation, and Karel Havlíček (1821-1854) dedicated his journalistic and critical talent to the democratic education of his countrymen.

Among the Southern Slavs (Serbs, Croats, and Slovenes) the Napoleonic wars had aroused a new national sentiment. Some Serbs under their Orthodox prince-bishop had maintained their independence from the Turks in the inaccessible highlands of the Black Mountains or Montenegro; in 1805 other Serbs in the valley of the Morava revolted against the Turks and established there an autonomous principality in 1830. The Serbs under Ottoman rule were culturally much more backward than the Serbs and other Southern Slavs who lived in the Habsburg domains. Among the latter, Croatians and Slovenes were incorporated for a short time by Napoleon into his empire; following his custom, he called the new provinces with the ancient Roman name Illyria. As a result, the national feeling awakened there among the Southern Slavs became known as Illyrian. Its leading spokesman was Ludevit Gaj (1809-1872), its greatest scholar Vuk Karadžić (1787-1864), who was foremost in creating a common literary language for the Croats and Serbs and in collecting their *pesme* or folk-songs. Illyrian nationalism soon gave way to the distinct and often conflicting national movements of Serbs, Croats, and Slovenes, but a feeling of close Southern Slav or Yugoslav affinity of these three peoples was preserved.

The Romanians inhabited the Turkish autonomous principalities of Moldavia and Wallachia under Orthodox princes of Greek descent appointed by the Sultan, and Transylvania, a part of Hungary where the Romanians or Vlachs, as they were often called, lived intermingled with Magyar and German settlers without, however, enjoying any of the rights and privileges reserved to these two peoples. Yet, it was from Transylvania that the national and cultural awakening of the Romanians started. In the eighteenth century the Romanians were all Greek Orthodox using the Cyrillic or Old-Slavic script and hardly conscious of the Latin origin of their language. In 1700 in the Transylvanian city of Alba Julia, an ancient Roman colony, Romanian priests joined Rome and established a Romanian Uniate Church. Under its influence Samuil Klein (1745-1806) introduced the Latin alphabet and emphasized the Roman origins of the native language. This supposed Roman origin endowed the Romanian people with the feeling of superiority over Magyars and Slavs, Turks and Greeks. They felt themselves an outpost of imperial Latin civilization in the East. A teacher, Gheorghe Lazar (1779-1823), brought this Latin spirit from Transylvania to Wallachia. As a result the new national spirit overcame there the Greek influence, and from 1822 on native princes were appointed as Turkish governors. Cultural and historical research starting from Alba Julia in the eighteenth century laid the foundations for Romanian nationalism; this nationalism in its turn brought about in 1918 the political unification of the former Turkish principalities with Transylvania in a ceremony conducted at Alba Julia.

The years before 1848 also witnessed the birth of an Ukrainian national movement and literature. In Kiev, Ukrainia's historical capital, then part of the Russian Empire, the poet, Taras Shevchenko (1814-1861), formed with his friends the society of St. Cyril and St. Methodius. The Russian government terminated its activities in 1847 by Shevchenko's arrest and exile. More fortunate was the Ukrainian national movement in the Austrian province of Galicia, where at the University of Lemberg (Lvov) a chair for Ukrainian language and literature was created and an Ukrainian press could develop.

Whereas the nationalist activities of Czechs and Croats, Romanians and Ukrainians, were before 1848 mostly confined to the cultural field, the Magyars in Hungary turned to transform this ancient multi-racial kingdom into a Magyar national state. In due consideration for its ethnically and linguistically composite character the official language of the kingdom had been Latin. In 1833 the Hungarian Diet changed the official language to Magyar and started the process of Magyarization of the Hungarian administration, which aroused the deep resentment of the non-Magyar nationalities, Slovaks and Croats, Serbs and Romanians. Great progress was made in the creation of a modern Magyar literature. Under the leadership of Lajos Kossuth (1802-1894), who edited the progressive newspaper *Pesti Hirlap,* the Magyar nationalists demanded constitutional reforms, liberal legislation, and national independence for Hungary, without, however, taking into account the similar nationalist demands of the non-Magyar peoples. Appealing to the conscience of liberal Europe for the rights of nationality against Habsburg domination, as far as they themselves were concerned, the Magyars were at the same time in no way willing to apply the same standard to other peoples. The "liberation" of the Magyars meant the "oppression" of the non-Magyar peoples within what the Magyars regarded as the historical frontiers of the medieval Hungarian kingdom. But it was not only in the case of the Magyars that nationalist aspirations clashed. It was this clash of nationalist revolutionary aspirations among themselves which defeated the 1848 revolutions in Central Europe.

The Spring of the Peoples. The signal in 1848 came again from Paris, where on February 24 the Second French Republic was proclaimed. In the following month revolutions broke out in Berlin and Vienna, in Prague and Budapest, in Milan and Venice. German, Italian, Slav, and Magyar nationalists in Central Europe from the North Sea to the Mediterranean greeted the dawn of a new day. The long winter of the Holy Alliance seemed broken, the regime of Metternich was overthrown, popular parliaments met, the peoples were in the ascendancy like an irresistible force, their Spring had come. But the promise and hope of this Spring ended soon in bitter disillusionment. 1848 was welcomed as the fulfilment of 1789. The proclamation of the republic in France was received in Europe as the fulfilment of the hope of the ages, as a universal message destined for all peoples and guaranteeing the peace of mankind. But the new age which emerged on the European continent as the result of the nationalist revolutions of 1848 was not a world of harmony and fraternity but of conflict and violence. Soon the new nationalism stressed collective power and unity far above individual liberty: it tended to mean independence from outside rather than freedom within. None of the new nationalities could resist, as soon as the opportunity offered itself, the temptation to assert its rule over ethnically disputed territory and populations. Nationalism changed in the middle of the nineteenth century from liberal humanitarianism to aggressive exclusivism, from the emphasis on the dignity of the individual to that on the power of the nation, from limitation and distrust of government to its exaltation.

In France the republic was overthrown not by the old monarchists or aristocrats but by Louis Napoleon, who in free elections received the overwhelming support of the people. The majority voted for him because he made the cause of nationalism and social progress his own. He was the candidate of all those who lamented the peaceful "anti-national" policy of Louis Philippe and who longed to see the glory of the victorious armies of 1793 and of Napoleon revived and to revenge Waterloo ard the treaties of 1815. Napoleon I while a prisoner in St. Helena had expressed his understanding and appreciation of nationalist movements. (*See Reading No. 9.*) His nephew, Louis Napoleon, had participated as a young man in the nationalist uprisings in Italy. After founding the Second French Empire as Napoleon III, he showed himself throughout his reign a friend of the revolutionary principle of nationality. In France herself no national problems were to be solved in 1848. France was a nation since 1789. The situation was different, however, in Central Europe. There the year 1848 meant the awakening of the nationalities and their first bitter clash.

At the beginning of 1848, Poles and Germans fraternized in the streets of Berlin, and Czechs and Germans in the streets of Prague. But as the revolution progressed it became clear that it meant in Central Europe less a fraternal longing for human liberty than a divisive nationalism. Individual liberty and constitutional guarantees were subordinated to the realization of nationalist aspirations. The revolutionary fervor was directed toward national goals rather than liberal ones. Wherever the two conflicted, nationalism prevailed. The first elected German Parliament, which met in May 1848 in Frankfort on the Main, disputed the frontiers of the German nation-state which it was about to create. Lands which were historically Danish or French or ethnically Polish or Czech were claimed for Germany. A German liberal, Wilhelm Jordan (1819-1904), made himself the spokesman of German claims to Polish territory. He appealed to "healthy" national egoism against "abstract" justice, to the right of conquest by plow and sword, and called all those Germans who saw the justice of the Polish point of view "traitors to their own people." By the end of 1848 the dream of the brotherhood of equal peoples in a universal order of democratic justice had given way to appeals based upon historical rights, the "reality" of power, and the supposed vital or strategic necessities of the nation. The liberal German historian, Friedrich Christoph Dahlmann (1785-1860), declared at Frankfort on January 23, 1849 that "The road of power was the only road which could satisfy and satiate the desire for liberty which was fomenting but which had not yet understood itself. For this desire does not want liberty alone, it thirsts much more for power which has so far not been granted it. Germany must at last become one of the political great powers of the European continent."

Looking back at the events of 1848, the English philosopher, John Stuart Mill, diagnosed the situation with unusual perspicacity in the following year. He complained that nationalism makes men indifferent to the rights and interests "of any portion of the human species, save that which is called by the same name and speaks the same language as themselves." He characterized the new feelings of exclusive nationalism and of appeals to historical rights as barbaric, and remarked bitterly that "in the backward parts of Europe and even (where better things might have been expected) in Germany, the sentiment of nationality so far outweighs the love of liberty that the people are willing to abet their rulers in crushing the liberty and independence of any people not of their race or language."

This change of the character of nationalism in the middle of the nineteenth century occurred not only among the Germans but among all the peoples of Central and Eastern Europe. The new spirit of violence, of glorification of heroic deeds, of the revival of a dim past and of its use as an inspirational source—phenomena which came to darken the horizon of the twentieth century—was first noticeable in 1848. No measure of Pope Pius IX, who had ascended the throne in 1846 as a liberal reformer, was so popular in Italy as his decision to send Papal troops to join the Sardinian army in the war against Catholic Austria. At the very outset of the war, on May 30, 1848, the Sardinian army, generally defeated in all its battles against Austria, won an insignificant and inconsequential victory at Goito. Forty-four years later the great Italian poet Giosuè Carducci (1835-1907), commemorating the victory in his poem "Piemonte," rapturously sang of "the smoke of blood rising from fields of battle." A growing popular impatience made violence and revolt in the service of the nation appear as highest moral values; nationalist self-sacrifice replaced the martyrdom of saints. The same spirit made itself felt outside Central Europe, in Ireland and later in Asia. Even the national anthem of Mexico written in 1854 is a resounding call to war. "Fatherland! Fatherland!" its last verse runs, "thy sons swear to breathe their last on thine altars, when the trumpet with its bellicose accent calls them to fight with valor. For thee the olive wreaths! For them a glorious remembrance! For thee a laurel of victory! For them an honorable grave!" The centenary of this poem of "roaring cannons" was celebrated in 1954 all over Mexico with unusual solemnity.

Scholars and writers were always at hand to produce historical and moral reasons for supporting the ambitions of their nation and to point out that their nation and its necessities presented a unique case to which general rules did not apply. In the welter of conflicting ethnic claims and counterclaims, national passions became overheated, historical scholarship often became subservient to nationalist aspirations, and individual freedom was neglected. Thus it was that the revolutions of 1848 all over Central Europe failed to strengthen the cause of liberty, in spite of the sincere idealism of many of its participants. Poles and Prussians, Danes and Germans, Czechs and Germans, Croats and Italians, Slavs and Magyars, Poles and Ukrainians, opposed each other bitterly. These nationalist struggles helped the absolutist powers of the Metternichian period to reassert themselves. The idealism of 1848 failed, largely because it aroused nationalist passions and lacked the wisdom of patience and compromise. Instead of constructive building it preferred enthusiastic declamation. By 1852 the Second French Republic was dead, and no visible progress had been achieved on the road to Italian and German unification. But the spirit of nationalism was in the air; its mainstay, the middle-classes, gained in numbers and economic strength; their nationalist aspirations were realized in the twelve years from 1859 to 1871, but they were realized not by revolutionary idealists but by the pre-nationalist governments and in their interests, not by the people on the barricades nor by votes in Parliaments, but on the battlefields of regular armies and by the wiles of international diplomacy. After 1848 nationalism entered the age of what has become known by German words—for the Germans played the leading role in this transformation—as the age of *Machtpolitik* and *Realpolitik,* a policy based on power and self-interest and not on humanitarian declarations.

NATIONALISM AND *REALPOLITIK*

The years between 1852 and 1878 marked a decisive step forward in the realization of national goals in Central Europe, no longer by popular revolutions and moralist propaganda but by governments, war, and diplomacy. The ideology of nationalism was now supported more and more by economic factors. Capitalism, industrialism, and the growing importance of the middle-class changed the social structure and the rhythm of life all over Central Europe. The old stillness and patriarchal order gave way before the new means of communication. Friedrich List (1789-1846), a German immigrant to the United States who was deeply impressed by American nationalism and economic progress, returned to Germany as United States Consul and opposed the dominant eighteenth century cosmopolitan theory of political economy, which then celebrated its triumph in the free trade movement in England. List wished to replace it by his new theory of the "national system of economy." He saw in the Customs Union (*Zollverein*), which Prussia started in 1828 and which most German states joined by 1834, an incarnation of the idea of national unity and the best approach to its realization. (*See Reading No. 10.*) He advocated high protective tariffs to facilitate Germany's rapid industrialization and to enable her to compete with Britain, the building of a net of railroads to forge a closer link among the German states, and the construction of a German navy to expand German trade on the high seas. List did not live to see the fulfilment of his projects. Discouraged by the lack of support of his countrymen he committed suicide. His program of large scale industrialization and railroad building was executed in France under Napoleon III, who in 1856, ten years after List's death, found himself at the height of his power and renown.

The Crimean War. The foreign policy of the Second French Empire was directed against the system established at the Congress of Vienna, which recalled to French minds not the long peace it established but the downfall of the First Empire. The Congress of Vienna had tried to erect dikes against the revolutionary force of nationalism. Napoleon III, with his past of an Italian revolutionary nationalism, became its spokesman. For different reasons liberal public opinion in Britain against the dynastic absolutism of the Holy Alliance also supported nationalism and constitutionalism among the peoples of Central Europe. Dynastic absolutism seemed equally distasteful to British constitutionalism and to revolutionary nationalism, though the two had little in common. In the Crimean War (1853-1856) France and Britain made common cause in the support of Turkey against Russia, whose Emperor Nikolai I (1825-1855) was regarded as the main supporter of dynastic absolutism all over Europe. In the course of the war Napoleon III encouraged the Italian kingdom of Sardinia to enter the Western coalition. Its Prime Minister, Count Camillo Cavour (1810-1861), seized gladly the opportunity though no immediate interest of his country was involved. But during the peace congress at Paris (1856) Cavour was able to voice Italian revindications against Austria and to cement his understanding with Napoleon III for the cause of Italian unification.

One of the factors leading to the Crimean War had been the occupation of the Danubian principalities of Moldavia and Wallachia (*see p.* 47) by Russian troops. In 1857 Napoleon III supported the demands of the diets of the two Turkish provinces for their autonomy and neutrality, their union under a foreign and hereditary prince, and the introduction of a constitution. The Turkish government rejected these demands, but in 1859 each of the principalities elected Alexandru Ioan Cuza (1820-1873) as ruler of the united principalities and he was recognized as such in 1861 by the Turkish government. When he resigned in 1866, Napoleon's support forced Turkey's acquiescence to the acceptance of Prince Charles of Hohenzollern-Sigmaringen as hereditary ruler of united Romania. Only after Napoleon's downfall, however, the complete independence of Romania was recognized by the Congress of Berlin (1878) and three years later Carol I assumed the royal title.

The Unification of Italy. The year 1859 was also of decisive importance in the unification of another "Latin" nation, Italy, and again Napoleon III acted as a godfather of this unification though its final stages, again, escaped his control. The 1840's witnessed the great debate about the ways and means of Italian unification. There seemed many insuperable problems: the multiplicity of historical sovereignties and traditions, the deep-seated differences in social structure between North and South, the fact that in a Catholic country the Pope, the head of the Universal Church, was a territorial prince and unwilling to have his more than one-thousand-year-old dominion included in a unified Italian nation. Was such a nation to be a federation or a unitarian state, a monarchy or a republic, founded with the cooperation of the Pope or against him? Carlo Cattaneo (1801-1869), a brilliant Milanese scholar, was a republican and a federalist. He clearly recognized that the autonomous development of the various parts of Italy alone could provide the soil for a fruitful development of democracy. Mazzini was a republican and a strict unitarian, pleading for a centralized Italy with Rome at its head. The Piedmontese Vincenzo Gioberti (1801-1852), a priest and philosopher, saw the future of Italy in a federation under the intellectual supremacy of the Papacy. Sardinian aristocrats like Count Cesare Balbo (1789-1853) and Cavour, who founded in 1847 *Il Risorgimento* as the organ for the Italian national movement, regarded Sardinia as its leader.

The events of 1848 disappointed all these hopes. In that year Charles Albert, king of Sardinia (1831-1849), took to the field against the Austrians. After the short-lived victory at Goito (*see p. 52*), he was acclaimed by his troops *"Viva il Re d'Italia!"* (Long live the king of Italy), but shortly thereafter his army was decisively defeated by the Austrians at Custozza (1848) and Novarra (1849). The restored Republic of St. Mark at Venice under Daniele Manin (1804-1857) was forced to capitulate before the Austrians in 1849. Pius IX, who reigned as Pope from 1846 to 1878, at first seemed to embody the hopes put into him by the Italian liberals and Gioberti. But the events of 1848-9 turned him into a determined opponent of liberalism and nationalism. In the Papal capital of Rome the nationalists on February 9, 1849 proclaimed a Roman Republic. Among its leaders was Mazzini, a native of Genoa, and Giuseppe Garibaldi (1807-1882), a native of Nice. But the Roman Republic was put down with the help of French troops; the Pope returned to Rome and regained his secular dominion; all over Italy the *ancien régime* was restored and the influence of Austria continued. The various solutions offered before 1848 for the unification of Italy were all defeated by 1849.

Sardinian Leadership. The only Italian state, however, where a return to the *ancien régime* did not occur after 1849 was Sardinia. The new king, Victor Emmanuel II, who followed his father in 1849, retained upon the advice of Cavour and of the Marquis Massimo d'Azeglio (1798-1866) the constitutional regime introduced the previous year. As the only constitutional monarchy in Italy, Sardinia won the sympathy of the middle-classes all over the peninsula. Cavour's progressive economic reforms, inspired by the example of England, did even more to awaken confidence in Sardinian leadership. In 1858 Cavour concluded a secret alliance with Napoleon III against Austria. French arms helped Sardinia to receive Lombardy from Austria in 1859, but Cavour's subtle diplomacy outwitted Napoleon's more limited goals and succeeded in winning most of the rest of Italy for the Sardinian monarchy. 1860 was the critical year deciding the way of Italian unification. Under Garibaldi's leadership the famous expedition of the one thousand Red Shirts to Sicily, an island which formed part of the Kingdom of Naples, threatened to provoke a conflict between the radical republicans and the Sardinian monarchists. Cavour's energetic action decided the issue in favor of the latter and led to the annexation of most of the Papal states and of southern Italy to the Sardinian monarchy. As a liberal, and to please Napoleon III and English public opinion, Cavour arranged for plebiscites throughout the Italian states to make the unification of

Italy the democratic expression of the will of the people. At least in the South of Italy the plebiscites were far from corresponding to the people's desire, yet Victor Emmanuel II could assume the title of King of Italy (1861-1878) and the constitution of Sardinia became the constitution of the united kingdom. The triumph of Italian centralism and the high-handed methods of the Sardinians, however, could not integrate the South into the Italian nation or make democracy a living force throughout Italy.

When Cavour died in 1861, Venetia was still in the hands of the Austrians and Rome with the surrounding territory (*Latium*) under the sovereignty of the Pope. Cavour's successors concluded in 1866 an alliance with Prussia against Austria, and though the Italian forces were severely defeated by the Austrians at Custozza on land and at Lissa at sea, Prussian victory secured Venetia for Italy. Napoleon III had supported the Italian-Prussian alliance; but he alienated Italian nationalist opinion by his support of the temporal power of the Pope. Twice, in 1862 and in 1867, Garibaldi led expeditions for the capture of Rome which was defended by French forces. Only when the French withdrew from Rome as the result of the Franco-German War of 1870, did the Italian forces enter Rome on September 20, 1870. After a plebiscite Rome was annexed to Italy against the bitter protest of the Pope who regarded himself henceforth as "the prisoner of the Vatican," and Rome became the capital of the Kingdom of Italy. Even then certain Italian speaking territories remained outside the new nation-state: Trieste, Istria, and Trentino formed part of Austria, the Ticino was a Swiss canton, Nice and Corsica belonged to France. Many Italian nationalists regarded them as *terra irredenta* (unredeemed soil) and were eager to achieve their "redemption," while other Italian nationalists looked to the restoration of the Roman Empire and led Italy into warlike, costly, and futile adventures in Ethiopia and Libya.

The Unification of Germany. Italy's example in 1859 stimulated the revival of nationalism in Germany. The year 1848 had brought Germany bitter disappointments too. The nationalists there faced similar problems:

the multiplicity of historical sovereignties and traditions; the differences between North and South; and the religious problem expressed in the antagonism between Protestants and Catholics. The question whether Germany was to become a centralized state or a federation, a republic or a monarchy, was undecided. But there was in Germany one fundamental difference from the situation in Italy: no great foreign power played a decisive role in Germany, on the contrary, among the German states there were two great European powers, and their jealousies and competition added to the difficulties of finding a solution according to the hearts of the German nationalists. Some of them adhered to a *grossdeutsch* solution, a Great Germany, which would include the Austrian dominions, others preferred the *kleindeutsch* solution, a Little Germany which would exclude Austria and unite the rest of Germany around Prussia. In the 1860's Prussia imposed her solution upon Germany as Sardinia had done in the case of Italy.

Prussia's Leadership. Again there were important similarities in the two cases. Sardinia and Prussia were frontier territories which had played only an insignificant role in the cultural development of Italy and Germany. Turin, Sardinia's capital, was outshone by almost any other city in Italy as an intellectual and artistic center; Berlin, Prussia's capital, achieved intellectual distinction only very late in German history. Both countries were ruled by ambitious dynasties which looked for their chief support to the army and to the aristocracy. But there the similarities ended. Sardinia's army was weak and accustomed to defeats, Prussia's army was renowned for its military spirit. To accomplish the unification of Italy, Sardinia had to rely in every case, in 1859, 1866, and 1870, on foreign help; Prussia achieved her goal unaided from outside. Sardinia formed only about one-tenth of united Italy and the national center of gravity soon shifted from Turin to Rome. Sardinia was absorbed in Italy. Prussia formed about two-thirds of the united Germany and the center of the nation remained evermore strongly in Berlin; it was Prussia which absorbed the rest of Germany and filled it with its authoritarian and militarist spirit.

Therein lay another difference: Cavour was a liberal who looked admiringly to England and the West. He eagerly sought the cooperation of the middle-classes and legitimized his conquests by parliamentary resolutions and plebiscites. Otto von Bismarck (1815-1898), a scion of the Prussian agrarian nobility and Prussia's counterpart of Cavour, despised Western liberalism and parliamentary constitutionalism. He became Prussian Prime Minister in 1862 to support the Crown in its constitutional struggle with the Prussian House of Representatives over the control and the enlargement of the army. Against violent liberal opposition he upheld the king and the army against the parliament and the people. The liberal opposition waned when Bismarck succeeded in three short and victorious wars—which made wars appear profitable for national strength and well-being—in aggrandizing Prussia, ousting Austria from the German *Bund,* and establishing a new German Empire under Prussia's leadership. This new Empire (*Reich*) was created on the battlefield, and proclaimed—a case unique in history—on the soil of the defeated enemy by the victorious German princes assembled in the Hall of Mirrors of the famous royal palace of Versailles, at the gates of the French capital which was surrounded and besieged by German troops.

The leading historians of Protestant Germany, above all Heinrich von Treitschke (1834-1896), helped to mobilize national enthusiasm behind Prussia and to popularize Hegel's theory of the nation-state as the source of all law and ethics, as a super-personality, whose essence is power (*Macht*). When the war of 1870 broke out, Treitschke wrote: "It does not become the German to repeat the commonplaces of the apostles of peace and of the priests of Mammon, nor to shut his eyes to the cruel truth that we live in an age of wars." Bismarck's victories confirmed most Germans in their belief in the superiority of their conservative monarchy over Western democracy. The declaration by the grand old man of German historical writing, Leopold von Ranke (1795-1886), that Prussia's "true destiny is to be and to remain a military monarchy," seemed confirmed by the events. "It is impossible," Ranke had written, "not to submit to what is historically necessary." Bismarck's *Realpolitik* succeeded not only in the field of diplomacy and war, but even more disastrously in the field of the German mind. German unity and power were achieved at the expense of liberal constitutionalism and political freedom.

Bismarck himself was primarily a Prussian monarchist, not a German nationalist. He rejected German "irredentism," the program of the pan-Germans or *Alldeutsche,* which worked to include all German-speaking peoples, who lived in the Austrian and Russian Empires, in Switzerland and Holland, in the new German Empire. But by the annexation of French Alsace-Lorraine in 1871 against the will of the population, who in spite of race and language wished to remain politically French, he inflamed French nationalism. The Germans based their claim upon Alsace-Lorraine on historical rights and ethnic solidarity. They rejected the principle of self-determination. "These provinces are ours by the right of the sword," Treitschke wrote; "and we will rule them in virtue of a higher right, in virtue of the right of the German nation to prevent the permanent estrangement from the German Empire of her lost children. We desire, even against their will, to restore them to themselves." It was against this theory that the French scholar, Ernest Renan (1823-1890), defined in 1882 the liberal concept of nationality in his famous lecture *"Qu'est-ce qu'une Nation?" (See Reading No. 11.)*

Nationalism in the Balkans. After the unification of Italy and Germany there came the turn of the Christian nationalities in the Ottoman Empire. The Greeks were not satisfied with their frontiers established in 1831. Greek irredentists fomented uprisings in Thessaly, Epirus, and on the island of Crete. In 1876 insurrections broke out among the Slav populations of the Turkish provinces of Bulgaria and Bosnia-Herzegovina. Serbia and Montenegro came to the help of the Bosnian insurgents and declared war against Turkey. But Serbia was decisively defeated. It was saved from the consequences by the intervention of Russia, which declared war on Turkey in April 1877 and officially espoused the cause of the Bulgarians. Russian military might and international diplomacy settled in 1878, in the Congress of Berlin, the fate of the Balkan peoples. Romania, Serbia, and Montenegro were declared independent nations. The Bulgarians became an autonomous principality under Turkish suzerainty; Austria was given a mandate to administer Bosnia-Herzegovina; Macedonia, which was disputed between Bulgarians, Serbs, and Greeks, remained part of Turkey.

Among the Turks the closer contact with the West produced a liberal nationalist reform movement which tried to modernize the medieval religious despotic empire. A new literature was created; Turkish writers like Ibrahim Sinasi (1826-1871), who was the first to translate French poetry and to pioneer in private Turkish journalism, and Namik Kemal (1840-1888), who wrote a stirring patriotic play *Vatan* (Fatherland), awakened in the Turks a modern national consciousness. Supported by these "Young Turks," Midhat Pasha (1822-1884) was able in 1876 to introduce a liberal constitution for the Turkish Empire and Western education was encouraged; but the first Turkish parliament which opened in March 1877 was quickly dissolved and the absolutist rule of the Sultan and the medieval character of the Empire were restored.

Some liberal Turkish patriots succeeded in escaping abroad and carried on their agitation from there, often in cooperation with the spokesmen of other nationalities of the Ottoman Empire living in exile. Though they had to wait for thirty years before they could realize some of their ideas—in a successful revolution in 1908 they reintroduced the Turkish constitution—they represented in the late 1860's and early 1870's the first indigenous movement for the modernization of an Asian state under the impact of European nationalism. A similar attempt though with much greater success was made during the same period at the opposite end of Asia, in Japan, where the Meiji Emperor (1867-1912) created a modern nation-state. The task of reform was much easier in Japan than in Turkey. In Japan it was done by a revolution from above and in a country which was ethnically and religiously homogeneous. The Japanese followed the model of Prussia both in the military and authoritarian character of the nation and in the efficiency of administrative, economic, and educational reforms. On the other hand, the Young Turks tried like the Italians before 1860 and the Russians before 1905 to carry through nationalist reforms against their government. Most of them were intellectuals who found the source of their inspiration in the Third French Republic and in French literature. They were faced with the great difficulty that the Turkish Empire was inhabited by a great variety of peoples of different ethnic origin and religious allegiance. In the period of their rule (1908-1918) the Young Turks were unable to solve the contradiction between the multi-national Empire which they wished to preserve and the modern nation-state which they wished to create.

Nationalism in the United States.   The period of the wars of Italian and German unification (1859-1871) coincided with a similar struggle for national unity in North America. National unity achieved in 1789 was by no means secure. During the war against Britain (1812), the New England States had voiced strong disaffection and the Hartford Convention (1814) emphasized the sovereignty of the states and the antagonism of sectional interests.   The following decades brought two decisive developments. American westward imperial expansion was regarded by many American nationalists as the unfolding of manifest destiny. (*See Reading No. 12.*) It strengthened the consciousness of a common glorious future. In the same period, however, the antagonism between South and North grew: the North insisted above all on national unity, the South stressed the precedence of self-determination and of the liberty of the individual states. The South felt exploited by the economically stronger North. This antagonism was expressed at the Jefferson Day Dinner in 1830. President Andrew Jackson (1767-1845) offered the toast to "Our Union: it must be preserved." Vice-President John C. Calhoun (1782-1850) responded, "The Union, next to our liberty, most dear. May we always remember that it can only be preserved by distributing equally the benefits and burdens of the Union."

Thirty years later the conflict had become "irrepressible." The Southern states, conscious of their own nationality, based on the existence of a civilization and a social structure different from those of the North, claimed the right of self-determination which the thirteen states had exercised in 1775. The North regarded the secession as "insurrection." When the North tried to impose unity the War between the States ensued. After four years of bitter struggle—the most protracted and costly war fought anywhere between 1815 and 1914—the superiority of the North in population and economic power decided the issue. In spite of its patriotism and its military valor the South was defeated, not only by the material superiority of the North, but by the obsoleteness of its own national idea. In the climate of liberal opinion in which the United States originated in the eighteenth century (*see p.* 19) it was impossible to establish a nation based upon feudal ideas of hierarchical authority.

After the victory of the North the democratic and federal character of the Union was preserved, and the Southern states were soon readmitted to full constitutional participation. The reconstruction period under the leadership of Northern radicals kept Southern resentment alive and created serious problems for American democracy. Yet, the American national idea based upon individual liberty and tolerance proved in the long run strong enough to overcome not only sectional differences but to fuse millions of immigrants of the most varied ethnic and religious backgrounds into a national whole. Individual liberty and tolerance endowed America with a unique power of voluntary assimilation and of creating a spiritual homogeneity at a time when the European continent, with the exception of Switzerland, followed the opposite pattern. (*See Reading No. 13.*) In Europe peoples of different religious and ethnic backgrounds entered in the middle of the nineteenth century a period of bitter nationality conflicts which led to unending tensions and wars and impeded or destroyed the progress of liberty and tolerance.

NATIONALIST CONFLICTS AND PAN-MOVEMENTS

Austria-Hungary. Prussia's victory over Austria in 1866 eliminated the Habsburgs from Germany and Italy where they had exercised leadership for many centuries. Yet, the Habsburg monarchy reentered a closer relationship with Germany, when Bismarck in 1879 concluded his alliance with Austria. This alliance, directed at France, was extended in 1882 to include Italy; it established a Central-European axis, Berlin-Vienna-Rome, through which Bismarck hoped to maintain German hegemony on the European continent. He was careful to avoid antagonizing Russia; Prussian-Russian friendship had been an important traditional factor in the past. But Austria's exclusion from Germany and Italy turned her attention towards the Balkans, where it conflicted with Russian imperial ambitions. Austria's acquisition of Bosnia-Herzegovina (*see p.* 62) increased the tension between the two powers.

The defeat in the war of 1866 caused also an internal reorganization of the Austrian monarchy. Hungary achieved, under the leadership of Ferencz Deák (1803-1876) and Baron Jószef Eötvös (1817-1871), independence in 1867, remaining connected with Austria only through the person of the monarch and a common foreign and military policy. However, within Hungary the Magyars who did not form a majority of the population, exercised supreme control over their Slav and Romanian subjects. The government under Kálmán Tisza (1830-1902, prime-minister 1875-1890) deprived the minorities even of the right of using their language in schools or in the administration originally conceded to them under the more conciliatory regime of Deák. The extreme policy of Magyarization was even followed in Croatia which on account of its historical rights had received in 1868 an autonomous position within Hungary with its own Diet and the right of using the Croatian language. To strengthen the Croatian position, Bishop Josip Juraj Strossmayer (1815-1905) founded the Yugoslav Academy in Zagreb, the Croatian capital, and promoted cooperation between Croatians and Serbs in opposition to the Magyars.

Different was the situation in Austria. There from the beginning the equality of nationalities and languages was constitutionally recognized and progressively put into practice. The long premiership of Count Edward von Taaffe (1833-1895, premier 1879-1893) was especially favorable to the progress of Austria's non-German population. But the nationalist radicalization of the Austrian Germans under Georg von Schönerer (1842-1921), and of the Czechs under the Young Czechs who assumed leadership in 1891, prevented the working of the democratic process in Austria despite the introduction of general suffrage in 1907.

The Russian Empire. Much less fortunate was the position of the various nationalities in the Russian Empire. The uprising of the Poles in 1863 was sternly repressed. A policy of extreme Russification followed not only towards the Poles, but also towards Ukrainians and all the other nationalities, even against the Baltic Germans and the Finns who until then had enjoyed a privileged position and the recognition of their historical rights. The Polish middle-classes under the leadership of Roman Dmowski (1864-1939) tried to arrive at a compromise with Russia and hoped to unite the Prussian dominated parts of Poland with Russian Poland as an autonomous and equal partner within the Russian Empire. On the other hand, Jozef Pilsudski (1867-1935) organized the Polish workers for a revolutionary nationalist fight for Polish independence from Russia. Polish literature prospered and had a great share in arousing the Polish national consciousness. A Polish scholar, Alexander Brückner, surveying the developments of a century concluded in 1901 his *History of Polish Literature:* "The national consciousness does not limit itself any longer, as it did in 1801, to the nobility and some isolated middle-class men, it has penetrated into the peasantry, even to the Jews . . . In spite of the lack of political independence it is thanks to its literature that the Polish nation can proudly say of itself: *E pur si muove.*"

Whereas the Poles in Russia and Prussia suffered bitter oppression, they enjoyed full freedom in Austria. No higher Polish education was allowed in the two other countries; the Austrian government, however, maintained two Polish universities in Lemberg and Cracow and the latter historical city was also the seat of a famed Polish academy of sciences. Similarly, Ukrainian intellectual and literary life which was completely suppressed in Russia, found a refuge among the Austrian Ukrainians who founded in Lemberg in 1873 the Shevchenko Society to encourage the development of national literature. There Mykhailo Hrushevsky (1866-1934) began in 1898 the publication of his *History of the Ukraine.* But Russian oppression, although intensified after 1881, did not achieve its goal. In the second half of the nineteenth century a remarkable national awakening took place among many nationalities of the Russian Empire, especially among Finns and Estonians, Latvians and Lithuanians. The local peasant vernaculars were developed into literary languages and took their place besides Swedish (in Finland) and German (in the Baltic Provinces). Elias Lönnrot (1802-1884) founded in 1831 the Finnish Literary Society, edited the *Kalevala,* the Finnish national epic, and fought for the equality of Finnish with Swedish in Finland. The "fennomen" carried the day over the "svecomen"; today the large majority of the population in Finland speaks Finnish, but the Swedish language though spoken only by a small urban minority retains full equality in democratic Finland.

Nationalism in Western Europe.   The struggle for linguistic equality was also successfully carried on within the framework of a democratic society by the Flemish speaking Belgians against the formerly dominant French language. In the awakening of Flemish national sentiment a growing modern literature played a similar role as among the Catalans in northeastern Spain, where Bonaventura Carlas Aribau (1798-1862) published in 1833 his *"Oda a la Patria."* Nationalist movements in Catalonia and in the Basque provinces fought for the federal re-organization of Spain, a trend supported by Francisco Pí y Margall in his book *Las Nacionalidades* (1877). These hopes were partly realized in the short-lived Spanish republic (1931-1939) which brought regional autonomy to Catalans and Basques, but the victorious dictatorship of Generalissimo Francisco Franco reintroduced the oppressive centralization.

Nationality conflicts in democratic Northern Europe found their solution in peaceful separation: the Norwegians, united in 1814 with the Swedes, established themselves in 1905 as an independent nation; Iceland united with Denmark since 1380 became independent in 1918. The Nordic nations (Denmark, Iceland, Norway, Sweden, and partly, Finland) have preserved, in spite of their independence, a strong feeling of solidarity and an inclination to cooperation; a Pan-Scandinavian movement for closer integration of which the great Norwegian writer, Henrik Ibsen (1828-1906), was a leading spokesman has not been able, however, to establish a Nordic federation.

The Irish Problem. While Irish leaders like Charles Stewart Parnell (1846-1891) and John Edward Redmond (1856-1918) fought successfully in cooperation with British liberals for Irish Home Rule by constitutional means—William Ewart Gladstone (1809-1898) introduced the First Home-Rule Bill in the British Parliament in 1886 and in 1914 the Third Home-Rule Bill became law—other Irishmen turned to violence to achieve the separation of Ireland from Britain. The Irish Republican Brotherhood—also called Fenians after legendary heroes of old—was widespread in the 1860's both in Ireland and among the Irish in the United States. But the progressive liberalization of the Irish administration and the rapid improvement in the economic situation of the Irish peasantry resulted in a sharp decline of the political nationalist movement before the turn of the century. Under these circumstances the nationalists turned to cultural and educational activities to arouse nationalist sentiments. The Gaelic Athletic Association was founded in 1884 to revive Irish games. More important became the efforts to revive the Gaelic language. In 1893 Douglas

Hyde (1860-1949), an Irish Protestant of English descent, became the first president of the Gaelic League, which stressed the necessity for "de-Anglicizing the Irish nation" and for resuscitating the Gaelic language and the ancient Celtic traditions. (*See Reading No. 14.*) Pride in the racial past was fanned by poets and orators. Had not the Celtic race once peopled most of Europe, "established itself in Greece and burned infant Rome?" Even a Pan-Celtic movement, to unite Gael, Welsh, and Bretons, was adumbrated in those years. Yet, the Gaelic League was unable to displace English as the leading language among the Irish. The great Irish literary renaissance (1890-1920) expressed itself in English: William Butler Yeats (1865-1939), John Millington Synge (1871-1909), James Joyce (1882-1941), and the Abbey Theater made Ireland and Dublin world famous. But by its emphasis on Irish separateness the Gaelic movement contributed to the revival of Irish nationalism in the twentieth century. In 1899 Arthur Griffith (1872-1922), a member of the Irish Republican Brotherhood, became editor of *The United Irishman* and helped found in 1905 *Sinn Fein* (Ourselves). The movement added an emphasis on economic nationalism (*see Reading No. 15*) to that on cultural and political nationalism. British initial defeats in the Boer War had helped this revival of the Fenian spirit in 1899; British initial defeats in World War I supplied the background for the Easter 1916 Uprising in Dublin and the proclamation of the Irish Republic. After British victory in World War I, Arthur Griffith could realize Sinn Fein's aspirations by signing the treaty of December 6, 1921, which created the Irish Free State as a virtually independent nation.

Balkan Nationalism. The disintegration of the Ottoman Empire and the ensuing struggles among its presumptive heirs did not come to an end with the settlement of 1878 (*see p. 61*). Nationalist unrest continued in the Balkans. The new Christian nations not only tried to undermine the continuous existence of Turkey in Europe but fought each other, each one desiring to expand according to the greatest limits of its past. Their principal object of discord was Macedonia. The Internal Macedonian Revolutionary Organization (IMRO) in Bulgaria, the nationalist aspirations of Premier Nikola Pašić (1845-1926) in Serbia, and of Prime Minister Eleutherios Venizelos (1864-1936) in Greece were instrumental in bringing about the two Balkan Wars (1912-1913), which became the immediate prelude to World War I. Having defeated the Turks in the First Balkan War, and the Bulgarians in the Second Balkan War, the Serbs regarded themselves as the Piedmont or Prussia for the unification of all Southern Slavs, of whom a great number lived in Austria-Hungary and in Bosnia-Herzegovina (see p. 65). The assassination of the Austrian heir to the throne in Sarajevo, Bosnia's capital, on June 28, 1914 by Serbian nationalists led to Austrian retaliatory measures. The Serb-Austrian clash broadened into a conflict between Pan-Germanism and Pan-Slavism. The Germans and Magyars in the Habsburg monarchy had been Germany's loyal allies since 1879. On the other hand, the Serbs were supported by the Russians who regarded themselves as the head of the Pan-Slav movement and as the protector of all the Slavs, especially against the German *Drang nach Osten* (Pan-German expansion eastward).

Pan-Germanism. The Pan-German Union (*Alldeutscher Verband*) was founded in 1891 by Ernst Haase (1846-1908) and Heinrich Class (1868-1953). Many of their ideas were inspired by Arndt, List, and Treitschke. The Pan-Germans demanded above all a greater German *Lebensraum* (living-space), overseas colonies, and a big navy. Their emphasis on a policy of ruthless national egoism and expansionism influenced wide circles who did not become members of the union itself and did not look primarily toward the creation of a vast colonial empire. They were more concerned with the fate of their "racial brethren" outside the frontiers of the German Empire, especially in Austria-Hungary. Many Pan-Germans renewed Arndt's demands for the "union" of the Swiss, the Dutch and even the Scandinavians with Germany in a great racial Nordic brotherhood. The Austrian Pan-Germans under Schönerer (see p. 66) accepted and promoted this program; in their bitter fight against the racially "inferior" Slavs and Jews they became Hitler's teachers. World War I, when Germany, Austria-Hungary, Turkey and Bulgaria were allied, seemed to provide the opportunity for the creation of a *Mitteleuropa* (Central Europe) unified under German leadership. After 1890, the date of Bismarck's dismissal, Pan-German thought exercised a growing influence upon the public opinion and even upon governmental policy in Germany. This influence reached its open climax in Hitler's Germany.

Pan-Slavism. Pan-Germanism was primarily a movement for the expansion of Prussian-German power through the incorporation of other German speaking peoples, even against their will, into a greater Germany, which in population, economic resources, and territorial size would afford a sufficient basis for German world leadership. Similarly, Pan-Slavism was primarily a movement for the expansion of Great Russian power by the incorporation of other Slav-speaking peoples, even against their will, into a greater Russia, which in population and economic resources would afford a sufficient basis for Russian world domination, or, as it was called in the nineteenth century, a Russian universal monarchy. (*See Reading No. 16.*) In both cases it was assumed that "racial" or linguistic affinity resulted in an affinity of civilization and political ideology and in a desire for union. In reality, no cultural affinity existed among the various Slav-speaking peoples. Polish civilization had less in common with Russian civilization than with that of Catholic Europe. In spite of all Pan-Slav theory, Slav peoples frequently felt more bitter hostility against each other than against non-Slav peoples. The feeling of Poles against Russians, of Ukrainians against Poles, of Serbs against Bulgars, supply convincing examples of *Erbfeindschaft* (hereditary and hateful enmity) between Slav neighbors. Though Pan-Germanism and Pan-Slavism were based on fictitious premises, nevertheless they exercised an emotional impact on many Germans and many Russians and were among the principal causes leading to the two World Wars in the present century.

Pan-Slavism started originally among the Slavs in Austria. The first Pan-Slav Congress with Palacký (*see p.* 39) in the chair met in June 1848 in Prague to demand the transformation of the Habsburg monarchy into a federation of equal peoples among whom the various Slav nationalities would have formed a majority.

Only after the Austro-Hungarian compromise of 1867 (*see p.* 65) had made clear the failure of federalization, did the Czechs whose leaders had been very critical of Russia (*see Reading No. 17*) turn to Russia, "the big brother." In 1867 the Second Pan-Slav Congress met in Moscow and claimed Russian leadership of the Slav world. Most Pan-Slavs shared the Slavophil faith of Russian messianism, according to which the Russian people were chosen by God to lead mankind to salvation. The Russians were proclaimed to be the truly Christian people, guardians of Orthodoxy (the true faith), devoted to peace and social justice, and called to spread this gospel to all the nations. The great Russian writer, Feodor Dostoevsky (1821-1881), was one of the many adherents of Slavophilism and Pan-Slavism. (*See Reading No. 18.*) The Russian communists, who in November, 1917, under the leadership of Lenin (Vladimir Ulyanov, 1870-1924), overthrew the short-lived democratic regime which the Russian Revolution of March, 1917, had established, revived Russian nationalist messianism. They proclaimed the Russians the truly Socialist people, guardians of Marxism (the true faith), devoted to peace and social justice, and called to spread this gospel to all nations. In 1945 they realized the most daring dreams of nineteenth century Russian Pan-Slavs, uniting all the Slavs under Russian leadership and extending their borders to the Oder River and the Adriatic Sea. They defeated the Pan-Germanism of Adolf Hitler (1889-1945), who as leader of the German nation, had in 1941 realized the most daring dreams of his Pan-German forerunners.

Pan-Asianism. The first Pan-Asian Empire was created by the Mongols, who at the death of Ghengiz Khan in 1227 ruled from the China Sea to the Dnieper River. Later on the Celestial Empire (China) appeared to its people identical with the world and civilization. "From within and from without, all lands are subject to China." At the end of the sixteenth century Hideyoshi Toyotomi decided to challenge Chinese world leadership on behalf of Japan. In a letter to the Portuguese Viceroy of Goa in India he promised that "after completing our heavenly mission of conquering China, we shall readily find a road by which to reach your country. Our warships and fighting men will accomplish the work entrusted to them regardless both of distance and the sort of warriors they may conquer." In the twentieth century Japan set out again for the conquest of China and beyond, convinced that she was "a divine country ruled over by the Son of Heaven" and that the Imperial Principle must be propagated over the Seven Seas and extended over the five continents in fulfilling "Japan's mission of peace." It was under the slogan of Pan-Asianism or "Asia for the Asians" that Japan tried to organize the population and resources of the vast lands from the Eastern shores of Africa to the Western Pacific as basis of Japanese world leadership. After Japan's defeat in 1945 the mantle of Pan-Asian leadership has fallen again to China. Like the other two great Pan-movements of the twentieth century, Pan-Germanism and Pan-Slavism, Pan-Asianism completely broke with the Western liberal tradition and turned to totalitarianism.

— 7 —

RACIALISM AND TOTALITARIANISM

Biological Nationalism. The latter part of the nineteenth century saw the rapidly growing prestige of the biological sciences. In a vulgarized form, they together with the Darwinian "struggle for survival," exercised a potent influence on nationalism. Whereas the Western concept of nationality was a political concept based upon free individuality, ancient "natural" tribalism was now revived in modern forms; it based nationality, and man's political and spiritual allegiance upon ancestry or "blood," supposedly most deeply imbedded in, and determining, human nature. Arthur de Gobineau (1816-1882) first systematized the new biological nationalism in his *Essai sur l'inégalité des races humaines* (1853-1855). According to him "blood" was of supreme importance; the human races were unequal in creative ability; civilization could not be communicated and, therefore, backward races could not reach a higher level. The "chosen" people was the Teutonic or German race; as racial ability depended upon "purity of blood," intermarriage was detrimental to civilization. Gobineau encouraged the cult of ancestor worship as a means for the preservation of purity of the higher races and the fulfilment of their leadership mission.

Anti-Semitism in France. The racial theory in Continental Europe manifested itself above all in anti-Semitism. It went hand in hand with a rejection of individualism and liberalism, which were thought responsible for the decline of Europe and which made Jewish emancipation and assimilation successful. The anti-Semites regarded the Jews as "alien" in their European homelands; Palestine was proclaimed their true fatherland; their exclusion from the political and cultural life of their countries was deemed beneficial to restore racial and spiritual integrity. In France Edouard Drumont published in 1886 *La France Juive;* the anti-Semites suspected the existence of a Jewish "plot," often in cooperation with the Anglo-Saxons, Germans or Protestants, to ruin traditionalist and Catholic France. The agitation came into the open in the Dreyfus Affair. Captain Alfred Dreyfus, the only Jewish officer on the French General Staff, was sentenced in 1894 for pro-German espionage. A bitter fight was waged about his innocence: his adversaries claimed that national self-interest and security (*sacro egoismo*) took precedence over "abstract" justice and objective considerations.

Charles Maurras (1868-1952) and Maurice Barrès (1862-1923) first formulated clearly the principles of integral nationalism which rejected humanitarian liberalism as old-fashioned in favor of exclusive national self-interest and speedy decisive action. Maurras demanded that French interests be considered paramount, *France d'abord* (France first), and proclaimed the necessity of nationalist action, *action française,* against deliberation and compromise. Barrès believed that France's salvation lay in a close national community of thought and feeling, beyond all class divisions and individualist non-conformity. All Frenchmen must be fused into a living unity by the recognition of their common deep roots in ancestral generations and by a return to the ancestral soil. Men lost their ethical and spiritual bearing, when they became "uprooted," as Barrès called it in his novel *Les Déracinés.* Nationalism, according to nationalists who stress "blood" and ancestors, was a determinism; the individual was not free but inescapably motivated by his biological inheritance, by *"la terre et les morts,"* as Barrès called it, by *"Blut und Boden,"* as Hitler phrased it.

Jewish Nationalism. It was during the Dreyfus Affair, and as a result of the anti-Semitism experienced there, that Theodore Herzl (1860-1904), an Austrian journalist, wrote his pamphlet *Der Judenstaat* (1896). In it he demanded for the "people without a land" a "land without a people." At that time he did not know that in Russia, as a result of the anti-Semitic pogroms of 1881, the *Hoveve Zion* (Lovers of Zion) had agitated for the return of the Jews to their ancestral soil in Palestine and the first pioneers had left to settle in that country to "redeem" (*geulah*) the land. Historical Zion became the goal of a modern nationalism. Herzl now assumed the leadership of the movement. A world-wide Zionist Organization was created and the first Zionist Congress met in Basel, Switzerland, in 1897 to demand the creation of a Jewish homeland in Palestine, secured by international law. Palestine was then a Turkish province; its people predominantly Arabs.

In World War I, twenty years after the first Congress, Arthur Balfour, on behalf of the British government, promised to use their best endeavors to facilitate "the establishment in Palestine of a national home for the Jewish people, it being clearly understood that nothing will be done which may prejudice the civil and religious rights of existing non-Jewish communities in Palestine, or the rights and political status enjoyed by Jews in any other country." The number of Jewish immigrants into

Palestine was small between 1919 and 1933. The new settlers succeeded in reviving Hebrew as a national language, and though there was no prospect of a Jewish majority in the country, Jewish cultural life was flowering. The situation changed in World War II. Hitler's anti-Semitism after 1933 induced many European Jews to look for refuge in Palestine. Nazi massacres of millions of Jews strengthened Jewish nationalism. The existence of a large Arab majority, eager to defend the national character of their homeland and to exercise their right of "self-determination," was the main hindrance for the establishment of a Jewish state. The Palestinian Arabs were supported by the neighboring Arab countries and the Islamic peoples. The issue was decided in a war between the Palestinian Jewish settlers and the Arab states; in May, 1948, Jewish victory resulted in the creation of the state of Israel.

Anti-Semitism in Germany.   Gobineau's racial theories had only a very limited influence in France. In the Dreyfus Affair the liberal forces prevailed. Few French intellectuals accepted racialism. Leading French historians like Michelet and Renan stressed racial intermingling as the fertile basis of French nationalism and the indispensable foundation of a liberal policy. Louis Joly wrote in his *Du Principe des Nationalités* (*On the Principle of Nationalities,* 1863) that stress on ancestors was contrary to the principles of 1789. "The idea of an association of men which is not constituted on the sympathies and hatreds stemming from common descent is superior to one based upon the recognition of these 'natural' sympathies and hatreds. The fusion of races, as it happened in France, Britain, and the United States, is one of the great beneficial factors of history. The leading powers in the world are the very ones where the various nationalities and racial strains which entered into their formation have been extinguished as far as possible and have left few traces." Alexis Comte de Tocqueville (1805-1859) wrote to Gobineau that his essay on the inequality of the human race was hostile to individual liberty and added prophetically that its ideas had a chance in France only if they came back there from abroad, especially from Germany. For the situation was different in Germany.

There leading artists and scholars espoused the cause of anti-Semitism and endowed it with an appearance of dignity. Richard Wagner (1813-1883) devoted great efforts to the spread of anti-Semitism (*see Reading No. 19*), and the most renowned historian of the period, Heinrich von Treitschke (1834-1896), published in 1879 an article *The Jews are our Misfortune,* which served as a rallying banner for the German anti-Semitic movement.

Germany became the fatherland of modern anti-Semitism; there the systems were thought out and the slogans coined. German literature was the richest in anti-Jewish writing. As early as 1815 Friedrich Rühs, professor of history at the University of Berlin, asked that the "Hebrew enemy" should wear a special sign on his garment to make him easily recognizable. In 1881 Eugen Dühring, a social philosopher, wrote a book, *The Jewish Question as a Racial, Ethical and Cultural Problem. With a World Historic Reply.* In it he suggested those "remedies" which Adolf Hitler was to apply. At the same time Adolph Stöcker, an influential Protestant cathedral and court preacher in Berlin, and Adolph Wagner, professor of political economy at the University of Berlin, led the "Christian Social Workmen's Party" in opposition to bourgeois liberalism and proletarian Marxism which they regarded both as inspired and dominated by Jews. In 1899 Richard Wagner's son-in-law, Houston Stewart Chamberlain (1855-1927), published his *The Foundations of the Nineteenth Century,* which became the "scientific source for Alfred Rosenberg's *Der Mythus des 20. Jahrhunderts* (*The Myth of the Twentieth Century,* 1930), in which he elaborated Hitler's racial theories. Anti-Semitism and a mystical anti-Western and anti-liberal concept of German *Kultur* (civilization) (*see Reading No. 20*) prepared the German people for the willing acceptance of Hitler's totalitarian and racial nationalism.

Totalitarian Nationalism. Charles Maurras' integral nationalism stressed the authority and absolute precedence of the national community over the individual and the need of determined action by a closely-knit, disciplined and well-armed vanguard, an élite which would seize power at the decisive moment. He believed the modern

West's liberal democracy, as developed in England, doomed. These theories had little influence in France except for the brief period of the regime of Marshal Henri Pétain which imposed itself upon France in 1940 in the wake of German victory. But they found a receptive soil in countries where Western democracy had scant opportunity for taking root. World War I caused the collapse of the traditional authorities and of the social order over most of Eastern and Central Europe. It opened the road to the rise of totalitarianism. In November, 1917, Nikolai Lenin (1870-1924) led a closely-knit, disciplined, and well-armed vanguard to overthrow the short-lived democratic regime which the Russian Revolution of March, 1917, had established in cooperation with the West. Lenin now erected the first totalitarian state directed against Western democracy. He was a follower of the internationalism of Karl Marx (1818-1883), who had expected a socialist world state based upon the union of the proletarian class of all countries. Under Lenin's leadership the Russian Empire was transformed into the Union of Soviet Socialist Republics, which it was hoped would expand to include the entire globe. Within the Soviet Union the various nationalities received territorial autonomy and the right to use and develop their own language. They were assured complete equality. But within a totalitarian state national liberty was as unthinkable as individual liberty: all persons and all groups had absolutely to conform to the one uniform pattern imposed by the Communist Party and doctrine. In the Soviet Union itself the Great Russian element numerically and culturally predominated. In the 1930's and 1940's it reasserted its dominant position more and more openly and in the later years of Josef Stalin (1879-1953), Lenin's successor, the Slavophil tendencies of stressing the unique and peculiar character of the Russian people and of its world mission (*see p.* 72) were revived. As a result the opposition of the many non-Russian nationalities of the vast Soviet Empire against Moscow's domination grew, especially among the Ukrainians in the west and among the Mohammedan peoples in Soviet Central Asia.

    Fascism.   Whereas Communism, the first and most

extreme totalitarian movement, was in its original ideology not connected with nationalism, Fascism, the other great authoritarian mass movement in opposition to modern middle-class civilization, was from the beginning an inflammation of nationalism. It came first to power in Italy under the leadership of Benito Mussolini (1883-1945) with the "March on Rome" in October, 1922. Fascism no longer believed as Mazzini did in the harmony of various national interests. It dedicated itself to the preparation for the "inevitable" struggle that forms the life of nations. It called for dynamic national growth, for an increased population for the sake of national strength, and for the military preparedness of the whole population. Mussolini called the Italian people to its mission of restoring Rome's ancient glories, and he stimulated the cult of the Roman imperial past in every possible way. Fascism absolutized nationalism. The nation became the supreme arbiter, its service the one supreme duty. Only actions, thoughts, and sentiments which help to increase the power of the nation are regarded as good by Fascism. The absolute devotion to the nation becomes the guiding principle of all Fascist education, which like Communist education wishes to determine every thought and every sentiment of the people. (*See Reading No. 21.*)

Fascism was originally regarded as an Italian phenomenon but by 1936 Fascist principles had become accepted, to a varying degree, by the governments of many countries in Central and Eastern Europe and had even penetrated into Latin America and Asia. There were variations in the doctrinal concepts and in the external symbols according to the peculiar national traditions of each country. In Romania Corneliu Zelia-Codreanu founded in 1927 a Legion of the Archangel Michael for the religious and racial renovation of Christian Romania; the Legion later developed into the terrorist organization of the Iron Guard, and when disbanded by the government constituted itself as a party *Totul Pentru Tara* (Everything for the Fatherland). In Greece General Joannes Metaxas established on August 4, 1936 a Fascist regime, inaugurating the "Third Hellenic Civilization," with the Spartan salute as its symbol. In the same year the Falangists in Spain revived the dream of recreating the great Spanish Empire of the golden century, which had attempted to impress its Catholic civilization upon the whole world and which had ruled in the Americas and in the South Seas. Similarly, in Japan patriotic terrorist organizations of young officers and students tried to stamp out the influences of Western liberalism and commercialism and to bring Japan back to the old faith and the ancient virtues. In Latin America the Integralistas in Brazil and the Peronistas in Argentina fanned the flame of native nationalism and imperialism in opposition to the liberal and commercial civilization of the United States.

On October 25, 1932, Mussolini assured his audience at Milan of the coming world leadership of Fascist Italy. "Today with a fully tranquil conscience, I say to you, that the twentieth century will be the century of Fascism, the century of Italian power, the century during which Italy will become for the third time the leader of mankind." Mussolini thus shared Mazzini's hope for a "Third Rome," the Rome of the Italian People which would exercise world leadership as the Rome of the Caesars and the Rome of the Popes had done in antiquity and in the Middle Ages. But the hope for Italian world leadership was futile. The Third Reich of National Socialism, the German form of Fascism which had come to power under Adolf Hitler (1889-1945) in January, 1933; the Japanese brand of imperial Fascism which gained the upper hand there in 1936; Russian totalitarianism with its center at Moscow, the "Third Rome" of the Slavophils (*see p.* 72) were more potent competitors for world leadership than Italy. In all these cases totalitarian nationalism widened into the ambition of world imperialism, fundamentally different from the limited and liberal nineteenth century imperialism. The new nationalism "justified" its merciless struggle with its passionate hatreds and cold-blooded liquidations by appealing to the necessities of history, to "God-ordained" nationalist missions, or to the evocation of a distant past.

— 8 —

WORLD-WIDE NATIONALISM

After the First World War. The Peace Congress of Vienna in 1814 tried to contain the revolutionary forces of nationalism. Yet throughout the following century these forces grew in intensity and expanded into ever new countries until the peace treaties of 1919 marked the complete breakdown of the system established at Vienna. All over Central and Central-Eastern Europe new nation-states sprang up and older nation-states which had come to existence in the nineteenth century were enlarged according to the principles of national self-determination. Yet, the hopes of the generation of 1848 that national independence would lead to peace and liberty—hopes largely shared by United States' opinion and by President Woodrow Wilson—were not fulfilled. Within the context of the intellectual traditions and the social structure of the modern West, nationalism had represented a movement for a more open society and the pursuit of individual happiness, for the security of civil liberties and the unfettering of thought. After the Second World War, nationalism lost much of its hold on the West. The trend toward supranational cooperation developed rapidly; Western European Union and the Atlantic Community held greater promise for securing peace and for broadening individual liberty than nationalism. On the other hand, in the East, Communism stressed national sovereignty as never before; there nationalism became the dominant and exclusive force. When nationalism spread to Eastern Europe and later to Asia, to lands with traditions different from those in the West and frequently hostile to modern Western ways, nationalism tended toward the closed society, in which the individual counted for less than the strength and authority of the national whole. Nationalism was considered a panacea for solving all problems and its impatient penchant for action and violence made it susceptible to Communist influences.

The "liberation" of many nationalities in the twentieth century did not strengthen the trend to peace and liberty. Nationalities which had demanded release from oppression often became oppressors themselves. Innumerable disputes about historical and natural frontiers sprang up. Long established security systems disintegrated before new foundations for peace were laid on solid ground. Some new and enlarged nation-states—-Poland, Czechoslovakia, Italy, Yugoslavia, and Romania—contained embittered minorities. A great and potentially fruitful innovation were the international agreements after the First World War which stipulated, for the assurance of protection of minorities, the right of supervision and intervention by the League of Nations. However, nationalism prevented this protection from becoming effective. Even the dominant nationalities of some of the new nation-states— Czechs and Slovaks in Czechoslovakia, Serbs and Croats in Yugoslavia—felt hostile to each other in spite of their close racial and linguistic affinity. The mutual animosities and jealousies among the new nation-states hindered their political and economic cooperation; this facilitated the conquest of Central and Central-Eastern Europe first by National Socialist Germany, then by Communist Russia. National independence and sovereignty multiplied and sanctified after, and as a result of, two World Wars, have not turned out to be reliable formulas for greater individual freedom and more secure international peace.

Nationalism in the Middle East. The First World War completed the disintegration of the Ottoman Empire. On its ruins Greek nationalism wished to recreate the Great Greece of antiquity and of the Byzantine Empire. Greek armies landed in 1919 in western Asia Minor (Anatolia), the site of famous Hellenic cities of the past and a country with a considerable and prosperous population of the Greek Orthodox faith. The invasion of this Turkish heartland aroused a new feeling of nationalism among the Turkish peasants. Under the leadership of Mustafa Kemal, later called Kemal Atatürk (1881-1938), they routed the Greeks in 1922. The victory secured for Turkey national independence and equality unknown for a long time. As part of the peace treaty a compulsory exchange of populations was carried through, Greek subjects of the Mohammedan faith had to leave for Turkey, Turkish subjects of the Greek Orthodox faith, by far more numerous and wealthier, were removed to Greece. Even with the bitter memories left by war and expatriation, as well as the political and religious hostility of many centuries, the Turkish and Greek governments were able, by definitely abandoning expansionist aspirations and all ambitions for the restoration of former greatness, to establish friendly relations between the two nations and to secure their close political and military cooperation. Equally important were Atatürk's domestic reforms. He changed the medieval religious structure of state and society, transformed Turkey into a modern secular republic, introduced European codes of law, and laid the foundations for a progressive Westernization and democratization of Turkish life. His example was followed, as far as the much more backward conditions allowed, in neighboring Iran (Persia), and exercised an influence on other Islamic peoples, whose status changed rapidly after 1920.

On the eve of the First World War, only three independent Islamic states existed. Two of them, Turkey and Persia, were deeply "sick" and shaky, the third one, Afghanistan, was primitive and inaccessible. Forty years later Turkey and Iran were consolidated to a degree unforeseen in 1914, Afghanistan was on the way to modernization, and a whole string of independent Mohammedan nations, the existence of which few would have anticipated in 1914, had come into being from North Africa to the South Seas—Libya, Egypt, Saudi Arabia, Jordan, Syria, Iraq, Pakistan, and Indonesia. But in spite of a consciousness of Islamic affinity, politically nationalism was the stronger force. Attempts to revive the Caliphate (which Mustafa Kemal abolished in Turkey in 1924) as a pan-Islamic movement based upon the Mohammedan Holy City of Mecca and under Arab leadership—the Arabs were the original supporters of Islam and of the Caliphate—failed. Nationalism and jealousies among the various Islamic states and leaders were too strong for the political efficacy of the religious tie. Only among

the Arabic states was a closer relationship established
based upon community of language and tradition and
upon common hostility to, and fear of, Israel.

Nationalism in Asia.   The Middle East had been in
contact with the West for many centuries: Islam and
Christianity have common foundations in Judaism and in
the Hellenic civilization. Different was the case in India
and the Far East. There real contact with the West is
hardly two centuries old. It was a contact forced upon
Asia by Europe. From the wars of the Persian Empire
against Greece to the incursions of Huns and Mongols
and finally to the siege of Vienna by the Ottoman imperial
armies, Europe had been under attack by aggressive Asian
powers. Only in recent times the trend has been reversed.
Western progress and the lethargy which had befallen
Eastern civilizations made it possible for European control to spread in the eighteenth and nineteenth centuries
over the globe, and with it came Western methods of
political and economic organization. Western beliefs in
freedom and rationality influenced the leading strata of
non-Western populations, first in Russia, then in Asia,
and aroused them from tradition-bound ways of life.
Western skill in administration, integrity of the judicial
system and ordered liberty were partly assimilated by
non-Western elites; at the same time Western superiority,
often arrogantly asserted, aroused deep resentment.
Through contact with the modern West, Asian civilizations and peoples were revitalized. As the very result of
Westernization and the resulting native renascence the
brief period of Western imperial expansion has recently
reached its end.

In this historical process England was the leading
power. Her liberal civilization, which in preceding centuries had influenced the growth of constitutional liberty
in Europe, infused a new spirit into Asia and later into
Africa. England introduced constitutional reforms in her
colonies and increased the facilities for education and
economic development. She set the example of complete
emancipation of dependent peoples by giving independence to Egypt (1922, completed 1936) and to Iraq
(1932), an example followed by the United States in
1934 when Congress promised to grant independence to

the Philippine Islands after a transitional period of twelve years. This process reached its fulfillment after the Second World War, when India, Pakistan, Ceylon, and Burma became independent. At home as abroad Britain offered the example of a political organization which adapted itself to changing public sentiment with flexibility and without doctrinaire theorizing, and which derived its vigor from ideas apt to promote orderly evolution and individual liberties everywhere.

Nationalism in India.   British rule brought a powerful ferment above all to India, a sub-continent in which the Far Eastern and the Islamic civilizations met. There British policy and methods first aroused the desire for individual liberty and self-government, formerly unknown in the Orient. In 1835 the English historian, Thomas Macaulay (1800-1859), as chairman of the Committee of Public Instruction in India proposed to base Indian education upon the study of the natural sciences and of the growth of liberty from ancient Greece to modern England. "It may be that the public mind of India may so expand under our system that it may outgrow that system and our subjects having been brought up under good government may develop a capacity for better government, that having been instructed in European learning, they may crave for European institutions. I know not whether such a day will ever come but if it does come it will be the proudest day in the annals of England."

The Indian National Congress.   Exactly fifty years later, at the end of 1885, the first Indian National Congress met in Bombay. It was founded upon the suggestions of an English liberal, a former member of the Indian Civil Service, in order to merge in one national whole all the different and hitherto hostile elements that make up the population of India; to direct the process of rebirth of the nation so evolved, intellectually, morally, socially, and politically; and to strengthen the tie that binds Britain and India by changing whatever is unjust or injurious to India. For the first time in Asia the Congress created a public platform for voicing political aspirations, representing the nation as a whole above all formerly unbridgeable differences of race and caste, religion, language, and province. For nowhere was racial and caste segregation as strict and cruel as in Hindu India, a country without a common language, without a common political tie before the one created by British administration and education. Though the membership of the Congress was overwhelmingly Hindu, nevertheless in its first thirty years three Mohammedans, four Englishmen, and one Parsee were its Presidents, one Englishman twice and the Parsee three times. The invitation to attend the Congress declared: "Indirectly this Congress will form the germ of a Native Parliament, and, if properly conducted, will constitute in a few years an unanswerable reply to the assertion that India is still wholly unfit for any form of representative institutions." The President in his opening speech defined the aim of the Congress as "the eradication by direct friendly personal intercourse of all possible race, creed or provincial prejudices amongst all lovers of their country, and the fuller development and consolidation of those sentiments of national unity that had their origin in their beloved Lord Ripon's ever memorable reign." (Lord Ripon, the most popular nineteenth century viceroy, filled that office from 1880 to 1884.)

In the twentieth century the leadership of the Congress shifted from the liberal Westerners to the radical Indophils whose first leader was Bal Gandahar Tilak (1856-1920). They turned for inspiration to the Hindu past and to the orthodox masses and aroused a fierce and semi-religious nationalism. Tilak's work was continued, though with a shift to an emphasis on non-violence, by the Indian National Congress under the leadership of Mohandas Karamchand Gandhi (1869-1948). His way of life and his moral appeal succeeded in arousing the Indian peasant masses. By 1935 when the British for the first time officially envisaged dominion status for India, the Congress had truly become a "native Parliament" representing the nation and followed by the Hindu masses. Hardly more than a decade later India was an independent nation. (*See Reading No. 22.*) Yet, the Indian Mohammedans did not join it. They demanded their independence from Hindu rule. In opposition to the Congress they created the Indian Moslem League and adopted, under the leadership of Mohammed Ali Jinnah

(1876-1948), the policy of establishing a separate Muslim nation (Pakistan).

Nationalism in the Far East. In the half century from 1885 to 1935 the whole political outlook in Asia changed. The decisive event which caused the change was Japan's victory over Russia in 1905. It demonstrated the possibility of the triumph of a "backward" people, by means of Western technique and organization, over a great European military power which until then had conquered more Asian territory than any other "white" empire and threatened to control Mongolia, Manchuria, northern China, and all of Korea. This unexpected victory awakened new hopes and stirred the peoples of Asia and Africa into a new self-consciousness. The small Far Eastern island kingdom had after an effort of half a century attained an equal footing with the Western nations and now matched or outdid them in the pursuit of its own colonial and imperial policy. Should not other "backward" peoples follow this example? A number of nationalist reform movements swept Asia in the wake of Japan's victory. In Turkey (*see p. 63*), Persia, and China, age-old theocratic autocracies crumbled under the impact of nationalist revolutionary movements. Of the greatest importance was the Chinese Revolution led by Sun Yat-sen (1866-1925) who established the Kuomintang (National People's Party) and who formulated in his *San Min Chu I* the Three Principles of the People which were to guide the building-up of a Chinese nation. In January, 1919, he called upon "Chinese patriots" to follow his example in taking an oath: "I truthfully and sincerely take this public oath that from this moment I will destroy the old and build the new, and fight for the self-determination of the people, and will apply all my strength to the support of the Chinese Republic and the realization of democracy through the Three Principles, . . . for the progress of good government, the happiness and perpetual peace of the people, and for the strengthening of the foundations of the state in the name of peace throughout the world."

But in China as in other Oriental countries no foundations for liberal democracy and modern nationhood existed. The cohesive forces of the traditional order were destroyed, before new ones emerged. A long period of chaos was to follow. The situation was different in Japan and Turkey where the old ruling class preserved its vitality and guided the transformation, and in India and Ceylon where many decades of British administration had trained a native civil service and a large educated class of high ability, of great learning and integrity. Even with the political chaos in China, the closer contact with the West produced there, in an atmosphere traditionally satiated with scholarship, a brilliant cultural renaissance. Students educated abroad initiated upon their return a "tidal wave" of creative thinking, which, though it lasted only for a decade, from 1916 to 1926, changed the face of Young China. Up to that time all Chinese instruction was on traditional classical lines conducted in a language that had not been spoken for two thousand years and that was unintelligible to the people. In an article in the monthly *Hsin Ching Nien* (The New Youth) Hu Shih, modern China's leading scholar, advocated the use of the spoken language for literary purposes. This living "national language" was first made popular by the Chinese students using it in 1919 in their patriotic struggle against the Japanese. It rapidly became the instrument of public instruction and of the mass education movement. At Peking National University, Hu Shih and his fellow scholars, young men trained in the West, started a critical scrutiny of China's cultural heritage. With an unusual openmindedness and insight they tried to fuse Western values with an appreciation of China's best heritage. "Despite the universal distress," Richard Wilhelm wrote in 1927, "a colossal work, which the rest of the world has hardly any notion of, has been accomplished in China in the course of a few years, namely, the formation of a uniform language and uniform schools. The Chinese schools now constitute a means for welding together the entire Chinese people by a single method, into a single cultural community such as has never yet existed in all the thousands of years of Chinese history."

Chinese nationalism under the leadership of Chiang Kai-shek (b. 1886), Sun Yat-sen's successor as leader of the Kuomintang, and Korean nationalism under the veteran nationalist Syngman Rhee (b. 1875) fought for

national independence and unity against Japanese attempts to establish domination over the whole Far East.
The Japanese did not succeed, but the social and moral
chaos in the wake of their conquests and defeats prepared
the way for an authoritarian Communist nationalism.
Was Communism not an ally against imperialism and
Western capitalism? (*See Readings Nos. 22 and 23.*) Its
authoritarian pattern fitted native traditions better than
individual liberty; the underdeveloped peoples, wishing
for full equality, rejoiced at the prospect of following
Russia's road to heavy industrialization and economic independence.

World-Wide Nationalism. The twentieth century
since 1945 has become the first period in history in which
the whole of mankind has accepted one and the same
political attitude, that of nationalism. Its rise everywhere
implied an activization of the people and the demand for
a new ordering of society. But everywhere nationalism
differs in character according to the specific historic conditions and the peculiar social structure of each country.
World-wide nationalism has, however, not simplified the
task of creating a cohesive and cooperative human society. Ambitions among Asian and African peoples
threaten to clash as they have among European nations.
China has in no way been willing to grant national independence to Tibet or to the Mohammedan peoples in
Sinkiang; on the contrary, it is trying to reassert its
former imperial influence in Korea and Annam. Chinese
settlers throughout Southeast Asia and Indian settlers in
Eastern Africa, both enjoying the protection of their lands
of origin, may create difficulties recalling imperial conflicts of the recent past. With the promotion under British
leadership of new African nations in Nigeria and the Gold
Coast to independence and with the cultural and social
emancipation of the Indian element in many Latin American countries—a process in which Mexico through the
new Constitution of January 31, 1917, and the "Aztec
renaissance" has led the way—nationalism has become
the determining political and cultural force among all the
races and civilizations on earth.

Recrudescence of Nationalism. Nationalism in the
late 1960's shows its strength not only among Asian,

African, and Latin American peoples. Britain set an example in Asia in 1947 by declaring India, Pakistan, Ceylon, and Burma independent, and within practically a decade the political map of Asia has been completely changed under the propelling force of nationalism. In Africa, Britain again set the example in 1957 with the independence of Ghana, the British colony of the Gold Coast, and within a few years more than twenty former African colonies achieved the status of independent nation-states, though in many of them the survival of tribalism complicated the formation of nations. The aggression against Egypt by Israel, France, and Britain in 1956 to overthrow the nationalist regime of Gamal Abdul Nasser strengthened the latter's hold on Egypt and on the imagination of Arab peoples from Iraq to Algeria. The "new" nationalism in the less developed countries became "socialistic"; the popular governments recognized the state's obligation to promote the welfare of the masses and to combat the age-old poverty and illiteracy.

But nationalism showed its surprising strength also in the Communist countries. The former monolithic character of a supra-national ideology directed and authoritatively interpreted by Moscow gave way to the desire and right of every Communist country and party to follow its "own" road to "socialism," independent from Moscow and often critical of Moscow, a road rooted in the national traditions and conditions of the country. The two great Communist powers, Soviet Russia and China, vied openly for leadership among the Communist nations and parties; their competition threatened at some time to lead to an open break. Smaller countries, like Yugoslavia and Rumania, declared their neutrality between Russia and the capitalist countries and pursued their purely national interests. Small Communist Albania openly attacked Soviet Russia in the most violent way. With Nikita Khrushchev's process of de-Stalinization, an irreversible process of disintegration, in the name of nationalism, of the formerly unified supra-national Communist bloc set in.

Among the Western nations the process of integrating non-Communist Europe and the Atlantic community suffered a setback in the mid-1960's because of the revival of nationalism. Nationalism became dominant in France under President Charles de Gaulle (b. 1890), who stressed the absolute independence of his nation from West and East and claimed for it the leadership of Europe, and nationalism grew in strength in the German Federal Republic with the demand for the recognition of the frontiers of the German Reich of 1937. Greece and Turkey faced each other as adversaries over the future of Cyprus, where after December 1963 the Greek majority tried to control the Turkish minority. In Belgium the Flemish- and the French-speaking parts of the population renewed their mutual distrust and hostility. In Canada there was a strong separatist movement among the Catholic French-speaking Canadians of Quebec province.

The United Nations. The only recognized meeting ground for all races, nations, and ideologies·is the United Nations, which in its twenty years of existence has shown a much greater vitality and universality than the League of Nations did. There all nations enter more and more into an open discourse, which follows the methods evolved by the Western parliamentary tradition, and where the small nations are heard on equal terms with the great powers. The United Nations represents the realization of the entirely new situation which has emerged from World War II, where nationalism has become worldwide but where the deadly destructiveness of total weapons and, thanks to the new means of communication, the neighborly interdependence of all peoples on this shrinking earth demand a new and less bellicose attitude.

Part II

READINGS

— Reading No. 1 —

MACHIAVELLI: *AN EXHORTATION TO LIBERATE ITALY FROM THE BARBARIANS*[1]

In the famous 26th (final) chapter of The Prince, *which Machiavelli wrote in 1513 while exiled from his native Florence, he appealed to the Medici rulers of Florence—a member of the Medici family was then Pope Leo X—to liberate Italy.*

✦   ✦   ✦

When I take a review of the subject matter treated of in this book, and examine whether the circumstances in which we are now placed would be favourable to the establishment of a new government, honourable alike to its founder and advantageous to Italy, it appears to me that there never was, nor ever will be, a period more appropriate for the execution of so glorious an undertaking.

If it was necessary that the people of Israel should be slaves to Egypt, in order to elicit the rare talents of Moses, that the Persians should groan under the oppression of the Medes, in order to prove the courage and magnanimity of Cyrus; and that the Athenians should be scattered and dispersed, in order to make manifest the rare virtues of Theseus, it will be likewise necessary, for the glory of some Italian hero, that his country should

[1] Niccolò Machiavelli, *The History of Florence together with The Prince,* a new translation, London: Bell and Daldy, 1872, pp. 483-87.

be reduced to its present miserable condition, that they should be greater slaves than the Israelites, more op- pressed than the Persians, and still more dispered than the Athenian; in a word, that they should be without laws and without chiefs, pillaged, torn to pieces, and enslaved by foreign powers.

And though it has sometimes unquestionably happened that men have arisen, who appeared to be sent by Heaven to achieve our deliverance; yet jealous fortune has ever abandoned them in the midst of their career; so that our unfortunate country still groans and pines away in the expectation of a deliverer, who may put an end to the devastations in Lombardy, Tuscany, and the kingdom of Naples. She supplicates Heaven to raise up a prince who may free her from the odious and humiliating yoke of foreigners, who may close the numberless wounds with which she has been so long afflicted, and under whose standard she may march against her cruel oppressors.

But on whom can Italy cast her eyes except upon your illustrious house, which, visibly favoured by Heaven and the church, the government of which is confided to its care, possesses also the wisdom and the power necessary to undertake so glorious an enterprise? And I cannot think that the execution of this project will seem difficult if you reflect on the actions and conduct of the heroes whose examples I have above adduced. Though their exploits were indeed wonderful, they were still but men; and al- though their merit raised them above others, yet none of them certainly were placed in a situation so favourable as that in which you now stand. You have justice on your side; their cause was not more lawful than yours, and the blessing of God will attend you no less than them. Every war that is necessary is just; and it is humanity to take up arms for the defence of a people to whom no other resource is left.

All circumstances concur to facilitate the execution of so noble a project, for the accomplishment of which it will only be necessary to tread in the steps of those great men whom I have had an opportunity of mentioning in the course of this work. For though some of them, it is true, were conducted by the hand of God in a wonderful manner, though the sea divided to let them pass, a cloud directed their course, a rock streamed with water to assuage their thirst, and manna fell from heaven to appease their hunger, yet there is no occasion for such miracles at present, as you possess in yourself sufficient power to execute a plan you ought by no mean neglect. God will not do everything for us; much is left to ourselves, and the free exercise of our will, that so our own actions may not be wholly destitute of merit.

If none of our princes have hitherto been able to effect what is now expected from your illustrious house, and if Italy has continually been unfortunate in her wars, the evil has arisen from the defects in military discipline, which no person has possessed the ability to reform.

Nothing reflects so much honour on a new prince as the new laws and institutions established under his direction, especially when they are good, and bear the character of grandeur. Now it must be acknowledged that Italy soon accommodates herself to new forms. Her inhabitants are by no means deficient in courage, but they are destitute of proper chiefs; the proof of this is in the duels and other individual combats in which the Italians have always evinced consummate ability, whilst their valour in battles has appeared well-nigh extinguished. This can only be attributed to the weakness of the officers, who are unable to ensure obedience from those who know, or think they know, the art of war.

If therefore your illustrious house is willing to regulate its conduct by the example of our ancestors, who have delivered their country from the rule of foreigners, it is necessary, above all things, as the only true foundation of every enterprise, to set on foot a national army; you cannot have better or more faithful soldiers, and though every one of them may be a good man, yet they will become still better when they are all united, and see themselves honoured, caressed, and rewarded by a prince of their own.

It is therefore absolutely necessary to have troops raised in our own country, if we wish to protect it from the invasion of foreign powers. The Swiss as well as the Spanish infantry are highly esteemed, but both have defects which may be avoided in the formation of our troops, which would render them superior to both of those powers. The Spaniards cannot support the shock of cavalry, and the Swiss cannot maintain their ground against infantry that is equally resolute with themselves.

It is necessary therefore to institute a military force possessing neither the defects of the Swiss or the Spanish infantry, and that may be able to maintain its ground against the French cavalry, and this is to be effected, not by changing their arms, but by altering their discipline. Nothing is more likely to make a new prince esteemed, and to render his reign illustrious.

Such an opportunity ought eagerly to be embraced, that Italy after her long sufferings, may at least behold her deliverer appear. With what demonstrations of joy and gratitude, with what affection, with what impatience for revenge, would he not be received by those unfortunate provinces, who have so long groaned under such odious oppression. What city would shut her gates against him, and what people would be so blind as to refuse him obedience? What rivals would he have to dread? Is there one Italian who would not hasten to pay him homage? All are weary of the tyranny of these barbarians. May your illustrious house, strong in all the hopes which justice gives our cause, deign to undertake this noble enterprise, that so, under your banners, our nation may resume its ancient splendour, and, under your auspices, behold the prophecy of Petrarch at last fulfilled.

> *Virtù contr'al furore*
> *Prendera l'arme et sia il combatter corto*
> *Che l'antico valore*
> *Ne gl'Italici cuor non è ancor morto.*

> When virtue takes the field,
> Short will the conflict be,
> Barbarian rage shall yield
> The palm to Italy:
> For patriot blood still warms Italian veins,
> Though low the fire, a spark at least remains.

— Reading No. 2 —

MICHELET: *ON THE UNITY OF THE FATHERLAND*[2]

Michelet, who wrote a History of the French Revolution and a History of France from the point of view of the nationalism of 1789, dedicated some famous pages to the description of the "spontaneous organization of France" from July, 1789, to July, 1790, under the impact of "the new principle" and "the new religion" of patriotism.

✓   ✓   ✓

I have related fully the resistance offered by the old principle,—the parliaments, the nobility, and the clergy; and I am now going to expound, in a few words, the new principle, and state briefly the immense fact, by which their resistance was confounded and annihilated. The fact, admirably simple in its infinite variety, is the spontaneous organization of France. . . . The great national facts, in which France has acted in concord, have been accomplished by immense, invincible, and, for that very reason, by no means violent, powers. They have excited less attention, and passed almost unperceived. . . .

France was born and started into life at the sound of the cannon of the Bastille. In one day, without any preparation or previous understanding, the whole of France, both cities and villages, were organized at the same time. The same thing happens in every locality: the people go to the communal house, take the keys and assume the power in the name of the nation. The electors (everybody was an elector in 1789) form committees, like that

[a] Jules Michelet, *Historical View of the French Revolution, from its Earliest Indications to the Flight of the King in 1791,* tr. by C. Cocks, new ed., London: S. Bell and Sons, 1890, Book III, chaps, X-XII, pp. 382-403.

of Paris, which will presently produce the regular municipalities. . . .

Nothing of all this existed in the winter of 1789: there
were neither any regular municipalities nor any depart-
ments: no laws, no authority, no public power. Everything, one would think, is about to fall into chaos; and
this is the hope of the aristocracy . . . "Ah! you wanted
to be free. Look about you, and enjoy the order you
have created." To this what reply is made by France? At
that formidable crisis, she becomes her own law; and,
without any assistance, springs, with a powerful will, over
the chasm between one world and the other, passes without stumbling the narrow bridge over the abyss, without
heeding the danger, with her eyes fixed on the goal. She
advances courageously through that dark winter, towards
the wished-for spring which promises a new light to the
world.

All that had been believed painful, difficult, and insur-
mountable, becomes possible and easy. People had asked
themselves how the sacrifice of provincial sentiments,
reminiscences, and inveterate prejudices, was to be accomplished. "How," said they, "will Languedoc ever
consent to cease to be Languedoc, an interior empire
governed by its own laws? How will ancient Toulouse
descend from her capitol, her royalty of the South? And
do you believe that Brittany will ever give way to France,
emerge from her barbarous language and obstinate
character? You will sooner see the rocks of Saint
Malo and Penmarck change their nature and become
soft."

But lo! the native land appears to them on the altar,
opening her arms and wishing to embrace them. . . .
And they all rush towards her and forget themselves, no
longer knowing on that day to what province they belong. . . . Like children gone astray, and lost till then,
they have at length found a mother; they had been so
humble as to imagine themselves Bretons, Provencaux.
No, children, know well that you were the sons of
France; she herself tells you so; the sons of that great
mother, of her who is destined, in equality, to bring forth
nations.

Is all this a miracle? Yes, and the greatest and most

simple of miracles, a return to nature. The fundamental
basis of human nature is sociability. It had required a
whole world of inventions against nature to prevent men
from living together. Interior custom-duties, innumerable
tolls on roads and rivers, an infinite diversity of laws and
regulations, weights, measures, and money, and rivalry
carefully encouraged and maintained between cities,
countries, and corporations,—all these obstacles, these old
ramparts, crumble and fall in a day. Men then behold
one another, perceive they are alike, are astonished to
have been able to remain so long ignorant to one another,
regret the senseless animosity which had separated them
for so many centuries, and expiate it by advancing to
meet and embrace one another with a mutual effusion of
the heart. . . .

In those immense assemblies wherein people of every
class and every communion have but one and the self-
same heart, there is something more sacred than an altar.
No special form of worship can confer holiness on the
most holy of holy things,—man fraternizing in the presence of God. All the old emblems grow pale, and the
new ones that are essayed have but little signification.
Whether people swear on the old altar, before the Holy
Sacrament, or take the oath before the cold image of
abstract liberty, the true symbol is elsewhere. The beauty,
the grandeur, the eternal charm of those festivals, is that
the symbol is a living one. The symbol for man is man.
All the conventional world crumbling to pieces, a holy
respect possesses him for the true image of God. He does
not mistake himself for God: he has no vain pride. It is
not as a ruler or a conqueror, but in far more affecting
and serious attributes that man appears here. The noble
harmonious sentiments of family, nature, and native land,
are sufficient to fill these festivals with a religious, pathetic
interest. . . .

Dauphiné, the serious and valiant province which
opened the Revolution, made numerous confederations of
the whole province, and of the towns and villages. The
rural communes of the frontier nearest to Savoy, close to
the emigrants, and tilling the ground in the neighborhood
of their guns, did but have still finer festivals. They had
a battalion of children, another of women, and another

of maidens, all armed. At Maubec they filed along in good order, headed by a banner, bearing and handling their naked swords with that graceful skill peculiar to the women of France. I have related elsewhere the heroic example of the women and maidens of Angers. They wanted to depart and follow the young army of Anjou and Brittany marching for Rennes, to take their share in that first crusade of liberty, to feed the combatants, and take care of the wounded. They swore they would never marry any but loyal citizens, love only the valiant, and associate for life only with those who devoted theirs to France. . . .

Women are kept back from public life; and people are too apt to forget that they really have more right to it than any. The stake they venture is very different from ours; man plays only his life; but woman stakes her child. She is far more interested in acquiring information and foresight. In the solitary sedentary life which most women lead, they follow, in their anxious musings, the critical events of their country, and the movements of the armies. The mind of this woman, whom you believe to be entirely occupied with her household duties, is wandering in Algeria, sharing all the privations and marches of our young soldiers in Africa, and suffering and fighting with them. But, whether called or not, they took the most active part in the *fêtes* of the confederations. . . .

Nobody was able to absent himself from the festival, for no one was a mere spectator; all were actors, from the centenarian to the new-born infant; and the latter more so than any. He was carried like a living flower among the flowers of the harvest, offered by his mother, and laid upon the altar. But it was not the passive part of an offering alone that he had to perform; he was active also; he was accounted a person; took his civic oath by the lips of his mother; claimed his dignity as a man and a Frenchman; was put at once in possession of his native land, and received his share of hope. Yes, the child, the future generation, was the principal actor. At a festival in Dauphiné, the commune itself is crowned, in the person of its principal magistrate, by a young child. Such a hand brings good fortune. These youths, whom I now behold under the anxious eye of their mother, will, in two years' time, at the age of fifteen or sixteen, depart in arms, full of military enthusiasm; the year '92 will have summoned them, and they will follow their elders to Jemmapes. These future soldiers of Austerlitz. Their hand has brought good fortune; they have accomplished the good omen, and crowned their native land; and even today, though feeble and pale, France still wears that eternal crown, and overawes nations.

How great and happy the generation born amidst such things, and whose first gaze was gladdened by that sublime spectacle! Children brought and blessed at the altar of their native land, devoted by their weeping, but resigned and heroic mothers, and bestowed by them on France. Oh! those who are thus born can never die. You received on that day the cup of immortality. Even those among you whom history has not mentioned, nevertheless fill the world with your nameless living spirit, with that great unanimous idea which, sword in hand, they extended throughout the world. I do not believe that the heart of man was at any period more teeming with a vast and comprehensive affection, or that the distinctions of classes, fortunes, and parties, were ever so much forgotten. In the villages, especially, there are no longer either rich or poor, nobles or plebeians; there is but one general table, and provisions are in common; social dissensions and quarrels have disappeared; enemies become reconciled; and opposite sects, believers and philosophers, Protestants and Catholics fraternize together. . . .

Man who, in our old churches, never saw his fellows' face, saw them here,—saw himself for the first time, and from the eyes of a whole people received a spark of God. He perceived nature, seized it again, and found it still sacred: for in it he perceived his God. And he called that people and that country by the name he had found,— Native Land. And however large this *Patria* may be, he enlarges his heart so as to embrace it all. He beholds it with the eyes of the mind, and clasps it with the longings of desire. Ye mountains of our native land, which bound our sight, but not our thoughts, be witness that if we do not clasp in one brotherly embrace the great family of France, it is already contained in our hearts.

. . . Ye sacred rivers, ye holy islands, where our altar was erected, may your waters, murmuring beneath the current of the spirit, go and proclaim to every sea and every nation, that, today, at the solemn banquet of liberty, we would not have broken bread, without having invited them, and that on this day of happiness, all humanity was present in the soul and wishes of France!

This faith, this candour, this immense impulse of concord, after a whole century of dispute, was a subject of great astonishment for every nation; it was like a wonderful dream, and they all remained dumb and affected. Several of our confederations had imagined a touching symbol of union, that of celebrating marriages at the altar of the native land. Confederation itself, a union of France with France, seemed a prophetic symbol of the future alliance of nations, of the general marriage of the world. Another symbol, no less affecting, appeared at these festivals. Occasionally they placed upon the altar a little child whom everybody adopted, and who, endowed with the gifts, the prayers, the tears of the whole assembly, became the relation of everybody. That child upon the altar is France, with all the world surrounding her. In her, the common child of nations, they all feel themselves united, and all participating heartily in her future destiny, are anxiously praying around her, full of fear and hope. . . . Not one of them beholds her without weeping. How Italy wept! and Poland! and Ireland! (Ah! sister sufferers. remember that day forever!). . . . Every oppressed nation, unmindful of its slavery at the sight of infant liberty, exclaimed: "In thee I am free!"

━ Reading No. 3 ━

HERDER: GERMANS AND SLAVS³

In the sixteenth book of his Ideas for the History of Mankind *(1784-1791), Herder discussed the peoples of Northern Europe.*

✔   ✔   ✔

As we now proceed, to discuss the peoples of the northern section of the Old World, who are our ancestors and from whom we have received our customs and constitutions, I think it necessary first to plead for the right to tell the truth. For what would be the use if we were allowed to write freely about the peoples of Asia or Africa, but would have to veil our opinion about peoples and periods, which concern us much more than everything that has been long buried in the dust beyond the Alps and the Taurus? History demands truth, and a philosophy of the history of mankind demands at least the love of impartial truth. . . .

Rather we shall look into the mirror of truth, we shall recognize ourselves in it, and if we find ourselves still covered with some of the barbaric ornaments of our ancestors, we shall exchange them for civilization and humanitarianism, the only true ornaments of the human race. Before we enter the edifice, which has become famous under the name of the European Republic and has become memorable or terrible by its effects upon the whole globe, let us first get acquainted with the peoples, who by their activities or suffering have contributed to the building of this great temple. . . .

(*After discussing in section I the origins and character of the Basques and Celts, Herder took up in section II*

³Johann Gottfried von Herder, *Sämtliche Werke*, Stuttgart and Tübingen: Cotta, 1853, vol. XXX, pp. 3, 16 ff., 23 ff., 30 ff.

the Finns, Latvians, and Prussians. This section con-
cludes:)

Surrounded by German, Slav and Finn peoples, the peace-loving Latvians could neither expand nor achieve a higher degree of civilization. Like their Prussian neighbors, they became ultimately most famous by the acts of violence which all these Baltic peoples suffered partly from the newly Christianized Poles and partly from the (German) Teutonic Knights. Humanity shudders at the blood that was shed there in long and wild wars, in which the old Prussians were almost entirely exterminated, while the Courlanders and Latvians were enslaved, a yoke which they still carry. Perhaps it will take centuries to free them from the yoke and to bring them instead of the horrors, by which these quiet peoples were robbed of their land and liberty, the enjoyment of a better liberty. But long enough have we dwelled with these displaced, subjected, or exterminated peoples: let us see now those who displaced and subjugated them.

German People

We pass now to the family of peoples which more than all others have contributed to the weal and woe of this continent—be it by reason of their tallness and bodily strength, their bold, enterprising hardiness and valor, their heroic sense of duty that moved them to march after their chiefs wherever they might lead and to divide conquered countries as spoils of war, or also by reason of their far-flung conquests and the constitution laid down everywhere after the German model. From the Black Sea throughout Europe German arms have spread terror: from the Volga to the Baltic there extended once a Gothic empire: in Thrace, Moesia, Pannonia, Italy, Gaul, Spain, even in Africa diverse German peoples had their seats and founded empires at diverse times. . . . Even now, thanks partly to the princes whom they have set upon all the thrones of Europe, partly to their own founding of these thrones, they rule, to a greater or lesser extent, all four continents of the earth, be it by outright possession or by means of industry and trade. Since there is no effect without a cause, this tremendous chain of effects must also have its cause.

(1) This cause must not be sought in the nation's character alone; the course of their achievements grew out of their position, both physical and political, and the combination of a host of circumstances unparalleled in any other northern people. Since early times Germans served in the Roman army and furnished the choicest men for the emperor's bodyguard; even more, when the sorely pressed empire was unable to maintain itself, it was German armies that fought for hire against anyone, even their own brethren. Through this service that lasted for centuries, many of their peoples acquired, not only a military expertness and discipline to which other barbarians had to remain strangers, but also a taste for conquests and expeditions of their own which were gradually suggested to them by the example of the Romans and by their own acquaintance with Roman weakness.

(2) The long resistance which many peoples of our German land had to offer the Romans, was bound to fortify them in their powers and in their hatred for an hereditary foe who gloried more in triumphs over them than in other victories.

(3) With such a permanently warlike constitution the Germans must necessarily be deficient in some other virtues, which they were not loth to sacrifice to their chief inclination, or their chiefest need: war. To agriculture they did not apply themselves too well; nay, in some tribes they redistributed lands every year to prevent anyone from finding some enjoyment in his own possessions and in the better cultivation of the soil. Some tribes, especially to the east, did long remain Tartaric people of hunters and herdsmen. The favorite idea of these nomads was the crude idea of common pastures and common property, which they introduced into the institutions of the countries and empires conquered by them. Thus Germany long remained a forest filled with meadows, swamps, and marshes, where the aurochs and elk, German hero-animals, now extinct, dwelt close to the German hero-man. Sciences they did not know, and the few arts indispensable to them were practised by women and largely by kidnapped slaves. People of this sort must be pleased when, driven by revenge, poverty, boredom,

social ties, or some other motive, they could leave their dreary forests, seek after better regions, or serve for hire. Thus it went on land, thus on the sea—rather a Tartaric manner of life. . . .

Having embraced Christianity, the German peoples fought for it with the same true warrior's fealty with which they fought for their kings and their nobles; some of their own peoples, the Alemans, Thuringians, Bavarians, and Saxons, and beyond these, the poor Slavs, Prussians, Courlanders, Livonians, and Esths have known this to their cost. It is the German's glory that they stood firm against the later barbaric incursions as well: a living wall against which the mad fury of Huns, Hungarians, Mongols and Turks dashed itself to pieces. Thus it is they by whom the major part of Europe has been, not only conquered, cultivated, and arranged after their own manner, but protected and defended: otherwise that which has sprung up there could never have sprung up. Their stature among other peoples, their warriors' leagues and inborn character have become the foundations of Europe's culture, freedom, and safety. Will not their political position make them a contributing cause in the gradual progress of this culture? A witness of spotless integrity, history will report on this question.

Slavic Peoples

The Slavic peoples occupy a larger space on earth than they do in history, the cause being, among other things, that they lived farther distant from the Romans. We know of them as having lived first along the Don, later along the Danube—there mingling with Goths, here with Huns and Bulgars. With these they would set out to harass the Roman Empire, serving in most cases as mere auxiliary or vassal peoples. Despite the deeds they accomplished here and there, they never were an enterprising people of warriors or adventurers like the Germans; they rather followed after the latter and quietly occupied the sites and countries left vacant by them till finally they encompassed the immense stretch of territory that reaches from the Don to the Elbe, from the Baltic to the Adriatic Sea.

Everywhere they settled to take possession of land

abandoned by other peoples, to cultivate and to use it as colonists, herdsmen or plowmen. Thus, after all the previous devastations, migrations, and evacuations, countries would benefit by their tranquil, industrious presence. They loved agriculture stores of grain and cattle, and manifold domestic arts, and everywhere they began a useful commerce with the products of their land and their industry. Along the Baltic shore, from Lübeck onward, they had erected maritime cities, among which Vineta, on the island of Rugen, was a Slavic Amsterdam; in this way they associated also with the Prussians, Courlanders, and Letts, as the language of these peoples still shows. On the Dniepr they built Kiev, on the Volkhov, Novgorod, both of which soon grew into flourishing merchant cities, uniting the Black and Baltic Seas and conveying the products of the East to northern and western Europe. In Germany they engaged in mining, they knew how to smelt and pour metals, they prepared salt, produced linen, brewed mead, planted orchards, and after their manner, led a merry musical life. They were charitable, hospitable to excess, lovers of free country ways, yet submissive and obedient, averse to pillage and robbery. All this was no use to them against oppression, it conduced to it. As they never competed for dominion over the world and, lacking hereditary warrior princes, preferred instead to pay tribute if this left them to pursue their quiet life on their land, they have been sinned against by many nations, most of all by those of the German family.

Already under Charlemagne there began those wars of oppression whose obvious motive was commercial advantage, though Christian religion was used as a pretext. Plainly the heroic Franks must find it quite convenient to hold in bondage a nation proficient in farming and commerce, rather than learning and exercising these arts for themselves. What the Franks had begun, the Saxons completed: through entire provinces the Slavs were wiped out or made serfs, and their lands were distributed among bishops and noblemen. Their Baltic trade was destroyed by Germanic Norsemen, Vineta was brought to a sad end by the Danes, and their remainder in Germany resembles that which the Spaniards have made of the Peruvians. After centuries of subjugation and deepest bitterness

against their Christian masters and robbers, is it any
wonder that the soft character of this nation has been
debased to the cruel, treacherous sullenness of the bonds-
man? And nevertheless one may still discern everywhere
their ancient traits, more especially in countries where
they enjoy some freedom. This people has grown unhappy,' because in its love of tranquillity and domestic
industry, it was unable to give itself a permanent warlike
constitution, though in a hot defensive battle it may not
have lacked for bravery. It was unfortunate that its
location among the earth's peoples brought it so close to
the Germans on one side, and on the other left its back
exposed to all attacks of oriental Tartars, nay Mongols,
under whom it has suffered greatly, endured much. Yet
the wheel of transmuting time runs its irresistible circle.
Most of these nations dwell in a region which, once fully
cultivated and opened to trade, will be Europe's finest.
Besides, one can hardly doubt that in European legislation and politics ever greater care must and will be given
to quiet industry, not to the spirit of war, and peaceful
intercourse will be promoted among peoples. Thus even
you, O submerged peoples that were once happy and
industrious, will finally rouse from your long, languid
slumber; delivered from your chains of bondage, you will
be able to possess and use your beautiful regions from
the Adriatic to the Carpathians, from the Don to the
Moldau, and will be free to celebrate there your ancient
festivals of quiet industry and trade.

Since many fine and useful contributions have been
made to the history of this people for several of its
regions, it is desirable to fill the gaps in our knowledge
of the others as well. The dwindling remnants of their
customs, songs, and legends should be collected, and
finally there should be painted a history of the family as
a whole, a history appropriate to the canvas of mankind.

General Considerations and Consequences

This is more or less a picture of the peoples of Europe.
What a multicolored and composite picture . . . Sea
voyages and long migrations of people on land finally
produced on the small continent of Europe the conditions
for a great league of nations. Unwittingly the Romans

had prepared it by their conquests. Such a league of nations was unthinkable outside of Europe. Nowhere else have people intermingled so much, nowhere else have they changed so often and so much their habitats and thereby their customs and ways of life. In many European countries it would be difficult today for the inhabitants, especially for single families and individuals, to say, from which people they descend, whether from Goths, Moors, Jews, Carthaginians or Romans, whether from Gauls, Burgundians, Franks, Normans, Saxons, Slavs, Finns or Illyrians, or how in the long line of their ancestors their blood had been mixed. Hundreds of causes have tempered and changed the old tribal composition of the European nations in the course of the centuries; without such an intermingling the common spirit of Europe could hardly have been awakened.

. . . Like the geological layers of our soil, the European peoples have been superimposed on each other and intermingling with each other, and yet can still be discerned in their original character. The scholars who study their customs and languages must hurry and do so while these peoples are still distinguishable: for everything in Europe tends towards the slow extinction of national character. But the historian of mankind should beware lest he exclusively favors one nationality and thereby slights others who were deprived by circumstances of chance and glory. From the Slavs too the German learned; the Welsh and the Latvians could perhaps have become Greeks, if their situation had been geographically different. We can be very happy that the Huns and the Bulgars did not occupy the Roman world, but a noble, chaste and loyal people like the Germans. It would however betray the ignoble pride of a barbarian, to therefore regard the Germans as God's chosen people in Europe, destined by its innate nobility to rule the world and to enslave other peoples. The barbarian rules and dominates; the educated conqueror educates.

No European people has become cultured and educated by itself. Each one tended to keep its old barbarian customs as long as it could, supported therein by the roughness of the climate and the need of primitive warfare. No European people for instance has invented its own alphabet; the whole civilization of northern, eastern and western Europe has grown out of seeds sown by Romans, Greeks and Arabs. It took a long time before this plant could grow in the hard soil and could produce its own fruit which at first lacked sweetness and ripeness. A strange vehicle, an alien religion, was necessary to accomplish by spiritual means that which the Romans had not been able to do through conquest. Thus we must consider above all this new means of human education, which had no lesser aim than to educate all peoples to become one people, in this world and for a future world, and which was nowhere more effective than in Europe.

— Reading No. 4 —

HEGEL: *THE STATE* [4]

In his Lectures on the Philosophy of History, *which Hegel delivered at the University of Berlin between 1823 and 1831 and which were only published after his death from lecture notes, he discussed the state as a decisive factor in history.*

✓   ✓   ✓

In the history of the World, only those peoples can come under our notice which form a state. For it must be understood that this latter is the realization of Freedom, i.e. of the absolute final aim, and that it exists for its own sake. It must further be understood that all the worth which the human being possesses—all spiritual reality, he possesses only through the State. For his

[4] Georg Wilhelm Friedrich Hegel, *Lectures on the Philosophy of History,* tr. by J. Sibree, London: G. Bell & Sons, 1890, pp. 40 f., 70.

spiritual reality consists in this, that his own essence—
Reason—is objectively present to him, that it possesses
objective immediate existence for him. Thus only is he
fully conscious; thus only is he a partaker of morality—
of a just and moral social and political life. For Truth
is the Unity of the universal and subjective Will; and the
Universal is to be found in the State, in its laws, its
universal and rational arrangements. The State is the
Divine Idea as it exists on Earth. We have in it, therefore,
the object of History in a more definite shape than before; that in which Freedom obtains objectivity, and lives
in the enjoyment of this objectivity. For Law is the
objectivity of Spirit; volition in its true form. Only that
will which obeys law, is free; for it obeys itself—it is
independent and so free. When the State or our country
constitutes a community of existence; when the subjective
will of man submits to laws—the contradiction between
Liberty and Necessity vanishes. The Rational has necessary existence, as being the reality and substance of things,
and we are free by recognizing it as law, and by following
it as the substance of our own being. The objective and
the subjective will are then reconciled, and present one
identical homogeneous whole. For the morality (*Sitt-
lichkeit*) of the State is not of that ethical (*moralische*)
reflective kind, in which one's own conviction bears sway;
this latter is rather the peculiarity of the modern time,
while the true antique morality is based on the principle
of abiding by one's duty (to the state at large.) An
Athenian citizen did what was required of him as it were
from instinct; but if I reflect on the object of my activity,
I must have the consciousness that my will has been
called into exercise. But morality is Duty—the substantial
Right—a "second nature" as it has been called; for the
first nature of man is his primary merely animal
existence. . . .

For the History of the World occupies a higher ground
than that on which morality has properly its position,
which is personal character—the conscience of individuals
—their particular will and mode of action; these have a
value, imputation, reward of punishment proper to themselves. What the absolute aim of Spirit requires and ac-
complishes—what Providence does—transcends the obli-

gation and the ascription of good or bad motives, which attach to individuality in virtue of its social relations. They who on moral grounds, and consequently with noble intention, have resisted that which the advance of the Spiritual Idea makes necessary, stand higher in moral worth than those whose crimes have been turned into the means—under the direction of a superior principle—of realizing the purposes of that principle. But in such revolutions both parties generally stand within the limits of the same circle of transient and corruptible existence. Consequently it is only a formal rectitude—deserted by the living Spirit and by God—which those who stand upon ancient right and order maintain. The deeds of great men, who are the Individuals of the World's History, thus appear not only justified in view of that intrinsic result of which they were not conscious, but also from the point of view occupied by the secular moralist. But looked at from this point, moral claims that are irrelevant must not be brought into collision with world-historical deeds and their accomplishment. The Litany of private virtues—modesty, humility, philanthropy and for-bearance—must not be raised against them. The History of the World might, on principle, entirely ignore the circle within which morality and the so much talked-of distinction between moral and politic lies not only in abstaining from judgments, for the principles involved, and the necessary reference of the deeds in question to those principles, are a sufficient judgment of them—but in leaving Individuals quite out of view and unmentioned. What it has to record is the activity of the Spirit of Peoples, so that the individual forms which that spirit has assumed in the sphere of outward reality might be left to the delineation of special histories. . . .

— Reading No. 5 —

GUIZOT: *HISTORICAL STUDIES*[5]

The study of history, especially that of documents and archives connected with national beginnings, plays a great role in the development of nationalism. François Guizot (1787-1874), who was himself a historian of renown, as minister of education played an important part in the establishment of the Society for the History of France.

✓   ✓   ✓

Our tastes easily become manias, and an idea which has long and powerfully possessed us, assumes an importance in our estimation to which vanity often lends too much faith. Nevertheless, the more I reflect, the more I feel convinced that I have not exaggerated to myself the interest which a nation ought to take in its own history; nor the advantage it gains in political intelligence as well as in moral dignity, by completely understanding and attaching itself to this subject. In the long course of successive generations, denominated a people, how rapidly each passes away! And in that short passage how narrowly is the horizon bounded! How insignificant is the place we occupy, and how little do we see with our own eyes! We require to magnify our thoughts, that we may be able to take a serious view of life. Religion opens the future and places us in presence of eternity. History brings back the past and adds to our own existence the lives of our fathers. When we turn to them, our perceptions rise and extend. When we thoroughly know them, we acquire a better knowledge and comprehension of ourselves. Our own destiny, our present situation, the circumstances which surround and the necessities which press upon us, become more clear and natural in our eyes.

[5] François Guizot, *Memoirs to Illustrate the History of My Time,* tr. by J. W. Cole, vol. III, London: Richard Bentley, 1860, pp. 161-69.

We not only gratify science and imagination, by thus associating ourselves with the events and persons that have preceded us on the same soil and under the same heaven, but we take from the ideas and passions of the day much of their narrow sourness. Amongst a people interested and well instructed in their own history, we are almost sure of finding a more wholesome and equitable judgment on their present affairs, the conditions of their progress, and their chances for the future.

The same idea and hope by which I had been governed and animated in my course of lectures at the Sorbonne, on the development of French civilization, followed me to the ministry of Public Instruction, and regulated my efforts to revive and expand the taste for, and study of, our national history. From this source, assuredly, I looked for no rapid or widely-spreading effect, either as to the abatement of political passions or the correction of popular prejudices. I knew too well already how deeply they are rooted, and that powerful and repeated blows from the hand of God Himself are necessary to extirpate them. But I expected that in Paris, in the first instance, in the centre of studies and ideas, and subsequently in various parts of France, a certain number of intelligent spirits would acquire more correct and impartial notions of the different elements of what French society is composed, of their mutual relations and rights, and of the value of their historical traditions in the new social combinations of our own days. I was not disheartened by the inevitable slowness of this intellectual progress, nor by the still more tardy effect of its public influence. There is pride in the pretension of reforming the errors of our time; those who indulge in it must be content with even a glimpse of success. They preach patience to nations in the pursuit of their desires; let them learn to practice patience themselves in their own labours and hopes.

Before 1830, I had obtained, not only with the public and by my lectures, but in the general system of public instruction, some important results in respect to the study of history. This study was not even named in the law which, under the Consulate, in 1802, had re-established secondary education. "In the lyceums will be taught," says the tenth article, "the classical languages, rhetoric, logic, moral philosophy, and the elements of mathematical and physical science." A step was made in the statute, by which the council of the University, in 1814, regulated the discipline and course of study in the colleges; instruction in history and geography was then introduced, but in a very accessory form. . . .

I was more impatient than anyone else to open new sources of wholesome strength and prosperity to the studies to which I was so warmly attached, and which I saw seriously endangered. Public feeling came to my assistance. If superior instruction in history had suffered a considerable check, the taste for historical researches and reflections was evidently extending, and afforded intellectual gratification, with the chance of literary fame, local or general, to many active minds who were neither attracted nor encouraged by political life. Several of my friends communicated to me their project for founding, under the title of Society of the History of France, an association specially devoted to the publication of original documents relative to our national history, and with a view to disseminate, either by correspondence regularly carried on, or by a monthly Bulletin, a general knowledge of the scattered and neglected labors of which it was the object. I hastened to give this plan my assent and cooperation. We met together on the 27th of June, 1833, to the number of twenty institutors; we arranged the bases of the association, and a little more than six months later, on the 23rd of January, 1834, the Society of the History of France, reckoning already one hundred members, formed itself into a general assembly, adopted definitive regulations, appointed a council to superintend its labours, and took the field in full activity. What it has since accomplished during twenty-five years is well known. It has printed seventy-one volumes of memoirs and unpublished documents, nearly all of the highest interest to our history, and some containing authentic discoveries, equally curious and important for the amateur and the professional scholar. . . .

GREEK NATIONAL ASSEMBLY: *PROCLAMATION OF INDEPENDENCE*[6]

*On January 27, 1822, "the first year of independence,"
the Greek National Assembly, which met in the ancient
seaport of Epidaurus near Argos to work out a provisional
constitution, issued the following manifesto to the peoples
of Europe.*

✓   ✓   ✓

We, descendants of the wise and noble peoples of
Hellas, we who are the contemporaries of the enlightened
and civilized nations of Europe, we who behold the advantages which they enjoy under the protection of the
impenetrable aegis of the law, find it no longer possible
to suffer without cowardice and self-contempt the cruel
yoke of the Ottoman power which has weighed upon us
for more than four centuries,—a power which does not
listen to reason and knows no other law than its own
will, which orders and disposes everything despotically
and according to its caprice. After this prolonged slavery
we have determined to take arms to avenge ourselves and
our country against a frightful tyranny, iniquitous in its
very essence,—an unexampled despotism to which no
other rule can be compared.

The war which we are carrying on against the Turk is
not that of a faction or the result of sedition. It is not
aimed at the advantage of any single part of the Greek
people; it is a national war, a holy war, a war the object
of which is to reconquer the rights of individual liberty,
of property and honor,—rights which the civilized people of Europe, our neighbors, enjoy today; rights of

ᵃ *British and Foreign State Papers,* London: J. Harrison and
Sons, 1829, vol. IX, pp. 629 ff.

which the cruel and unheard of tyranny of the Ottomans would deprive us—us alone—and the very memory of which they would stifle in our hearts.

Are we, then, less reasonable than other peoples, that we remain deprived of these rights? Are we of a nature so degraded and abject that we should be viewed as unworthy to enjoy them, condemned to remain crushed under a perpetual slavery and subjected, like beasts of burden or mere automatons, to the absurd caprice of a cruel tyrant who, like an infamous brigand, has come from distant regions to invade our borders? Nature has deeply graven these rights in the hearts of all men; laws in harmony with nature have so completely consecrated them that neither three nor four centuries—nor thousands nor millions of centuries—can destroy them. Force and violence have been able to restrict and paralyze them for a season, but force may once more resuscitate them in all the vigor which they formerly enjoyed during many centuries; nor have we ever ceased in Hellas to defend these rights by arms whenever opportunity offered.

Building upon the foundation of our natural rights, and desiring to assimilate ourselves to the rest of the Christians of Europe, our brethren, we have begun a war against the Turks, or rather, uniting all our isolated strength, we have formed ourselves into a single armed body, firmly resolved to attain our end, to govern ourselves by wise laws, or to be altogether annihilated, believing it to be unworthy of us, as descendants of the glorious peoples of Hellas, to live henceforth in a state of slavery fitted rather for unreasoning animals than for rational beings.

Ten months have elapsed since we began this national war; the all-powerful God has succored us; although we were not adequately prepared for so great an enterprise, our arms have everywhere been victorious, despite the powerful obstacles which we have encountered and still encounter everywhere. We have had to contend with a situation bristling with difficulties, and we are still engaged in our efforts to overcome them. It should not, therefore, appear astonishing that we were not able from the very first to proclaim our independence and take rank among the civilized peoples of the earth, marching

forward side by side with them. It was impossible to
occupy ourselves with our political existence before we
had established our independence. We trust these reasons
may justify, in the eyes of the nations, our delay, as well
as console us for the anarchy in which we have found
ourselves. . . .

— Reading No. 7 —

MAZZINI: ON THE UNITY OF ITALY[7]

*"In the faith of the reawakening of that people to
whom alone God has yet granted the privilege, in each
epoch of its own existence, of transforming Europe," to
quote Mazzini's own proud words about Italy, Mazzini
wrote in 1861 the following lines to prove that "unity
ever was and is the destiny of Italy."*

✓   ✓   ✓

(*The adversaries of Italian unity*) forgot the unanimous
shout of Italy raised by the insurgents of every province
ten years later, the earnest unitarian apostolate of our
secret societies during the years following those insurrections, and the blood shed by the martyrs of every
province of Italy, in the name of the common country.
Above all, they forgot the principle that no peoples ever
die, nor stop short upon their path, before they have
achieved the ultimate historical aim of their existence,
before having completed and fulfilled their mission. Now
the mission of Italy is pointed out by her geographical
conditions, by the prophetic aspirations of our greatest

[7] Giuseppe Mazzini, *Life and Writings of Joseph Mazzini*,
London: Smith, Elder and Co., 1890, vol. I, pp. 226-90.

minds and noblest hearts, and by the whole of our magnificent historical tradition, easily to be traced by anyone who will but study the life of our people, instead of the deeds of individuals or aristocracy. . . .

The nation never has existed, said they; therefore it can never exist. But we—viewing the question from the height of our ruling synthesis—declare: The nation has not as yet existed; therefore, it must exist in the future. A people destined to achieve great things for the welfare of humanity must one day or other be constituted a nation. And slowly, from epoch to epoch, our people has advanced towards that aim. But the history of our people and of our nationality, which is one and the same thing, has yet to be written. It is sadder to me than I can say to be compelled to carry with me to the tomb the unfulfilled desire of attempting it myself according to my own design. He who shall write it as it ought to be written, without burying the salient points of Italian progress beneath a multitude of minute details, and keeping in view the collective development of the Italian element from period to period, will be rewarded by the fact of having sustained the unity of the country upon the firm basis of history and tradition.

Having proved, by the testimony of our ancient records, and the vestiges of past religions, the absolute independence of our primitive civilization from the Hellenic (considerably posterior), the writer will then proceed to trace the origin of our nationality from those Sabellian tribes, dwelling, as I have said, round the ancient Amiternus; who, along with the Osques, Siculians, and Umbrians, first assumed the sacred name of Italy, and initiated the fusion of the different elements spread over the Peninsula, by planting their lance—the symbol of authority—in the valley of the Tibur, in the Campagna, and beyond. This was the first war of independence sustained by the Italian element, against that element (probably of Semitic origin) called by the ancients Pelasgic. . . . In the first period, Italy appears to assign to Rome her mission of unification, by declaring to her, I am yours, but on condition of your identifying your life with mine. . . .

The second epoch—initiated in the midst of the barbarian invasions—carried on with a pertinacity ensuring its triumph, that work of social fusion which has rendered us fit to be a nation at the present day. The unitarian movement continued even after the last liberties of Italy were destroyed by the fall of Florence, when all public life was silent and at an end, and all hope of country appeared extinguished beneath foreign domination, and the rule of the petty princes who were vassals of the foreigner. Yes; unity was and is the destiny of Italy. The civil primacy twice exercised by Italy—through the arms of the Caesars and the voice of the Popes—is destined to be held a third time by the people of Italy—the nation.

They who were unable forty years ago to perceive the signs of progress towards unity made in the successive periods of Italian life, were simply blind to the light of history. But should any, in the face of the actual glorious manifestation of our people, endeavour to lead them back to ideas of confederations, and independent provincial liberty, they would deserve to be branded as traitors to their country.

It matters little that it may not now be easy to determine what the mission—I believe it to be highly religious—of Italy is in the world. The tradition of two epochs of initiation, and the conscience of the Italian people, alike bear witness that such a mission exists; and even if the world did not indicate what that mission is, the fact of this instinct among the people of a national mission to be fulfilled, and a collective idea to be developed, would be enough to prove the necessity of one sole country, with one form of organization to embody and represent it. That form of organization is unity. Federalism implies a multiplicity of aims to be realised, and resolves itself, sooner or later, into a system of aristocracies or castes. Unity is the only security for equality, and the due development of the life of the people.

Italy therefore will be one. Her geographical conditions, language, and literature; the necessities of defence, and of political power; the desire of the populations, the democratic instincts innate in our people, the presentiment of a progress in which all the forces and faculties of the country must concur, the consciousness of an initiative in Europe, and of great things yet to be achieved by Italy for the world; all point to this aim. There is no obstacle in the way that may not be easily overcome, no objection that may not be historically and philosophically met and confuted.

— Reading No. 8 —

ACTON: *NATIONALITY*[8]

In 1862 the British historian Lord Acton (1834-1903) published an essay criticizing Mazzini's concept of political nationality.

✓   ✓   ✓

Whenever great intellectual cultivation has been combined with that suffering which is inseparable from extensive changes in the condition of the people, men of speculative or imaginative genius have sought in the contemplation of an ideal society a remedy, or at least a consolation, for evils which they were practically unable to remove . . . The eighteenth century acquiesced in this oblivion of corporate rights on the Continent, for the absolutists cared only for the State, and the liberals only for the individual. . . .

The old despotic policy which made the Poles its prey had two adversaries,—the spirit of English liberty, and the doctrines of that revolution which destroyed the French monarchy with its own weapons; and these two contradicted in contrary ways the theory that nations have no collective rights. At the present day, the theory of nationality is not only the most powerful auxiliary of

[8]Lord Acton, *Essays on Freedom and Power*, Glencoe. Illinois: The Free Press, 1948, pp. 166-95.

revolution, but its substance in the movements of the last three years. This, however, is a recent alliance, unknown to the first French Revolution. The modern theory of nationality arose partly as a legitimate consequence, partly as a reaction against it. As the system which overlooked national division was opposed by liberalism in two forms, the French and the English, so the system which insists upon them proceeds from two distinct sources, and exhibits the character either of 1688 or 1789.

Napoleon called a new power into existence by attacking nationality in Russia, by delivering it in Italy, by governing in defiance of it in Germany and Spain. The sovereigns of these countries were deposed or degraded; and a system of administration was introduced which was French in its origin, its spirit, and its instruments. The people resisted the change. The movement against it was popular and spontaneous, because the rulers were absent or helpless; and it was national, because it was directed against foreign institutions. In Tyrol, in Spain, and afterwards in Prussia, the people did not receive the impulse from the government, but undertook of their own accord to cast out the armies and the ideas of revolutionized France. Men were made conscious of the national element of the revolution by its conquests, not in its rise. The three things which the Empire most openly oppressed—religion, national independence, and political liberty—united in a short-lived league to animate the great uprising by which Napoleon fell. . . .

At first, in 1813, the people rose against their conquerors, in defence of their legitimate rulers. They refused to be governed by usurpers. In the period between 1825 and 1831, they resolved that they would not be misgoverned by strangers. The French administration was often better than that which it displaced, but there were prior claimants for the authority exercised by the French, and at first the national contest was a contest for legitimacy. In the second period this element was wanting. No dispossessed princes led the Greeks, the Belgians, or the Poles. The Turks, the Dutch, and the Russians were attacked, not as usurpers, but as oppressors—because they misgoverned, not because they were of a different race. Then began a time when the text simply was, that nations would not be governed by foreigners. Power legitimately obtained, and exercised with moderation, was declared invalid. . . . Now nationality became a paramount claim, which was to assert itself alone, which might put forward as pretexts the rights of rulers, the liberties of the people, the safety of religion, but which, if no such union could be formed, was to prevail at the expense of every other cause for which nations make sacrifices. . . . It was appealed to in the name of the most contradictory principles of government, and served all parties in succession, because it was one in which all could unite. Beginning by a protest against the dominion of race over race, its mildest and least-developed form, it grew into a condemnation of every State that included different races, and finally became the complete and consistent theory, that the State and the nation must be co-extensive.

The outward historical progress of this idea from an indefinite aspiration to be the keystone of a political system, may be traced in the life of the man who gave to it the element in which its strength resides—Giuseppe Mazzini. He found Carbonarism impotent against the measures of the governments, and resolved to give new life to the liberal movement by transferring it to the ground of nationality. Exile is the nursery of nationality, as oppression is the school of liberalism; and Mazzini conceived the idea of Young Italy when he was a refugee at Marseilles. In the same way, the Polish exiles are the champions of every national movement; for to them all political rights are absorbed in the idea of independence, which, however they may differ with each other, is the one aspiration common to them all.

In pursuing the outward and visible growth of the national theory we are prepared for an examination of its political character and value. The absolutism which has created it denies equally that absolute right of national unity which is a product of democracy, and that claim of national liberty which belongs to the theory of freedom. These two views of nationality, corresponding to the French and to the English systems, are connected in name only, and are in reality the opposite extremes of political thought. In one case, nationality is founded on the perpetual supremacy of the collective will, of which the unity of the nation is the necessary condition, to which every other influence must defer, and against which no obligation enjoys authority, and all resistance is tyrannical. The nation is here an ideal unit founded on the race, in defiance of the modifying action of external causes, of tradition, and of existing rights. It overrules the rights and wishes of the inhabitants, absorbing their divergent interests in a fictitious unity; sacrifices their several inclinations and duties to the higher claim of nationality, and crushes all natural rights and all established liberties for the purpose of vindicating itself.

Connected with this theory in nothing except in the common enmity of the absolute state, is the theory which represents nationality as an essential, but not a supreme element in determining the forms of the State. It is distinguished from the other, because it tends to diversity and not to uniformity, to harmony and not to unity; because it aims not at an arbitrary change, but at careful respect for the existing conditions of political life, and because it obeys the laws and results of history, not the aspirations of an ideal future. While the theory of unity makes the nation a source of despotism and revolution, the theory of liberty regards it as the bulwark of self-government, and the foremost limit to the excessive power of the State. . . .

The presence of different nations under the same sovereignty is similar in its effect to the independence of the Church in the State. It provides against the servility which flourishes under the shadow of a single authority, by balancing interests, multiplying associations, and giving to the subject the restraint and support of a combined opinion . . . Liberty provokes diversity, and diversity preserves liberty by supplying the means of organization. This diversity in the same State is a firm barrier against the intrusion of the government beyond the political sphere which is common to all into the social department which escapes legislation and is ruled by spontaneous laws . . . That intolerance of social freedom which is natural to absolutism is sure to find a corrective in the national diversities, which no other force could so efficiently provide. The co-existence of several nations under the same State is a test, as well as the best security of its freedom. It is also one of the chief instruments of civilisation; and, as such, it is in the natural and providential order, and indicates a state of greater advancement than the national unity which is the ideal of modern liberalism.

If we take the establishment of liberty for the realisation of moral duties to be the end of civil society, we must conclude that those states are substantially the most perfect which, like the British and Austrian Empires, include various distinct nationalities without oppressing them. Those in which no mixture of races has occurred are imperfect; and those in which its effects have disappeared are decrepit. A State which is incompetent to satisfy different races condemns itself; a State which labours to neutralise, to absorb, or to expel them, destroys its own vitality; a State which does not include them is destitute of the chief basis of self-government. The theory of nationality, therefore, is a retrograde step in history.

Nationality is more advanced than socialism, because it is a more arbitrary system. The social theory endeavours to provide for the existence of the individual beneath the terrible burdens which modern society heaps upon labour. It is not merely a development of the notion of equality, but a refuge from real misery and starvation. However false the solution, it was a reasonable demand that the poor should be saved from destruction; and if the freedom of the State was sacrificed to the safety of the individual, the more immediate object was, at least in theory, attained. But nationality does not aim either at liberty or prosperity, both of which it sacrifices to the imperative necessity of making the nation the mould and measure of the State. Its course will be marked with material as well as moral ruin, in order that a new invention may prevail over the works of God and the interests of mankind.

— Reading No. 9 —

NAPOLEON: *ON NATIONAL UNITY*[9]

In the conversations which Napoleon, while a prisoner at Saint Helena, held with the Count de las Cases, he spoke about his plans to promote the nationalism of the European peoples and the unity of Europe. These words had a great influence on European nationalists in the 1830's and 1840's. They also affected the inclinations and policies of Napoleon III.

✓ ✓ ✓

After alluding to some other subjects, the Emperor said, "One of my great plans was the re-uniting, the concentration, of those same geographical nations which have been separated and parcelled out by revolution and policy. There are in Europe, dispersed, it is true, upwards of thirty millions of French, fifteen millions of Spaniards, fifteen millions of Italians, and thirty millions of Germans; and it was my intention to incorporate these people each into one nation. It would have been a noble thing to have advanced into posterity with such a train, and attended by the blessings of future ages. I felt myself worthy of this glory!

"After this summary simplification, it would have been possible to indulge the chimera of the *beau ideal* of civilization. In this state of things, there would have been some chance of establishing, in every country, a unity of codes, principles, opinions, sentiments, views, and interests. Then, perhaps, by the help of the universal diffusion of knowledge, one might have thought of attempting, in the great European family, the application of the American Congress, or the Amphictyons of Greece; and then what a perspective of power, greatness, happiness, and

Count de las Cases, *Memoirs of the Life, Exile, and Conversations of the Emperor Napoleon*, London: Henry Colburn, 1836, vol. IV, pp. 104-08, 19 f.

prosperity! What a grand, what a magnificent, spectacle!

"The concentration of the thirty of forty millions of Frenchmen was completed and perfected; and that of the fifteen millions of Spaniards was nearly accomplished; for nothing is more common than to convert accident into principle. . . .

"With regard to the fifteen millions of Italians, their concentration was already far advanced: it only wanted maturity. The people were daily becoming more firmly established in the unity of principles and legislation; and also in the unity of thought and feeling, that certain and infallible cement of human concentration. The union of Piedmont with France, and the junction of Parma, Tuscany and Rome, were, in my mind, but temporary measures, intended merely to guarantee and promote the national education of the Italians. You may judge of the correctness of my views, and of the influence of common laws. The portions of Italy that had been united to France, though that union might have been regarded as the insult of conquest on our part, were, in spite of their Italian patriotism, the very parts that continued by far the most attached to us. Now that they are restored to themselves, they conceive that they have been invaded and disinherited; and so they certainly have been!

"All the South of Europe, therefore, would soon have been rendered compact in point of locality, views, opinions, sentiments, and interests. In this state of things, what would have been the weight of all the nations of the north? What human efforts could have broken through so strong a barrier?

"The concentration of the Germans must have been effected more gradually; and therefore I had done no more than simplify their monstrous complication. Not that they were unprepared for centralization; on the contrary, they were too well prepared for it, and they might have blindly risen in reaction against us, before they had comprehended our designs. How happens it that no German Prince has yet formed a just notion of the spirit of his nation, and turned it to good account? Certainly, if heaven had made me a Prince of Germany amidst the many critical events of our times, I should, infallibly, have governed the thirty millions of Germans

united; and, from what I know of them, I think I may
venture to affirm that, if they had once elected and proclaimed me, they would not have forsaken me, and I
should never have been at St. Helena."

Then, after some melancholy details and comparisons,
he thus resumed: "At all events, this concentration will
be brought about, sooner or later, by the very force of
events. The impulse is given; and I think that, since my
fall and the destruction of my system, no grand equi-
librium can possibly be established in Europe, except by
the concentration and confederation of the principal
nations. The sovereign who, in the first great conflict,
shall sincerely embrace the cause of the people, will find
himself at the head of all Europe, and may attempt
whatever he pleases."

Passing to other topics, he made many observations on
the Russian war. Among other things he said: "That war
should have been the most popular of any in modern
times. It was a war of good sense and true interests; a
war for the repose and security of all; it was purely
pacific and preservative; entirely European and continental. Its success would have established a balance of
power and would have introduced new combinations, by
which the dangers of the present time would have been
succeeded by future tranquillity. In this case, ambition
had no share in my views. In raising Poland, which was
the key-stone of the whole arch, I would have permitted
a King of Prussia, an Archduke of Austria or any other
to occupy the throne. I had no wish to obtain any new
acquisition; and I reserved for myself only the glory of
doing good, and the blessings of posterity. Yet this undertaking failed, and proved my ruin, though I never acted
more disinterestedly, and never better merited success. As
if popular opinion had been seized with contagion, in a
moment, a general outcry, a general sentiment, arose
against me. I was proclaimed the destroyer of kings,—I,
who had created them! I was denounced as the subverter
of the rights of nations—I, who was about to risk all to
secure them! And people and kings, those irreconcilable
enemies, leagued together and conspired against me!

— Reading No. 10 —

LIST: *NATIONALITY AND ECONOMY*[10]

In 1841 Friedrich List published The National System
of Economy, *in which he rejected the cosmopolitan foundations of eighteenth century economic doctrine.*

✓　　　　　✓　　　　　✓

More than thirty-three years have elapsed since I first
entertained doubts as to the truth of the prevailing theory
of political economy, and endeavoured to investigate
(what appeared to me) its errors and their fundamental
causes. . . .

I perceived that the popular theory took no account of
nations, but simply of the entire human race on the one
hand, or of single individuals on the other. I saw clearly
that free competition between two nations which are
highly civilised can only be mutually beneficial in case
both of them are in a nearly equal position of industrial
development, and that any nation which owing to mis-
fortunes is behind others in industry, commerce, and
navigation, while she nevertheless possesses the mental
and material means for developing those acquisitions,
must first of all strengthen her own individual powers, in
order to fit herself to enter into free competition with
more advanced nations. In a word, I perceived the distinction between cosmopolitical and political economy. . . .

When afterwards I visited the United States, I cast all
books aside—they would only have tended to mislead me.
The best work on political economy which one can read
in that modern land is actual life. There one may see
wildernesses grow into rich and mighty States; and progress which requires centuries in Europe, goes on there
before one's eyes, viz. that from the condition of the

[10] Friedrich List, *The National System of Political Economy*,
tr. by Samson S. Lloyd, London: Longmans, Green and
Co., 1885, pp. xxxix ff., 87, 97 ff., 320 ff., 332 ff.

mere hunter to the rearing of cattle—from that to agriculture, and from the latter to manufactures and commerce. There one may see how rents increase by degrees from nothing to important revenues. There the simple peasant knows practically far better than the most acute savants of the old world how agriculture and rents can be improved; he endeavours to attract manufacturers and artificers to his vicinity. Nowhere so well as there can one learn the importance of means of transport, and their effect on the mental and material life of the people.

That book of actual life, I have earnestly and diligently studied, and compared with the results of my previous studies, experience, and reflections.

And the result has been (as I hope) the propounding of a system which, however defective it may as yet appear, is not founded on bottomless cosmopolitanism, but on the nature of things, on the lessons of history, and on the requirements of the nations. . . .

I would indicate, as the distinguishing characteristic of my system NATIONALITY. On the nature of nationality, and the intermediate interest between those of individualism and of entire humanity, my whole structure is based. . . .

History everywhere shows us a powerful process of reciprocal action between the social and the individual powers and conditions. In the Italian and the Hanseatic cities, in Holland and England, in France and America, we find the powers of production, and consequently the wealth of individuals, growing in proportion to the liberties enjoyed, to the degree of perfection of political and social institutions, while these, on the other hand, derive material and stimulus for their further improvement from the increase of the material wealth and of the productive power of individuals. The real rise of the industry and power of England dates only from the days of the actual foundation of England's national freedom, while the industry and power of Venice, of the Hanse Towns, of the Spanish and Portuguese decayed concurrently with their loss of freedom. However industrious, thrifty, inventive and intelligent, individual citizens might be, they could not make up for the lack of free institutions. History also teaches that individuals derive the greater part of their productive powers from the social institutions and conditions under which they are placed. . . .

Quesnay (from whom the idea of universal free trade originated) speaks of cosmopolitical economy, i.e. of that science which teaches how the entire human race may attain prosperity; in opposition to political economy, or that science which limits its teaching to the inquiry how a given nation can obtain under the existing conditions of (the world) prosperity, civilization, and power, by means of agriculture, industry, and commerce.

Adam Smith treats his doctrine in a similarly extended sense, by making it his task to indicate the cosmopolitical idea of the absolute freedom of the commerce of the whole world in spite of the gross mistakes made by the physiocrats against the very nature of things and against logic. Adam Smith concerned himself as little as Quesnay did with true economics, i.e. that policy which each separate nation had to obey in order to make progress in its economical conditions. Although here and there he speaks of wars, this only occurs incidentally. The idea of a perpetual state of peace forms the foundation of all his arguments. . . .

If, as the prevailing school requires, we assume a universal union or confederation of all nations as the guarantee for an ever-lasting peace, the principle of international free trade seems to be perfectly justified. . . . Unquestionably the idea of a universal confederation and a perpetual peace is commended both by common sense and religion. If single combat between individuals is at present considered to be contrary to reason, how much more must combat between two nations be similarly condemned? The proofs which social economy can produce from the history of the civilization of mankind of the reasonableness of bringing about the union of all mankind under the law of right, are perhaps those which are the clearest to sound human understanding. . . .

A universal republic (in the sense of Henry IV, and of Abbe St. Pierre) i.e. a union of the nations of the earth whereby they recognize the same conditions of right among themselves and renounce self-redress, can only be realized if a large number of nationalities attain as nearly as possible the same degree of civilization, industry, political cultivation, and power. Only with the gradual formation of this union can free trade be developed, only as a result of this union can it confer on all nations the same great advantages which are now experienced by those provinces and states which are politically united. The system of protection, inasmuch as it forms the only means of placing those nations which are far behind in civilization on equal terms with the one predominating nation (which, however, never received at the hands of nature a perpetual right to a monopoly of manufacture, but which merely gained an advance over others in point of time), the system of protection regarded from this point of view appears to be the most efficient means of furthering the final union of nations, and hence also of promoting true freedom of trade. And national economy appears from this point of view to be that science which, correctly appreciating the existing interests and the individual circumstances of nations, teaches how every separate nation can be raised to that stage of industrial development in which union with other nations equally well developed, and consequently freedom of trade, can become possible and useful to it. . . .

From day to day it is necessary that the governments and peoples of Germany be more convinced that national unity is the rock on which the edifice of their welfare, their honor, their power, their present security and existence, and their future greatness must be founded. Thus from day to day the apostasy of these small maritime (German) states will appear more and more, not only to the states in the (German) Customs Union but to these small states themselves, in the light of a national scandal which must be got rid of at any price. Also, if the matter is considered intelligently, the material advantages of joining the Union are much greater for those states, than the sacrifice which it requires. . . .

The Union will foster their fisheries, secure special advantages to their shipping, protect and promote their foreign commercial relations by effective consular establishments and by treaties. Partly by their means it will found new colonies, and by their means carry on its own colonial trade. For a union of States comprising thirty-five million inhabitants (for the Union will comprise at least that number when it is fully completed) owing to an annual increase of one and a half percent in the population can easily spare two or three hundred thousand persons annually. For provinces abounding with well-informed and cultivated inhabitants who have a peculiar propensity to seek their fortune in distant countries, people who can take root anywhere and make themselves at home wherever unoccupied land is to be cultivated, are called upon by Nature to place themselves in the first rank of those nations who colonize and diffuse civilization. . . .

From a national point of view, we say and maintain that in reference to its geographical position, as well as in respect to its commercial and industrial circumstances, and to the origin and language of its inhabitants, Holland is a German province, which was separated from Germany at a period of German national disunion, without whose reincorporation in the German Union Germany may be compared to a house whose door belongs to a stranger. Holland belongs to Germany as much as Brittany and Normandy belong to France, and as long as Holland constitutes an independent kingdom of her own, Germany can attain independence and power as little as France would have been able to attain these if those provinces had remained in the hands of the English. The commercial power of Holland has declined due to the unimportance of the country. Notwithstanding the prosperity of her colonies, Holland will and must continue to decline because the nation is too weak to support the enormous expense of a large military and naval power. In her present position Holland cannot profit nearly as much from her colonial possessions as she could if they became a constituent part of the German Union, especially since she is too weak in the elements necessary for colonization—in population and in mental powers.

Nothing at this time so greatly impedes a closer union of the continent of Europe as the fact that its center still has not taken the position for which it is naturally fitted.

If, on the other hand, Germany could constitute itself with the maritime territories which appertain to it, with Holland, Belgium and Switzerland, as a powerful commercial and political whole—if this mighty national body

could fuse representative institutions with the existing
monarchical, dynastic and aristocratic interests, as far as
these are compatible with one another,—then Germany
could secure peace to the European continent for a long
time, and at the same time make herself the central point
of a durable Continental alliance. . . .

From this point of view we must also judge the extremely important question of slavery. We are very far
from ignoring that much philanthropy and good motives
lie at the root of the zeal with which England pursues
the goal of the emancipation of the Negroes, and that this
zeal does great honor to the character of the English
nation. But at the same time, if we consider the immediate effects of the measures adopted by England in
reference to this matter, we cannot get rid of the idea
that also much political motive and commercial interest
are mingled with it. These effects are: (1) That the
sudden emancipation of the blacks, through their rapid
transition from a condition of disorder and carelessness
little removed from that of wild animals to a high degree
of individual independence, the yield of tropical produce
in South America and the West Indies will be extremely
diminished and ultimately reduced to nothing, as the
example of St. Domingo incontestably shows, inasmuch
as there, since the expulsion of the French and Spaniards,
the production has greatly decreased from year to year,
and continues to do so. (2) That the free Negroes continually seek to obtain an increase in their wages, whilst
they limit their labour to the supply of their most indispensable wants; that hence their freedom merely leads
to idleness. (3) That, on the other hand, England possesses in the East Indies ample means of supplying the
whole world with colonial products. . . . (4) Finally, it
may be asserted, that by the emancipation of the slaves
England desires to hang a sword over the head of the
North American slave states, which is so much more
menacing to the Union the more this emancipation ex-
tends and the wish is incited among the Negroes of North
America to partake of similar liberty. The question if
rightly viewed, must appear to be a philanthropical experiment of doubtful benefit towards those on whose
behalf it was undertaken, and in any case must appear

as disadvantageous to those nations who rely on trade with South America and the West Indies.

If we only consider the enormous interests which the nations of the Continent have in common, as opposed to the English maritime supremacy, we shall be led to the conviction that nothing is so necessary to these nations as union, and nothing is so ruinous to them as Continental wars. The history of the last century also teaches us that every war which the powers of the Continent have waged against one another has led invariably to the increase of industry, of wealth, of navigation, of colonial possessions and of power to the insular supremacy. . . .

Thus, in a not very distant future, the natural necessity which now forces the French and Germans to establish a continental alliance against the British supremacy, will force the British to establish a European coalition against the supremacy of America. Then Great Britain will be compelled to seek and to find protection, security, and compensation against the predominance of America, and an equivalent for her lost supremacy, in the leadership of the United Powers of Europe.

— Reading No. 11 —

RENAN: *THE MEANING OF NATIONALITY*[11]

After the experience of the Franco-German War, Renan came to define nationalism and nationality according to the traditions of French liberalism. He did this in a lecture at the Sorbonne on March 11, 1882, "Qu'est-ce

[11] Ernest Renan, *Discours et Conferences,* Paris: Calman-Lévy, 1887, pp. 277-310.

qu'une Nation?" *In the introduction to his collected speeches, Renan wrote: "The piece in this volume to which I attach the greatest importance is the lecture 'What is a Nation?' I weighed each part with greatest care. It is my profession of faith regarding human affairs, and I hope that these twenty pages will be recalled when modern civilization founders as the result of the disastrous ambiguity of the words: nation, nationality, race."*

✔   ✔   ✔

I intend to analyze with you an idea which seems simple and clear but which lends itself to the most dangerous misunderstandings. . . . In our day one commits a serious error: one confounds nation and race, and one attributes to ethnographical or rather linguistic groups a sovereignty analogous to that of real peoples. Let us try for some precision in these difficult questions where the slightest confusion about the meaning of words, which are at the basis of our reasoning, can produce the most disastrous errors. . . .

Since the end of the Roman Empire, or rather since the dissolution of the empire of Charlemagne, Western Europe seems to be divided into nations. At certain times some of them have sought to exercise a hegemony over the others, without being able to arrive there in an enduring fashion. What Charles V, Louis XIV, Napoleon I could not achieve, nobody, probably, will be able to do in the future. The establishment of a new Roman Empire or a new empire of Charlemagne has become impossible. The division of Europe is too great for an attempt at universal domination not to provoke with speed a coalition which puts the ambitious nation back within its natural limits. . . .

Nations in this sense are something new in history. . . . What characterizes these various nations is the fusion of the populations which compose them. Nothing similar exists in Turkey, where the Turk, the Slav, the Greek, the Armenian, the Arab, the Syrian, the Kurd, are today as distinct as they were on the day of the conquest. . . . Even by the tenth century all the inhabitants of France are French. The idea of a difference of races in the population of France has completely disappeared with the French writers and poets after Hugues Capet. The distinction between the noble and the serf is highly emphasized, but this distinction is in no way an ethnic distinction. . . .

These great laws of the history of Western Europe become obvious if we contrast them with the events in Eastern Europe. Under the crown of St. Stephan, the Magyars and the Slavs have remained as distinct today as they were 800 years ago. In Bohemia, the Czech and the German elements are superimposed as water and oil in a glass. The Turkish policy of separating nationalities according to religion has had the most serious consequences: it caused the ruin of the Middle East. For, the essential element of a nation is that all its individuals must have many things in common, but must also have forgotten many things. Every French citizen must have forgotten the night of St. Bartholemew and the massacres in the thirteenth century in the South. There are not ten families in France who could prove their Frankish origin, and such a proof would be deficient because thousands of unknown mixed breedings could derange all genealogical systems. . . .

According to certain political theorists, the nation is above all the work of a dynasty representing an ancient conquest which was first accepted and later forgotten by the mass of the people. . . . Has such a law absolute validity? Certainly not. Switzerland and the United States, which arose as agglomerations of successive additions, have no dynastic basis. . . . One must therefore admit that a nation can exist without the dynastic principle, and even that nations which were formed by dynasties can separate themselves from them without losing their identity thereby. Against dynastic rights, the right of nationality has emerged. On what tangible fact could it be based?

I. Some people say that it could be based upon race. The artificial divisions created by the feudal past, by princely marriages and diplomatic congresses, have lapsed. What remains firm and permanent is the race of the people. It constitutes a legitimate right. According to this theory the Germans have the right to take back the scattered members of the Germanic family, even if these members do not seek annexation. Thus one creates a primordial right analogous to that of the divine right of kings. This is a very great fallacy whose dominance would ruin European civilization. . . .

To base one's policy on an ethnographical analysis means to establish it on a chimera. The noblest countries —England, France, Italy,—are those where the blood is most mixed. Germany is no exception. . . . Race as we historians understand it is something which is formed by history and undone by history. The study of race is of great importance for the study of the history of mankind, but it has no place in politics. . . . Will the Germans, who have raised the banner of ethnography so high, not see one day the Slavs analyze the names of the villages of Saxony and of Lusatia, seek the traces of populations long dead, and ask for an account of the massacres and the mass enslavement to which the Germans under their Ottonian emperors subjected their ancestors? It is good for all of us to know how to forget.

II. What we have said of race is as true of language. Language may invite us to unite, but it does not compel us to do so. . . . Languages are historical formations, which tell us very little about the race of those who speak them. In any event, they should not fetter human freedom when it concerns the fate of the group with whom we wish to unite for life or death. . . .

One abandons the great air which one breathes in the large camp of humanity in order to shut oneself up in conventicles of compatriots. Nothing could be worse for the mind; nothing could be more troublesome for civilization. Let us not abandon the fundamental principle that man is a rational and moral being before he is penned up in this or that language, before he is a member of this or that race, before he adheres to this or that culture. Above the French, German, or Italian culture, there is a human culture. Look at the great men of the Renaissance. They were neither French, Italian or German. By their intimacy with the spirit of antiquity, they had found the secret of the true education of the human mind, and they devoted themselves to it with all their heart. How well they acted!

III. Nor could religion offer a sufficient foundation for

the establishment of a modern nation. . . . One can be a Frenchman, an Englishman or a German, by being a Catholic, a Protestant, a Jew or an agnostic. Religion has become something individual; it concerns the conscience of each person. . . .

IV. The community of interests is certainly a strong tie among men. But are interests sufficient to create a nation? I do not believe it. The community of interests creates commercial treaties. Nationality is something sentimental too; it is body and soul at the same time; a custom-union is not a fatherland.

V. Geography, or as one says, the natural frontiers, certainly plays a considerable part in the division of nations. . . . Can we say, however, as certain people believe, that the frontiers of a nation are marked on the map, and such a nation has the right to adjudicate to itself what it regards as necesary to round off its contours, to reach some mountain or some river, to which one credits a kind of *a priori* quality? I do not know of any doctrine which would be more arbitrarily disastrous. With it one can justify all violence. One speaks of strategic reasons. Nothing is absolute; clearly, certain concessions must be made to necessity. But these concessions should not go too far. Otherwise everybody would demand what is strategically convenient to him, and a war without end would ensue. . . .

A nation is a soul, a spiritual principle . . . A nation is a great solidarity, created by the sentiment of the sacrifices which have been made and of those which one is disposed to make in the future. It presupposes a past; but it resumes itself in the present by a tangible fact: the consent, the clearly expressed desire to continue life in common. The existence of a nation is a plebiscite of every day, as the existence of the individual is a perpetual affirmation of life. I well know that this is less metaphysical than the divine right and less brutal than the alleged historical right . . . We have driven the metaphysical and theological abstractions from politics. What remains? Man remains, his desires and his wants. You will object to me that the secession and eventual crumbling of nations are the consequences of a system which praises the old organic entities at the mercy of the will of frequently unenlightened peoples. Clearly, in matters like these, no principles should be carried to excess. Principles of this kind can be applied only in a very general way. Human will changes, but what does not change here on earth? Nations are nothing eternal. They had a beginning, they will have an end. The European confederation will probably replace them. But this is not the law of the century in which we live. At present, the existence of nations is good and even necessary. Their existence is a guarantee of liberty which would be lost if the world had only one law and one master. . . .

— Reading No. 12 —

O'SULLIVAN: *MANIFEST DESTINY*[12]

John Louis O'Sullivan (1813-1895) published from 1837 to 1846 the United States Magazine and Democratic Review, *"to strike the hitherto silent string of the demo-cratic genius of the age and the country." There he published in July and August, 1845, an article "An-nexation" defending the annexation of Texas.*

✓   ✓   ✓

It is time now for opposition to the Annexation of Texas to cease, all further agitation of the waters of bitter-ness and strife, at least in connection with this question, —even though it may perhaps be required of us as a necessary condition of the freedom of our institutions, that we must live on for ever in a state of unpausing struggle and excitement upon some subject of party division or other. But, in regard to Texas, enough has

[12] *The United States Magazine and Democratic Review,* vol. XVII, no. LXXXV, July and August 1845.

now been given to Party. It is time for the common duty of Patriotism to the Country to succeed;—or if this claim will not be recognized, it is at least time for common sense to acquiesce with decent grace in the inevitable and the irrevocable.

Texas is now ours. Already, before these words are written, her Convention has undoubtedly ratified the acceptance, by her Congress, of our proffered invitation into the Union; and made the requisite changes in her already republican form of constitution to adapt it to its future federal relations. Her star and her stripe may already be said to have taken their place in the glorious blazon of our common nationality; and the sweep of our eagle's wing already includes within its circuit the wide extent of her fair and fertile land. She is no longer to us a mere geographical space—a certain combination of coast, plain, mountain, valley, forest and stream. She is no longer to us a mere country on the map. She comes within the dear and sacred designation of Our Country; no longer a *pays,* she is a part of *la patrie;* and that which is at once a sentiment and a virtue, Patriotism, already begins to thrill for her too within the national heart. . . .

Why, were other reasoning wanting, in favor of now elevating this question of the reception of Texas into the Union, out of the lower region of our past party dissensions, up to its proper level of a high and broad nationality, it surely is to be found, found abundantly, in the manner in which other nations have undertaken to intrude themselves into it, between us and the proper parties to the case, in a spirit of hostile interference against us, for the avowed object of thwarting our policy and hampering our power, limiting our greatness and checking the fulfillment of our manifest destiny to overspread the continent alloted by Providence for the free development of our yearly multiplying millions. This we have seen done by England, our old rival and enemy; and by France. . . .

It is wholly untrue, and unjust to ourselves, the pretence that the Annexation has been a measure of spoliation, unrightful and unrighteous—of military conquest under forms of peace and law—of territorial aggrandizement at the expense of justice, and justice due by a double sanctity to the weak. This view of the question is wholly unfounded, and has been before so amply refuted in these pages, as well as in a thousand other modes, that we shall not again dwell upon it. The independence of Texas was complete and absolute. It was an independence, not only in fact but of right. . . .

Texas has been absorbed into the Union in the inevitable fulfillment of the general law which is rolling our population westward; the connection of which with that ratio of growth in population which is destined within a hundred years to swell our numbers to the enormous population of two hundred and fifty millions (if not more), is too evident to leave us in doubt of the manifest design of Providence in regard to the occupation of this continent. It was disintegrated from Mexico in the natural course of events, by a process perfectly legitimate on its own part, blameless on ours; and in which all the censures due to wrong, perfidy and folly, rest on Mexico alone. And possessed as it was by a population which was in truth but a colonial detachment from our own, and which was still bound by myriad ties of the very heartstrings to its old relations, domestic and political, their incorporation into the Union was not only inevitable, but the most natural, right and proper thing in the world—and it is only astonishing that there should be any among ourselves to say it nay. . . .

California will, probably, next fall away from the loose adhesion which, in such a country as Mexico, holds a remote province in a slight equivocal kind of dependence on the metropolis. Imbecile and distracted, Mexico never can exert any real governmental authority over such a country. A population will soon be in actual occupation of California, over which it will be idle for Mexico to dream of dominion. They will necessarily become independent. Whether they will then attach themselves to our Union or not, is not to be predicted with any certainty. Unless the projected railroad across the continent to the Pacific be carried into effect, perhaps they may not; though even in that case, the day is not distant when the Empires of the Atlantic and Pacific would again flow together into one, as soon as their inland border should approach each other. But that great work, colossal as appears the plan on its first suggestion, cannot remain long unbuilt. Its necessity for this very purpose of binding and holding together in its iron clasp our fast settling Pacific region with that of the Mississippi valley—the natural facility of the route—the case with which any amount of labor for the construction can be drawn in from the overcrowded populations of Europe, to be paid in the lands made valuable by the progress of the work itself—and its immense utility to the commerce of the world with the whole eastern coast of Asia, alone almost sufficient for the support of such a road—these considerations give assurance that the day cannot be distant which shall witness the conveyance of the representatives from Oregon and California to Washington within less time than a few years ago was devoted to a similar journey by those from Ohio; while the magnetic telegraph will enable the editors of the "San Francisco Union," the "Astoria Evening Post," or the "Nootka Morning News" to set up in type the first half of the President's Inaugural, before the echoes of the latter half shall have died away beneath the lofty porch of the Capitol, as spoken from his lips.

Away then with all idle French talk of balances of power on the American Continent. There is no growth in Spanish America! Whatever progress of population there may be in the British Canadas, is only for their own early severance of their present colonial relation to the little island three thousand miles across the Atlantic; soon to be followed by Annexation, and destined to swell the still accumulating momentum of our progress. And whosoever may hold the balance, though they should cast into the opposite scale all the bayonets and cannon, not only of France and England, but of Europe entire, how would it kick the beam against the simple solid weight of the two hundred and fifty, or three hundred millions—destined to gather beneath the flutter of the stripes and stars, in the fast hastening year of the Lord 1945!

— Reading No. 13 —

SCHURZ: *LIBERAL PATRIOTISM*[13]

Carl Schurz (1829-1906), a German immigrant who had come to the United States after the Revolution of 1848, delivered a speech on "True Americanism" in Boston on April 18, 1859, after the victory of the American Party in Massachusetts. The party opposed the grant of complete equality to recent Irish Catholic immigrants. In his speech Schurz gave a definition of liberal nationalism.

✓　　　　✓　　　　✓

Whoever reads the history of this country calmly and thoroughly, cannot but discover that religious liberty is slowly but steadily rooting out the elements of superstition, and even of prejudice. It has dissolved the war of sects, of which persecution was characteristic, into a contest of abstract opinions, which creates convictions without oppressing men. By recognizing perfect freedom of inquiry, it will engender among men of different belief that mutual respect of true convictions which makes inquiry earnest and discussion fair. It will recognize as supremely inviolable, what Roger Williams, one of the most luminous stars of the American sky, called the sanctity of conscience. Read your history, and add the thousands and thousands of Romanists and their offspring together, who, from the first establishment of the colonies, gradually came to this country, and the sum will amount to many millions; compare that number with the number of Romanists who are now here, and you will find that millions are missing. Where are they? You did not kill them; you did not drive them away; they did not perish as the victims of persecution. But where are they? The

ᵃ Carl Schurz, *Speeches, Correspondence, and Political Papers,* ed. by F. Bancroft, New York: G. P. Putnam's Sons, 1913, vol. 1, pp. 58-72.

peaceable working of the great principles which called this Republic into existence, gradually and silently absorbed them. True Americanism, toleration, the equality of rights, has absorbed their prejudices, and will peaceably absorb everything that is not consistent with the victorious spirit of our institutions.

Oh, sir, there is a wonderful vitality in true democracy founded upon the equality of rights. There is an inexhaustible power of resistance in that system of government, which makes the protection of the individual rights a matter of common interest. If preserved in its purity, there is no warfare of opinions which can endanger it—there is no conspiracy of despotic aspirations that can destroy it. But if not preserved in its purity! There are dangers which only blindness cannot see, and which only stubborn party prejudice will not see.

Do not indulge in the delusion, that in order to make a government fair and liberal, the only thing necessary is to make it elective. When a political party in power, however liberal their principles may be, have once adopted the policy of knocking down their opponents instead of voting them down, there is an end of justice and equal rights. The history of the world shows no example of a more arbitrary despotism, than that exercised by the party which ruled the National Assembly of France in the bloodiest days of the great French Revolution. I will not discuss here what might have been done, and what not, in those times of a fearful crisis; but I will say that they tried to establish liberty by means of despotism, and that in her gigantic struggle against the united monarchs of Europe, revolutionary France won the victory, but lost her liberty.

Remember the shout of indignation that went all over the Northern States when we heard that the border ruffians of Kansas had crowded the free-State men away from the polls and had not allowed them to vote. That indignation was just, not only because the men thus terrorized were free-State men and friends of liberty, but because they were deprived of their right of suffrage, and because the government of that territory was placed on the basis of force, instead of equal rights. Sir, if ever the party of liberty should use their local predominance for the purpose of disarming their opponents instead of convincing them, they will follow the example set by the ruffians of Kansas, although legislative enactments may be a genteeler weapon than the revolver and bowie knife. They may perhaps achieve some petty local success, they may gain some small temporary advantage, but they will help to introduce a system of action into our politics which will gradually undermine the very foundations upon which our republican edifice rests. Of all the dangers and difficulties that beset us, there is none more horrible than the hideous monster, whose name is "Proscription for opinion's sake." I am an anti-slavery man, and I have a right to my opinion in Massachusetts as well as in South Carolina. You tell me that for my opinion they would mob me in South Carolina? Sir, there is the difference between South Carolina and Massachusetts. There is the difference between an anti-slavery man, who is a freeman, and a slaveholder, who is himself a slave.

Our present issues will pass away. The slavery question will be settled, liberty will be triumphant and other matters of difference will divide the political parties of this country . . .

— Reading No. 14 —

HYDE: *ON THE REVIVAL OF GAELIC*[14]

Douglas Hyde in 1892 delivered to the National Literary Society of Dublin a lecture on the necessity for de-Anglicizing Ireland which outlined the conception of nationality that was to dominate twentieth century Eire.

✓   ✓   ✓

[14] Dr. Douglas Hyde, *Revival of Irish Literature and other Addresses*, London: Fischer Unwin, 1894, pp. 117-31.

When we speak of "The Necessity for de-Anglicizing the Irish Nation," we mean it, not as a protest against imitating what is best in the English people, for that would be absurd, but rather to show the folly of neglecting what is Irish, and hastening to adopt, pell-mell, and indiscriminately, everything that is English, simply because it is English . . . If we take a bird's-eye view of our island to-day, and compare it with what it used to be, we must be struck by the extraordinary fact that the nation which was once, as everyone admits, one of the most classically learned and cultivated nations in Europe, is now one of the least so. . . .

I shall endeavour to show that this failure of the Irish people in recent times has been largely brought about by the race diverging during this century from the right path, and ceasing to be Irish without becoming English. I shall attempt to show that with the bulk of the people this change took place quite recently, much more recently than most people imagine, and is, in fact, still going on. I should also like to call attention to the illogical position of men who drop their own language to speak English, of men who translate their euphonious Irish names into English monosyllables, of men who read English books, and know nothing about Gaelic literature, nevertheless protesting as a matter of sentiment that they hate the country which at every hand's turn they rush to imitate.

I wish to show you that in Anglicizing ourselves wholesale we have thrown away with a light heart the best claim we have upon the world's recognition of us as a separate nationality. What did Mazzini say? That we ought to be content as an integral part of the United Kingdom because we have lost the notes of nationality, our language and customs. It has always been very curious to me how Irish sentiment sticks in this halfway house—how it continues apparently to hate the English, and at the same time continues to imitate them; how it continues to clamour for recognition as a distinct nationality and at the same time throws away with both hands what would make it so. . . .

What lies at the back of the sentiments of nationality with which the Irish millions seem so strongly leavened? . . . Of course it is a very composite feeling which prompts them; but I believe that what is largely behind it is the half unconscious feeling that the race which at one time held possession of more than half Europe, which established itself in Greece, and burned infant Rome, is now—almost extirpated and absorbed elsewhere —making its last stand for independence in this island of Ireland; and do what they may the race of to-day cannot wholly divest itself from the mantle of its own past. Through early Irish literature, for instance, we can best form some conception of what that race really was, which, after overthrowing and trampling on the primitive peoples of half Europe, was itself forced in turn to yield its speech, manners, and independence to the victorious eagles of Rome. We alone of the nations of Western Europe escaped the claws of those birds of prey; we alone developed ourselves naturally upon our own lines outside of and free from all Roman influence; we alone were thus able to produce an early art and literature, our antiquities can best throw light upon the pre-Romanized inhabitants of half Europe, and—we are our father's sons. . . .

What the battleaxe of the Dane, the sword of the Norman, the wile of the Saxon were unable to perform, we have accomplished ourselves. We have at last broken the continuity of Irish life, and just at the moment when the Celtic race is presumably about to largely recover possession of its own country, it finds itself deprived and stripped of its Celtic characteristics, cut off from the past, yet scarcely in touch with the present. It has lost since the beginning of this century almost all that connected it with the era of Cuchullain and of Ossian, that connected it with the christianizers of Europe, that connected it with Brian Boru and the heroes of Clontarf, with the O'Neills and O'Donnells, with Rory O'More, with the wild geese, and even to some extent with the men of '98. It has lost all that they had—language, traditions, music, genius and ideas. Just when we should be starting to build up anew the Irish race and the Gaelic nation—as within our own recollection Greece has been built up anew—we find ourselves despoiled of the bricks of nationality. The old bricks that lasted eighteen hundred years are destroyed; we must now set to, to bake new

ones, if we can, on other ground and of other clay . . .
In a word, we must strive to cultivate everything that
is most racial, most smacking of the soil, most Gaelic,
most Irish, because in spite of the little admixture of
Saxon blood in the north-east corner, this island is and
will ever remain Celtic at the core.

— Reading No. 15 —

GRIFFITH: *NATIONALITY AND ECONOMY*[15]

*Arthur Griffith, at the first annual convention of the
National Council of Sinn Féin on November 28, 1905,
delivered a speech about the need for the production and
use of home manufactures and the boycott of foreign
goods. Itself influenced by List, the Irish movement became a model for similar movements like the Indian*
swadeshi *propagating homespun cotton cloth or* khaddar.

✓   ✓   ✓

I am in economics largely a follower of the man who
thwarted England's dream of the commercial conquest of
the world, and who made the mighty confederation before which England has fallen commercially and is falling
politically—Germany. His name is a famous one in the
outside world, his works are the text books of economic
science in other countries—in Ireland his name is unknown and his works unheard of—I refer to Frederick
List, the real founder of the German Zollverein— . . .
Brushing aside the fallacies of Adam Smith and his
tribe, List points out that between the individual and

[15] Arthur Griffith in *The United Irishman,* December 9, 1905.

humanity stands, and must continue to stand, a great fact —the nation. The nation, with its special language and literature, with its peculiar origin and history, with its special manners and customs, laws and institutions, with the claims of all these for existence, independence, perfection, and continuance for the future, with its separate territory, a society which, united by a thousand ties of minds and interests, combines itself into one independent whole, which recognizes the law of right for and within itself, and in its united character is still opposed to other societies of a similar kind in their national liberty, and consequently can, only under the existing conditions of the world, maintain self-existence and independence by its own power and resources. As the individual chiefly obtains by means of the nation and in the nation, mental culture, power of production, security and prosperity, so is the civilization of the human race only conceivable and possible by means of the civilization and development of individual nations . . .

How are we to accord protection to and procure the development of our manufacturing arm? First, by ourselves individually—secondly, through our county, urban, and district councils, and poor law guardians, thirdly, by taking over control of those inefficient bodies known as harbour commissioners; fourthly, by stimulating our manufacturers and our people to industrial enterprise; and fifthly, by inviting to aid in our development, on commercial lines, Irish-American capital. In the first case, every individual knows his duty, whether he practises it or not —it is, unless where fraud is attempted, to pay if necessary an enhanced price for Irish goods, and to use whenever possible none but Irish goods. As to our public elective bodies which annually control the expenditure of our local taxation, their duty is the same. The duty of our harbour bodies is to arrange the incidence of port dues so that they shall fall most heavily on manufactured goods coming into the country, and to keep and publish a table of all goods imported and to whom consigned.

— Reading No. 16 —

DANILEVSKY: PAN-SLAVISM[16]

In his book Russia and Europe: An Inquiry into the Cultural and Political Relations of the Slav World and of the Germano-Latin World *(1869), Nikolai Danilevsky (1822-85) stated the incompatibility of Slav civilization with Western civilization, the great superiority of the former and its victory in the inevitable struggle between the two. For that purpose the Russians, the foremost Slav power, had to liberate and to unite all the Slavs and to conquer Constantinople and the (Middle) East.*

✦   ✦   ✦

In the preceding chapters, strictly speaking, I finished my self-appointed task. A special case—the course of the Schleswig-Holstein question as compared with the (Middle) Eastern question before the Crimean War—gave me the opportunity to discuss the hostility of Europe towards Russia and the Slav world. . . . This investigation led me to the conclusion that this hostility lies in the deep gulf separating the world of the Slavs and the Germano-Roman world—a gulf which reaches down to the very origins of the general stream of universal history.

I attempted to develop this theoretical approach and to supplement it with indications about the main differences between the Slavs and the Germano-Roman cultural-historical types, and about the fatal predicament to which this Westernization or Europeanization has led us, and the extent to which it is the cause of the disease from which Russia's social body suffers, a disease which is the source of all our social ills. Only historical events can remedy this disease and raise the spirit of our society, suffering from spiritual decay and abasement. The cure is possible and probable, because so far the disease has

[16] Hans Kohn, *The Mind of Modern Russia*, New Brunswick, N.J.: Rutgers University Press, 1955, pp. 195-210

luckily penetrated only the surface of the social structure. We can see such an event, or rather a whole series of events, endowed with a healthy dynamism, in the latest phase of the struggle known as the (Middle) Eastern question, whose origins are rooted in the general course of universal historical development. This struggle must shortly stamp its imprint upon an entire historical period. The importance of this inevitably approaching struggle forces us to try to understand the objections raised against the only decision useful to the Slav world— the full political liberation of all the Slav peoples and the formation of a Pan-Slav union under the hegemony of Russia. The Pan-Slav union will guarantee our success in this struggle.

Religious truth, in the eternal form of Christianity, was discovered and adopted with humility and exaltation by new peoples, who were rich in gifts of spiritual nature, among which one has to include ardent religious feelings. In this same religious doctrine there was, as its central tenet, the need to do away with slavery; and in reality, slavery appeared only as a transitory phase in the life of the Germano-Roman peoples. These peoples also revealed themselves richly endowed with political sense and an ability for cultural development: scientific, artistic, and industrial. They were not fated, however, to have these great gifts fully realized, due to the violence of their character. With them Roman love for power and Roman state structure fell upon a receptive soil. In this way, Christian truth was distorted, and the Church was transformed into the religiously political despotism of Catholicism. This church despotism in conjunction with feudal despotism, which took root in the violence of the German character, and with the despotism of scholasticism, which had taken its origin in a slavish attitude to the forms of ancient science, oriented all the history of Europe towards a severe struggle, ending in a three-fold anarchy. It comprised a religious anarchy, that is, Protestantism with the idea of basing religious truth upon personal authority; a philosophical anarchy, or an all-embracing skeptical materialism, which began to take on the character of a faith and little by little replaced religious conviction; and a socio-political anarchy, a contradiction between an ever growing political democratism and economic feudalism. As these anarchies are substantially the forerunners and instruments of decay, they cannot, of course, be considered viable investments in the treasury of mankind; and the Germano-Roman cultural-historical type cannot be considered a successful representative of the religious, or of the socio-economic aspect of cultural activity. . . .

On the other hand, . . . from an objective, factual viewpoint, the Russians and the majority of Slav peoples became, with the Greeks, the chief guardians of the living tradition of religious truth, Orthodoxy, and in this way they continued the high calling, which was the destiny of Israel and Byzantium: to be the chosen people. . . .

Whatever the future may bring we are entitled, on the evidence of the past alone, to consider the Slavs among the most gifted families of the human race in political ability. Here we may turn our attention to the special character of this political ability and show how it manifested itself during the growth of the Russian state. The Russians do not send out colonists to create new political societies, as the Greeks did in antiquity or the English in modern times. Russia does not have colonial possessions, like Rome or like England. The Russian state from early Muscovite times on has been Russia herself, gradually, irresistibly spreading on all sides, settling neighboring nonsettled territories, and assimilating into herself and into her national boundaries foreign populations. This basic character of Russian expansion was misunderstood because of the distortion of the original Russian point of view through Europeanization, the origin of every evil in Russia. . . .

In the socio-economic sphere, Russia is the only large state which has solid ground under its feet, in which there are no landless masses, and in which, consequently, the social edifice does not rest on the misery of the majority of the citizens and on the insecurity of their situation. In Russia, only, there cannot and does not exist any contradiction between political and economic ideals. This contradiction threatens disaster to European life . . . The factors that give such superiority to the Russian social structure over the European, and give it an unshakeable stability, are the peasants' land and its common ownership. On this health of Russia's socio-economic structure we found our hope for the great socio-economic significance of the Slav cultural-historical type. This type has been able for the first time to create a just and normal system of human activity, which embraces not only human relations in the moral and political sphere, but also man's mastery of nature, which is a means of satisfying human needs and requirements. Thus it establishes not only formal equality in the relations between citizens, but a real and concrete equality. . . .

The political independence of the race is the indispensable foundation of culture, and consequently all the Slav forces must be directed towards this goal. Independence is indispensable in two respects; without the consciousness of Slav racial unity, as distinct from other races, an independent culture is impossible; and without fruitful interaction between the Slav peoples, liberated from foreign powers and from their national divisions, diversity and richness of culture are impossible. A well-known example of the beneficial influence of unity is the relationship and interaction between the spiritual developments of Great Russia and the Ukraine.

The requisite preliminary achievement of political independence has still another importance in the cultural as well as in all other spheres: the struggle against the Germano-Roman world (without which Slav independence is impossible) will help to eradicate the cancer of imitativeness and the servile attitude towards the West, which through unfavorable conditions has eaten its way into the Slav body and soul. Only now has the historical moment for this cultural development arrived: only with the emancipation of the peasantry can the period of Russian cultural life begin, and her purely state period of life (which consisted in leading the people from tribal will to civil liberty) end. But first, as a *sine qua non* condition of success, strong and powerful Russia has to face the difficult task of liberating her racial brothers; for this struggle she must steel them and herself in the spirit of independence and Pan-Slav consciousness.

Thus, on the basis of our analysis of the preceding cultural-historical types and of the peculiarities of the

Slav world, we can maintain the fundamental hope that the Slav cultural-historical type will, for the first time in history, accomplish a synthesis of all aspects of cultural activity—aspects which were elaborated by its precursors on the historical scene, either in isolation or in incomplete union. We may hope that the Slav type will be the first to embody all four basic cultural activities, the religious, the political, the esthetic-scientific, and the socio-economic. . . .

— Reading No. 17 —

HAVLICEK: *THE DANGER OF PAN-SLAVISM* [17]

Karel Havlíček (1821-1856), the foremost Czech journalist, in 1846 after his return from a visit to Russia and Poland, wrote an article "Czech and Slav," in which he pointed out the dangers of Pan-Slavism for the Czechs.

✓   ✓   ✓

Simultaneously with the awakening of the national spirit and some higher activities in our (Austrian-Czech) fatherland, there came also the Slav idea, or rather this idea made itself felt again, but this time with greater strength and greater hope than before. As often happens, this Slav idea, like all other great and new ideas, became fashionable with us, so that some years ago almost everybody called himself a Slav, ashamed, as it were, of something as small as our Czech, Moravian, Silesian, or Slovak. Everybody called the Russians, Poles, Illyrians, and

[17] Hans Kohn, *The Mind of Modern Russia,* New Brunswick, N.J.: Rutgers University Press, 1955, pp. 83-90.

other Slavs his brothers and was concerned for their well-being, at least as much as for the growth of his own nation; and those who were the most practical ones felt in their heart the firm conviction that as time went on all eighty million Slavs (and all the other millions who meanwhile would accrue) would have in common one literary language, the same sympathies and all the other matters, which it is presently not advisable to discuss; in short that they all would become a single nation in the same sense in which the French and others were single nations. . . .

The purpose of this article is to correct these errors as far as possible in the minds of my countrymen, to remove the harmful, and thereby to strengthen the useful, aspects of the Slav idea. I consider that my words will become more acceptable if I prove them from my own life experience: if we wish to combat prejudices we can do it best if we acknowledge that we shared them formerly. One always believes an experienced man more.

I learned to know Poland and I did not like it. With a feeling of hostility and pride I left the Sarmation country, and in the worst cold season I arrived in a sleigh in Moscow, being warmed mostly by the Slav feeling in my heart. The freezing temperature in Russia and other aspects of Russian life extinguished the last spark of Pan-Slav love in me. Cosmopolitanism was always completely alien to me, and so I returned to Prague as a Czech, a simple determined Czech, even with some secret sour feeling against the name Slav, which a better knowledge of Russia and Poland had made suspect to me. After some time, when I had somewhat forgotten the unpleasant impression, I again quieted down, and I was able to balance my unpleasant personal experiences and my former poetic enthusiasm. In short, I formed for myself principles about Slavdom and Czechdom. and these I now wish to put before my readers for their consideration.

No decent man should be a cosmopolitan (who says that he loves everybody, loves nobody), and it would be ridiculous to feel Indo-European patriotism and to write enthusiastic poetry about it; equally invalid, though to a lesser degree, is a Pan-Slav patriotism. Should somebody object that the differences among the Slav nations are not so great as among the Romance or the Teutonic nations, then we must simply disagree. Even if there be slighter differences among the various Slav languages than among the various Teutonic and Romance languages (though the Dutch tongue is nearer to German than Russian is to Czech, and between French and Italian there is no greater difference than between Russian and Czech), we must not forget that nationality is determined not only by language but also by customs, religion, form of government, state of education, sympathies, and so on, and that the differences among the different nations are based upon these characters. If we take all that in due consideration, then we cannot say that Russians and Czechs, Poles and Russians, Illyrians and Poles, show a greater affinity than any two Teutonic or Romance nations. . . .

We cannot expect unity even among closely related Slav nations. On the contrary, the closer they live together the more disunity we may expect. Let us take the world as it is, and expect friendship and unity among people and nations only when this is advantageous for both sides. . . .

At the beginning, I sided with the Poles against the Russians. As soon as I recognized the true state of affairs in Poland, as soon as the veil which poetically hid from me the prosaic misery and corruption of the nation (that is, the Polish nobility) dropped from my eyes, my affection changed to dislike, and for a psychologically understandable reason the Russians appeared to me to be better than the Poles. This, however, did not last long. I soon recognized that Peter is like Paul, Russia like Poland. My Slav sympathy disappeared, and I learned to regard the Russians and the Poles, in spite of the affinity of language, origin, and customs, as nations alien to us Czechs. . . . We must not look on the Russian-Polish relations with such a blind eye as the greater part of Europe does; we should not think of an innocent lamb and a wolf, but know that there wolf meets wolf, and we shall say later that the lamb among them is the Ukrainian. The Poles themselves formerly tried to destroy Russia, and the Russians now try the opposite. . . . The Ukraine is the apple of discord which fate threw between these

two nations. . . . Thus the suppression of Ukrainian
liberty revenges itself on Poland and Russia. . . .

The Poles and the Russians buried the national spirit
of the Ukraine and began to divide the great body, and,
as generally happens in such cases, they began to fight
and have not yet ceased. Both the Russians and the Poles
regard the Ukrainian language as a dialect of their own
language. . . . Thus we have seen three great Eastern
Slav nations, each one of which hates the other two, and
also has a just reason for it. Nobody can speak reason-
ably of brotherhood there. Nevertheless, the Pan-Slav
idea has been accepted even by these nations. That might
seem to contradict me: in reality the way in which Poles
and Russians understood and accepted Pan-Slavism will
prove that they don't deserve our sympathy.

The Russians (and I do not speak here of the government, because I cannot know its trend of thought) have
taken up the idea of Pan-Slavism. In the whole world,
but above all in Europe, the Russians are either disliked
or rejected (and that almost always for good reasons): it
was therefore surprising but most agreeable to them to
find at least some friends in the West. Thus they declared
immediately their friendship and brotherhood with us
and the Illyrians but regarded themselves as the older
brother, as our commander. The Russian Pan-Slavs believe that we and the Illyrians would like to be under
their domination! ! They are firmly convinced that they
will one day control all Slav lands! ! ! They now look forward with joy to their future vineyards in Dalmatia.
These gentlemen have started everywhere to say and
write Slav instead of Russian, so that later they will again
be able to say Russian instead of Slav. . . .

But let us be equally cool towards the Poles. They are
like the Russians, but with tied hands. It is well known
that formerly the Poles did not wish to know anything of
the Slavs. Only when the Polish democrats and emigrants
in France came upon the happy thought that perhaps the
other Slavs could jointly with the Poles make light-
hearted revolutions and thus serve them in their poorly
calculated plans, did they begin to fraternize with us, and
in their easy and sanguine temper they began to imagine
how they would be the leaders among the Western liberal

Slavs and how we should fight for them against everyone they hate! . . .

Finally, it is also significant that the Russians and the Poles exclude each other from the ranks of the Slavs: Russian scholars have proved that the Poles descend from the non-Slav Sarmatians (and be it said quietly, that the Polish nobility thought so too, believing its blood superior to the Slav peasant blood), and the Poles on their part have proved that the Russians are of Mongol origin. . . .

What I wrote here stems from the reading of almost the whole literature on Pan-Slavism and from personal experiences. . . . and everything written here is my full conviction. The plain principles, once more summarized, are: the Slavs are not one nation but four nations as independent and unconnected as any other European nations. Each of these Slav nations stands for itself, and none is responsible for another; they share neither national honor nor national infamy. As the result of the great similarity of the Slav languages, it is useful and necessary for each Slav nation to pay as much attention to the literature of the others as possible, and to profit from their literature and languages and nationality. Only between the Czechs and the Illyrians can there be more far-reaching sympathies, because under present conditions one cannot be dangerous to the other but on the contrary useful. The Austrian monarchy is the best guarantee for the preservation of our and the Illyrian nationality, and the greater the power of the Austrian empire grows, the more secure our nationalities will be. It is impossible then for all Slavs to use one literary language, and therefore all efforts in this direction are meaningless, and, as a waste of time, harmful.

DOSTOEVSKY: *RUSSIAN MESSIANISM*[18]

Dostoevsky expressed his Russian nationalism not only in his journalism (The Diary of a Writer) *but also in his novels. In* The Possessed, *which he wrote 1870 to 1872, he made Shatov represent his Slavophil point of view in a famous discussion with the enigmatic Nikolai Stavrogin.*

✓   ✓   ✓

"Do you know," he began, with flashing eyes, almost menacingly, bending right forward in his chair, raising the forefinger of his right hand above him (obviously unaware that he was doing so), "do you know who are the only 'god-bearing' people on earth, destined to regenerate and save the world in the name of a new God, and to whom are given the keys of life and of the new world. . . . Do you know which is that people and what is its name?"

"From your manner I am forced to conclude, and I think I may as well do so at once, that it is the Russian people."

"And you can laugh, oh, what a race!" Shatov burst out.

"Calm yourself, I beg of you; on the contrary, I was expecting something of the sort from you." . . .

Shatov interrupted, waving his hand.

"Do you remember your expression that 'an atheist can't be a Russian,' that 'an atheist at once ceases to be a Russian'? Do you remember saying that?"

"Did I?" Nikolai Vsyevolodovitch questioned him back.

"You ask? You've forgotten? And yet that was one of the truest statements of the leading peculiarity of the

[18] Feodor Mikhailovich Dostoevsky, *The Possessed*, pt. II, chap. I. tr. by Constance Garnett, New York: Copyright by Macmillan Co., and used with permission.

Russian soul, which you divined. You can't have forgotten it! I will remind you of something else: you said then that 'a man who was not orthodox could not be Russian.' "

"I imagine that's a Slavophil idea."

"The Slavophils of to-day disown it. Nowadays, people have grown cleverer. But you went further: you believed that Roman Catholicism was not Christianity; you asserted that Rome proclaimed Christ subject to the third temptation of the devil. Announcing to all the world that Christ without an earthly kingdom cannot hold his ground upon earth, Catholicism by so doing proclaimed Antichrist and ruined the whole Western world. You pointed out that if France is in agonies now it's simply the fault of Catholicism, for she has rejected the iniquitous God of Rome and has not found a new one. That's what you could say then! I remember our conversations." . . .

Shatov bent forward in his chair again and again held up his finger for a moment.

"Not a single nation," he went on, as though reading it line by line, still gazing menacingly at Stavrogin, "not a single nation has ever been founded on principles of science or reason. There has never been an example of it, except for a brief moment, through folly. Socialism is from its very nature bound to be atheism, seeing that it has from the very first proclaimed that it is an atheistic organisation of society, and that it intends to establish itself exclusively on the elements of science and reason. Science and reason have, from the beginning of time, played a secondary and subordinate part in the life of nations; so it will be till the end of time. Nations are built up and moved by another force which sways and dominates them, the origin of which is unknown and inexplicable: that force is the force of an insatiable desire to go on to the end, though at the same time it denies that end. It is the force of the persistent assertion of one's own existence, and a denial of death. It's the spirit of life, as the Scriptures call it, 'the river of living water,' the drying up of which is threatened in the Apocalypse. It's the aesthetic principle, as the philosophers call it, the ethical principle with which they identify it, 'the seeking for God,' as I call it more simply. The object of every na-

tional movement, in every people and at every period of
its existence is only the seeking for its god, who must be
its own god, and the faith in him as the only true one.
God is the synthetic personality of the whole people,
taken from its beginning to its end. It has never happened that all, or even many, peoples have had one common god, but each has always had its own. It's a sign of
the decay of nations when they begin to have gods in
common. When gods begin to be common to several
nations the gods are dying and the faith in them, together with the nations themselves. The stronger a people
the more individual their god. There never has been a
nation without a religion, that is, without an idea of
good and evil. Every people has its own conception of
good and evil, and its own good and evil. When the same
conceptions of good and evil become prevalent in several
nations, then these nations are dying, and then the very
distinction between good and evil is beginning to disappear. Reason has never had the power to define good
and evil, or even to distinguish between good and evil,
even approximately; on the contrary, it has always mixed
them up in a disgraceful and pitiful way; science has
even given the solution by the fist. This is particularly
characteristic of the half-truths of science, the most terrible scourge of humanity, unknown till this century, and
worse than plague, famine, or war. A half-truth is a
despot such as has never been in the world before. A
despot that has its priests and its slaves, a despot to whom
all do homage with love and superstition hitherto incon-
ceivable, before which science itself trembles and cringes
in a shameful way. These are your own words, Stavrogin,
all except that about the half-truth; that's my own because I am myself a case of half-knowledge, and that's
why I hate it particularly. I haven't altered anything of
your ideas or even of your words, not a syllable."

"I don't agree that you've not altered anything," Stavrogin observed cautiously. "You accepted them with ardour, and in your ardour have transformed them uncon-
sciously. The very fact that you reduce God to a simple
attribute of nationality. . . ."

He suddenly began watching Shatov with intense and
peculiar attention, not so much his words as himself.

"I reduce God to the attribute of nationality?" cried Shatov. "On the contrary, I raise the people to God. And has it ever been otherwise? The people is the body of God. Every people is only a people so long as it has its own god and excludes all other gods on earth irreconcilably; so long as it believes that by its god it will conquer and drive out of the world all other gods. Such, from the beginning of time, has been the belief of all great nations, all, anyway, who have been specially remarkable, all who have been leaders of humanity. There is no going against facts. The Jews lived only to await the coming of the true God and left the world the true God. The Greeks deified nature and bequeathed the world their religion, that is, philosophy and art. Rome deified the people in the State, and bequeathed the idea of the State to the nations. France throughout her long history was only the incarnation and development of the Roman god, and if they have at last flung their Roman god into the abyss and plunged into atheism, which, for the time being, they call socialism, it is solely because socialism is, anyway, healthier than Roman Catholicism. If a great people does not believe that the truth is only to be found in itself alone (in itself alone and in it exclusively); if it does not believe that it alone is fit and destined to raise up and save all the rest by its truth, it would at once sink into being ethnographical material, and not a great people. A really great people can never accept a secondary part in the history of Humanity, nor even one of the first, but will have the first part. A nation which loses this belief ceases to be a nation. But there is only one truth, and therefore only a single one out of the nations can have the true God, even though other nations may have great gods of their own. Only one nation is 'god-bearing,' that's the Russian people, and . . . and. . . ."

"Certainly I'll ask differently," Nikolai Vsyevolodovitch looked coldly at him. "I only wanted to know, do you believe in God, yourself?"

"I believe in Russia. . . . I believe in her orthodoxy. . . . I believe in the body of Christ. . . . I believe that the new advent will take place in Russia. . . . I believe. . . ." Shatov muttered frantically.

"And in God? In God?"

"I . . . I will believe in God." . . .

"I'm sorry I can't feel affection for you, Shatov," Stavrogin replied coldly.

"I know you can't, and I know you are not lying. Listen. I can set it all right. I can 'catch your hare' for you."

Stavrogin did not speak.

"You're an atheist because you're a snob, a snob of the snobs. You've lost touch with your own people. A new generation is coming, straight from the heart of the people, and you will know nothing of it, neither you nor the Verhovenskys, father or son; nor I, for I'm a snob too—I, the son of your serf and lackey, Pashka. . . . Listen. Attain to God by work; it all lies in that; or disappear like rotten mildew. Attain to Him by work."

"God by work? What sort of work?"

"Peasants' work. Go, give up all your wealth. . . . Ah! you laugh, you're afraid of some trick?"

But Stavrogin was not laughing.

"You suppose that one may attain to God by work, and by peasants' work," he repeated, reflecting as though he had really come across something new and serious which was worth considering.

— Reading No. 19 —

RICHARD WAGNER: *THE JEWISH DANGER* [19]

In 1850 Richard Wagner published an (anonymous) article, "Judaism in Music." It first gave to extreme anti-Semitism the support of an artist of genius.

✓   ✓   ✓

[19] Richard Wagner, *Prose Works,* tr. by W. A. Ellis, London: Kegan, Paul, Trench, Trübner & Co., 1912, vol. III, pp 79-100.

If emancipation from the yoke of Judaism appears to us the greatest of necessities, we must above all prove our forces for this war of liberation. Now we shall never win these forces from an abstract definition of the phenomenon *per se,* but only from an accurate acquaintance with the nature of our involuntary feeling of an instinctive repugnance against the Jew's essential character. Through it, through this unconquerable feeling—if we avow it quite without ado—must there become plain to us what we hate in that essence; what we then know clearly, we can oppose; nay, through his very laying bare, may we even hope to rout the demon from the field, whereon he has only been able to maintain his stand beneath the shelter of a twilight darkness—a darkness we good-natured humanitarians ourselves have cast upon him, to make his look less loathesome.

The Jew—who, as everyone knows, has a God all to himself—in ordinary life strikes us primarily by his outward appearance, which, no matter to what European nationality we belong, has something disagreeably foreign to that nationality: instinctively we wish to have nothing in common with a man who looks like that. By far more weighty, nay, of quite decisive weight for our inquiry, is the effect the Jew produces on us through his speech; and this is the essential point about the Jewish influence upon music. The Jew speaks the language of the nation in whose midst he dwells from generation to generation, but he speaks it always as an alien. . . . Our whole European art and civilization, however, have remained to the Jew as a foreign tongue; for, just as he has taken no part in the evolution of the one, so has he taken none in that of the other; but at most the homeless wight has been a cold, nay more, a hostile on-looker. In this speech, this art, the Jew can only after-speak and after-patch—not truly make a poem of his words, an artwork of his doings. . . .

Alien and apathetic stands the educated Jew in the midst of a society he does not understand, with whose tastes and aspirations he does not sympathise, whose history and evolution have always been indifferent to him . . .

Now, our modern arts had likewise become a portion of this culture, and among them more particularly that art which is just the very easiest to learn—the art of music, and indeed that music which, severed from her sister arts, had been lifted by the force and stress of grandest geniuses to a stage in her universal faculty of expression where either, in new conjunction with the other arts, she might speak aloud the most sublime, or, in persistent separation from them, she could also speak at will the deepest bathos of the trivial. Naturally, what the cultured Jew had to speak, in his situation, could be nothing but the trivial and indifferent, because his whole artistic bent was in sooth a mere luxurious, and needless thing. At present no art affords such plentiful possibility of talking in it without saying any real thing, as that of music, since the greatest geniuses have already said whatever there was to say in it as an absolute separate-art. After this there was nothing left but to babble after; and indeed with quite distressing accuracy and deceptive likeness, just as parrots reel off human words and phrases, but also with just as little real feeling and expression as these foolish birds. Only in the case of our Jewish music-makers this mimicked speech presents one marked peculiarity—that of the Jewish style of talk in general, which we have more minutely characterised above. . . .

— Reading No. 20 —

WAGNER: GERMAN ART[20]

The following essay was written by Wagner in 1867, one year after Prussia defeated Austria at Königgrätz and set the stage for the Prussian unification of Germany. The

* Richard Wagner, *Prose Works*, tr. by William Ashton Ellis, London: Kegan, Paul, Trench, Trübner & Co., 1912, vol. IV, Art and Politics, pp. 43 f., 48 f., 58, 63, 107 f., 165 f.

last paragraph dates from 1878 and expresses Wagner's disappointment with the too "liberal" and "Judaized" new Germany of Bismarck.

✓   ✓   ✓

It is good and most encouraging for us, to find that the German spirit, when in the second half of the last century it raised itself from its deepest decay, did not require a new birth, but merely a resurrection: across two desert centuries it could stretch its hands to the same spirit, which then strewed wide its lusty seeds through all the Holy Roman Empire of the German nation. . . . Hail Winckelmann and Lessing, you who, beyond the centuries of native German majesty, found the German's kinsmen in the divine Hellenes, and laid bare the pure ideal of human beauty to the powder-bleared eyes of French civilised mankind! Hail to thee, Schiller, thou who gavest to the reborn spirit the stature of the "German youth," who stands disdainful of the pride of Britain, the sensuous wiles of Paris! Who was this *"deutsche Jüngling?"* Has anyone heard of a French, an English *"Jüngling?"* And yet how plain and clear beyond mistake, we understand this "German *Jüngling!"* This youth, who in Mozart's virginal melodies beshamed the Italian capons; in Beethoven's Symphony grew up to courage of the man, for dauntless, world-redeeming deeds! And this stripling it was, who threw himself at last upon the battle-field when his princes had lost everything, Empire, country, honour; to reconquer for the folk its freedom, for the princes even their forfeit thrones. And how was this *"Jüngling"* repaid? In all history there is no blacker ingratitude, than the German princes' treachery to the spirit of their people; and many a good, a noble and self-sacrificing deed of theirs, will it need to atone for that betrayal. We hope for those deeds, and therefore let the sin be told right loudly! . . .

The only thing left over from the time of Germany's revival, was the military organization retained by Prussia: with this last remnant of the German spirit, uprooted everywhere else, the Prussian crown won the battle of Königgrätz, to all the world's amazement, after the lapse of half a century. So great was the terror at this host in every European Ministry of War, that anxious longing needs must seize the French commander-in-chief himself, regarded as the mightiest of them all, to introduce a something like this *"Landwehr"* into his so rightly famous army. We have seen, not long ago, how the whole French people kicked against the thought. So that French civilisation has not accomplished what the downtrod German spirit so quickly and so lastingly succeeded in: the formation of a true folk-army. . . .

Ever since the regeneration of European folk-blood, the German has been the creator and inventor, the Latin the modeller and exploiter: the true fountain of continual renovation has remained the German nature. In this sense, the dissolution of the "Holy Roman Empire of the German Nation" gave voice to nothing but a temporary preponderance of the practically-realistic trend in European culture; if this latter now has reached the bottom of sordidest materialism, by a most natural instinct the nations turn back to the fount of their renewing; and, strange to say, they there find the German Reich itself in an almost inexplicable state of suspended animation, yet not a victim to advanced decay, but engaged in a very obvious inner struggle towards its noblest resurrection. . . .

Here came to consciousness and received its plain expression, what *German* is: to wit, the thing one does for its own sake, for the very joy of doing it; whereas utilitarianism, namely the principle whereby a thing is done for sake of some personal end, ulterior to the thing itself, was shown to be un-German. The German virtue herein expressed thus coincided with the highest principle of aesthetics, through it perceived, according to which the 'objectless' alone is beautiful, because, being an end in itself, in revealing its nature as lifted high above all vulgar ends it reveals that whose sight and knowledge alone makes life worth living; whereas everything that serves an end is hideous, because neither its fashioner nor its onlooker can have aught before him save a disquieting conglomerate of fragmentary material, which is first to gain its meaning and elucidation from its employment for some vulgar need. None but a great nation, confiding with tranquil stateliness in its unshakable might, could ripen such a principle within itself, and apply it for the happiness of the whole world: for it assuredly presupposes a solid ordering of every relation that serves life's necessary ends; and it was the duty of the political powers to found that order in this lofty, world-redeeming sense,—that is to say: Germany's princes should have been as German, as were her great masters. . . .

After all that had gone before, it now had really become a difficult matter, to rule in Germany. As the governments made it a maxim to judge their German peoples by the measure of French events, there also soon arose adventurers to teach the downtrod German folk-spirit to apply French maxims to its estimate of the governments. Every new Parisian revolution was promptly 'mounted' in Germany: of course, for every new spectacular Paris opera had been mounted forthwith at the Court-theatres of Berlin and Vienna, a pattern for all Germany. I have no hesitation about styling the subsequent revolutions in Germany entirely un-German. "Democracy" in German is purely an alien and translated thing. It exists merely in the newspapers; and what this German press is, one must find out for oneself. But untowardly enough, this translated Franco-Judaico-German democracy could really borrow a deceptive cloak, from the misprised and maltreated spirit of the German folk. To secure a following among the people, "democracy" aped a German mien; and *"Deutschthum,"* "German spirit," "German honesty," "German freedom," "German morals," became catchwords disgusting no one more than him who had true German culture, who had to stand in sorrow and watch the singular comedy of agitators from a non-German people pleading for him without letting their client so much as get a word in edgewise. The astounding unsuccessfulness of the so loud-mouthed movement of 1848 is easily explained by the curious circumstance that the German found himself, and found his name, so suddenly represented by a race of men quite alien to him. . . .

— Reading No. 21 —

MUSSOLINI: *THE DOCTRINE OF FASCISM*[21]

Benito Mussolini himself expressed the political doc trines of fascism in an article in the Enciclopedia Italiana *in 1932; it was republished in an official translation in a somewhat changed form.*

✓   ✓   ✓

Thus many of the practical expressions of Fascism, such as party organization, educational systems, discipline, can only be understood when considered in relation to its general attitude towards life. Fascism does not see in the world only those superficial, material aspects in which man appears as a self-centered individual, standing alone, subject to natural laws and instincts which urge him towards a life of selfish momentary pleasure; it does not only see the individual, but also the nation and the country; individuals and generations bound together by a moral law, moral traditions and a mission which, repressing the instinct for life enclosed in a brief circle of pleasure, builds up a higher life founded on duty, a life free from the limitations of time and space, in which the individual may achieve that purely spiritual existence in which his worth as a man consists, by self-sacrifice, in the renunciation of self-interest, by death itself. . . .

Fascism wants men to be active and to engage in activity with all their energy; it requires that they should be manfully aware of the difficulties besetting them and ready to face them. Life is conceived as a struggle in which a man is bound to win for himself a really worthy place, first of all by fitting himself physically, morally and

■ Benito Mussolini, *The Doctrine of Fascism*, tr. by E. Cope. third edition, Florence: Vallechi publishers, 1938, pp. 10-25, 30-40, 49.

intellectually, and to have the necessary qualities for winning it. As it is for the individual, so is it for the nation, and for all mankind. Hence the high value of culture in all its forms, religious, scientific and artistic, and the outstanding importance of education. Hence also the essential value of work, by which man subdues nature and creates the human world in its economic, political, ethical and intellectual aspects.

This positive conception of life is obviously an ethical one. It covers the entire field of reality as well as the human activities which master it. No action is exempt from moral judgment; no activity can be deprived of the value which a moral purpose confers on all things. Therefore life, as conceived by the Fascist, is serious, austere, religious; all its manifestations take place in a world sustained by moral forces and subject to spiritual responsibilities. The Fascist disdains an easygoing life.

The Fascist conception of life is a religious one in which man is viewed in his permanent relation to a higher law, endowed with an objective will transcending the individual and raising him to conscious membership of a spiritual society. Those who perceive nothing beyond opportunist considerations in the religious policy of the Fascist Regime, fail to realize that Fascism is not only a system of government, but also and chiefly a system of thought. . . .

Being anti-individualistic, the Fascist system of life stresses the importance of the State and recognizes the individual only in so far as his interests coincide with those of the State, which stands for the consciousness and the universality of man as an historic entity. It is opposed to classic Liberalism which arose as a reaction to absolutism and exhausted its historical function when the State became the expression of the consciousness and the will of the people. Liberalism denied the State in the name of the individual; Fascism reasserts the rights of the State as expressing the real essence of the individual. And if liberty is to be the attribute of living men and not that of abstract dummies invented by individualistic Liberalism, then Fascism stands for liberty and for the only liberty worth having, the liberty of the State and of the individual within the State. The Fascist conception of the State is all-embracing; outside of it no human or spiritual values may exist, much less have any value. Thus understood, Fascism is totalitarian and the Fascist State, as a synthesis and a unit which includes all values, interprets, develops and lends additional power to the whole life of a people.

A nation, as expressed in the State, is a living, ethical entity only in so far as it is progressive. Inactivity means death. Therefore the State does not only stand for Authority which governs and confers legal form and spiritual value on individual wills, but it is also Power which makes its will felt and respected beyond its own boundaries, thus affording practical evidence of the universal character of the decisions necessary to ensure its development. This implies organization and expansion, potential if not actual. . . .

Fascism, in short, is not only a lawgiver and a founder of institutions, but an educator and a promoter of spiritual life. It does not merely aim at remoulding the forms of life, but also their content, man, his character and his faith. To achieve this purpose it enforces discipline and makes use of authority, entering into the mind and ruling with undisputed sway. Therefore it has chosen as its emblem the Lictors' rods, the symbol of unity, strength and justice. . . .

Yet if anybody cares to read over again the faded minutes of the meetings at which the Italian *Fasci di Combattimento* were founded, he will not find a doctrine, but a series of hints, pointers, forecasts which, after being freed from unavoidable contemporary confusion, were to develop in a few years' time into a series of theoretical positions entitling Fascism to rank as a political doctrine differing from all others, past or present.

"If the bourgeoisie"—I stated at that time—"believe that they have found in us their lightning conductors, they are mistaken. We must go towards the people. . . . We wish the working classes to accustom themselves to the responsibilities of management, so that they may realize that it is no easy matter to run a business. . . . We will fight both technical and spiritual rear-guardism. . . . Now that the succession of the Regime is open we must not be faint-hearted. We must rush forward; when the present Regime is superseded we must take its place. The right to the succession is ours, for we urged the country to enter the war and we led it to victory. . ". . . The existing forms of political representation cannot satisfy us; we want direct representation of all separate interests. . . . It may be objected that this programme implies a return to the guilds. No matter! . . . I therefore hope this assembly will accept the economic claims advanced by National Syndicalism. . . ."

Fascism is definitely and absolutely opposed to the doctrines of Liberalism, both in the political and in the economic sphere. The importance of Liberalism in the XIX century must not be exaggerated for present-day controversial purposes, nor should we make of one of the many theories which flourished in that century, a religion for mankind for the present and for all time to come. It is symptomatic that throughout the 19th century the religion of Liberalism was totally unknown to so highly civilized a people as the Germans, except for a single case, which has been described as the "ridiculous Parliament of Frankfort" which lasted just one season. Germany attained her national unity outside Liberalism and in opposition to Liberalism, a doctrine which seems to be foreign to the German temperament, an essentially Monarchist one, whereas Liberalism is the historic and logical prelude to anarchy. The three stages in the achievement of German unity were the three wars of 1864, 1866 and 1870, directed by such "Liberals" as Moltke and Bismarck. And Liberalism played a very minor part in building up Italian unity, if we compare it to the contribution made by Mazzini and Garibaldi who were not Liberals. But for the intervention of the illiberal Napoleon III we would not have had Lombardy, and without that of the illiberal Bismarck at Sadowa and Sedan very probably we would not have had Venetia in 1866, nor would we have entered Rome in 1870. . . .

The Fascist negation of Socialism, Democracy, Liberalism should not, however, be interpreted as implying a desire to drive the world backwards to positions occupied prior to 1789. Monarchist absolutism is of the past, and so is Church rule. Dead and done for are feudal privileges and the division of society into closed, secluded castes.

Neither has the Fascist conception of authority anything in common with that of the police-ridden State.

The State educates its members to citizenship, makes them aware of their mission, urges them to unity; its justice harmonizes their divergent interests; it hands down to future generations the conquests of the mind in the fields of science, art, law, human solidarity; it leads them up from primitive tribal life to imperial rule, the highest expression of human power. The State hands down to future generations the memory of those who laid down their lives to ensure its safety or to obey its laws; it sets up as examples and records for future ages the names of captains who enlarged its territory and of the men of genius who have made it famous. Whenever respect for the State declines and the disintegrating and centrifugal tendencies of individuals and groups prevail, nations are heading for decay. . . ."

If Liberalism spells individualism, Fascism spells collectivism. The Fascist State, however, is an unique and original creation. It is not reactionary but revolutionary, for it anticipates the solution of certain universal problems which have been raised elsewhere in the political field by the disgregation of parties, the usurpation of powers by parliaments, the irresponsibility of assemblies; in the economic field by the increasingly numerous and important functions discharged by trade unions and trade associations with their disputes and agreements, affecting both capital and labour; in the ethical field by the need felt for order, discipline, obedience to the moral principles of patriotism.

Fascism desires the State to be strong and organic, based on solid foundations of popular support. The Fascist State lays claim to rule in the economic field no less than in others; it makes its action felt throughout the length and breadth of the country by means of its corporate, social and educational institutions, and all the political, economic and spiritual forces of the nation, organized in their respective associations, spread all over the State. . . .

Today I hold that Fascism as an idea, a doctrine, a realization, is universal; it is Italian in its particular institutions, but it is universal by reason of its nature.

Therefore anyone may foresee a Fascist Europe drawing inspiration for her institutions from the doctrine and practice of Fascism; Europe, in other words, giving a Fascist turn to the solution of problems which beset the modern State, the Twentieth Century State which is very different from the States existing before 1789, and the States formed immediately after. Today Fascism answers to universal requirements.

— Reading No. 22 —

NEHRU: *SOCIALISM AND NATIONALISM* [22]

Jawarharlal Nehru (b. 1889), Gandhi's successor as President of the Indian National Congress and first Prime Minister of the Republic of India (Bharat), published in 1936 his Autobiography *in England, where the book went through fourteen printings within three years. In a shortened form it was published in the United States in 1941. In the following extract Nehru discusses socialism and nationalism, the importance of the Congress and of Gandhi.*

✓ ✓ ✓

I had long been drawn to socialism and communism, and Russia had appealed to me. Much in Soviet Russia I dislike—the ruthless suppression of all contrary opinion, the wholesale regimentation, the unnecessary violence (as I thought) in carrying out various policies. But there was no lack of violence and suppression in the capitalist

[22] Jawaharlal Nehru, *Toward Freedom*, New York: John Day, 1941, pp. 229-33. Reprinted by permission.

world, and I realized more and more how the very basis and foundation of our acquisitive society and property was violence. Without violence it could not continue for many days. A measure of political liberty meant little indeed when the fear of starvation was always compelling the vast majority of people everywhere to submit to the will of the few, to the greater glory and advantage of the latter.

Violence was common in both places, but the violence of the capitalist order seemed inherent in it; while the violence of Russia, bad though it was, aimed at a new order based on peace and cooperation and real freedom for the masses. With all her blunders, Soviet Russia had triumphed over enormous difficulties and taken great strides toward this new order. While the rest of the world was in the grip of the depression and going backward in some ways, in the Soviet country a great new world was being built up before our eyes. Russia, following the great Lenin, looked into the future and thought only of what was to be, while other countries lay numbed under the dead hand of the past and spent their energy in preserving the useless relics of a bygone age. In particular, I was impressed by the reports of the great progress made by the backward regions of Central Asia under the Soviet regime. In the balance, therefore, I was all in favor of Russia, and the presence and example of the Soviets was a bright and heartening phenomenon in a dark and dismal world.

But Soviet Russia's success or failure, vastly important as it was as a practical experiment in establishing a communist state, did not affect the soundness of the theory of communism. The Bolsheviks may blunder or even fail because of national or international reasons, and yet the communist theory may be correct. On the basis of that very theory it was absurd to copy blindly what had taken place in Russia, for its application depended on the particular conditions prevailing in the country in question and the stage of its historical development. Besides, India, or any other country, could profit by the triumphs as well as the inevitable mistakes of the Bolsheviks. Perhaps the Bolsheviks had tried to go too fast because, surrounded as they were by a world of enemies, they feared external aggression. A slower tempo might avoid much of the misery caused in the rural areas. But then the question arose if really radical results could be obtained by slowing down the rate of change. Reformism was an impossible solution of any vital problem at a critical moment when the basic structure had to be changed, and, however slow the progress might be later on, the initial step must be a complete break with the existing order, which had fulfilled its purpose and was now only a drag on future progress. . . .

Russia apart, the theory and philosophy of Marxism lightened up many a dark corner of my mind. History came to have a new meaning for me. The Marxist interpretation threw a flood of light on it, and it became an unfolding drama with some order and purpose, howsoever unconscious, behind it. In spite of the appalling waste and misery of the past and the present, the future was bright with hope, though many dangers intervened. It was the essential freedom from dogma and the scientific outlook of Marxism that appealed to me. It was true that there was plenty of dogma in official communism in Russia and elsewhere, and frequently heresy hunts were organized. That seemed to be deplorable, though it was not difficult to understand in view of the tremendous changes taking place rapidly in the Soviet countries when effective opposition might have resulted in catastrophic failure. The great world crisis and slump seemed to justify the Marxist analysis. While all other systems and theories were groping about in the dark, Marxism alone explained it more or less satisfactorily and offered a real solution.

As this conviction grew upon me, I was filled with a new excitement, and my depression at the nonsuccess of civil disobedience grew much less. Was not the world marching rapidly toward the desired consummation? There were grave dangers of wars and catastrophes, but at any rate we were moving. There was no stagnation. Our national struggle became a stage in the longer journey, and it was as well that repression and suffering were tempering our people for future struggles and forcing them to consider the new ideas that were stirring

the world. We would be the stronger and the more disciplined and hardened by the elimination of the weaker
elements. Time was in our favor. . . .

The policy of the British Government in India had
resulted in ranging the socially reactionary classes in
opposition to political independence. That was inevitable,
and I welcomed the clearer demarcation of the various
classes and groups in India. But was this fact appreciated
by others? Apparently not by many. It was true that there
were a handful of orthodox communists in some of the
big cities, and they were hostile to, and bitterly critical
of, the national movement. The organized labor movement, especially in Bombay and, to a lesser extent, in
Calcutta, was also socialistic in a loose kind of way, but
it was broken up into bits and suffering from the depression. Vague communistic and socialistic ideas had spread
among the intelligentsia, even among intelligent Government officials. The younger men and women of the Congress, who used to read Bryce on democracies and Mor-
ley and Keith and Mazzini, were now reading, when they
could get them, books on socialism and communism and
Russia. The Meerut Conspiracy Case had helped greatly
in directing people's minds to these new ideas, and the
world crisis had compelled attention. Everywhere there
was in evidence a new spirit of inquiry, a questioning and
a challenge to existing institutions. The general direction
of the mental wind was obvious, but still it was a gentle
breeze, unsure of itself. Some people flirted with fascist
ideas. A clear and definite ideology was lacking. Nationalism still was the dominating thought.

It seemed clear to me that nationalism would remain
the outstanding urge, till some measure of political freedom was attained. Because of this the Congress had been,
and was still (apart from certain labor circles), the
most advanced organization in India, as it was far the
most powerful. During the past thirteen years, under
Gandhiji's leadership, it had produced a wonderful awakening of the masses, and, in spite of its vague bourgeois
ideology, it had served a revolutionary purpose. It had
not exhausted its utility yet and was not likely to do so
till the nationalist urge gave place to a social one. Future
progress, both ideological and in action, must therefore

be largely associated with the Congress, though other avenues could also be used. . . .

But Congress at present meant Gandhiji. What would he do? Ideologically he was sometimes amazingly backward, and yet in action he had been the greatest revolutionary of recent times in India. He was a unique personality, and it was impossible to judge him by the usual standards, or even to apply the ordinary canons of logic to him. But, because he was a revolutionary at bottom and was pledged to political independence for India, he was bound to play an uncompromising role till that independence was achieved. And in this very process he would release tremendous mass energies and would himself, I half hoped, advance step by step toward the social goal.

— Reading No. 23 —

SUN YAT-SEN: *A MESSAGE TO SOVIET RUSSIA*[23]

On his deathbed, in March 1925, the leader of the Kuomintang, Sun Yat-sen, addressed the following letter to the Central Executive Committee of the Union of Soviet Socialist Republics.

✓   ✓   ✓

Dear Comrades:

While I lie here in a malady against which men are powerless, my thoughts are turned towards you and towards the fates of my Party and my country.

[23] *The New York Times,* May 24, 1925.

You are the head of the union of free republics—that heritage left to the oppressed peoples of the world by the immortal Lenin. With the aid of that heritage the victims of imperialism will inevitably achieve emancipation from that international regime whose foundations have been rooted for ages in slavery, wars, and injustice.

I leave behind me a Party which, as I always hoped, will be bound up with you in the historic work of the final liberation of China and other exploited countries from the yoke of imperialism. By the will of fate I must leave my work unfinished, and hand it over to those who, remaining faithful to the principles and teachings of the Party, will thereby be my true followers.

Therefore I charge the Kuomintang to continue the work of the revolutionary nationalist movement, so that China, reduced by the imperialists to the position of a semi-colonial country, shall become free.

With this object I have instructed the Party to be in constant contact with you. I firmly believe in the continuance of the support which you have hitherto accorded to my country.

Taking my leave of you, dear comrades, I want to express the hope that the day will come when the U.S.S.R. will welcome a friend and ally in a mighty, free China, and that in the great struggle for the liberation of the oppressed peoples of the world both those allies will go forward to victory hand in hand.

With fraternal greetings,
Sun Yat-sen

— Reading No. 24 —

MAO TSE-TUNG: *A NATIONAL POPULAR CULTURE* [24]

In 1941 Mao Tse-tung issued a basic program "for the Marxists of China." It stressed the national character of Chinese Marxist culture.

✶   ✶   ✶

The culture of New Democracy is national in character. It opposes imperialist oppression, and advocates the dignity and independence of the Chinese nation. It belongs to our nation, and possesses its characteristics. It unites with the socialist culture and New Democratic culture of other nations, establishes with them relations of mutual absorption and mutual development, and serves with them mutually as part of the new culture of the world. But it can never unite with the imperialist culture of other nations, because it is a revolutionary, national culture. To be sure, China should absorb abundantly the progressive culture of foreign nations as raw material for her own cultural food. Such absorption was not sufficient in the past. What we find useful today we must absorb, not only from the present socialist or New Democratic cultures of other nations, but also from ancient cultures, e.g., from the cultures of the various capitalist countries in the period of enlightenment. These foreign materials we must treat as we treat our food. We submit our food to the mouth for chewing

[24] Mao Tse-tung, "The Politics and Culture of New Democracy," January 15, 1941, section XV.

and to the stomach and intestines for digestion, add to it saliva, pepsin and other secretions of the intestines to separate it into the essence and the residue, and then absorb the essence of our nourishment and pass off the residue. In somewhat similar manner, we should subject our cultural materials to the process of discrimination and should absorb everything conditionally. The idea of "unconditional Westernization" is a wrong one. China has suffered a lot by blindly absorbing foreign materials before. Chinese Communists should never break this rule even in the application of Marxism. We must unify appropriately the general truth of Marxism and the concrete practice of the Chinese revolution, i.e., we must adopt the national form before we can find Marxism useful and should never subjectively or mechanically apply it. Subjective and formal Marxists are only playing with Marxism and the Chinese revolution, and there is no place for them in the revolutionary ranks of China. China's culture should have its own form, the national form. The national form, plus the New Democratic content, is our new culture today.

The culture of New Democracy is scientific in character. It opposes all feudal and superstitious thoughts, and advocates "searching for truth from concrete facts," it advocates objective truth as well as the unity of theory and practice. . . .

The culture of New Democracy is popular in character. It should serve the purpose of the toiling masses, which occupy more than 90 per cent of the whole Chinese population, and should gradually become their own culture. . . .

This national, scientific, and popular culture is the anti-imperialist, anti-feudal culture of the people, the culture of New Democracy, the culture of New San Min Chi I, the culture of the Chinese nation. . . .

— Reading No. 25 —

THE UGANDA FLAG[25]

Characteristic of the new African nationalism is the stanza from the poem "Fly Higher and Higher the Uganda Flag."

Our fight for land will never cease.
It was ours and it will be ours,
    forever and ever.
We do not fear those who speak
    behind our backs.
If they scorn us, they will not be
    here forever.
We look for the day to arrive
When great jubilation will reign
    everywhere.
And the children of black men
    throughout the world
Will know happiness in the
    return of their rights.

* *Uganda Renaissance*, vol. IV, no. 1, January 1961.

A SHORT BIBLIOGRAPHY

Ahmad, Jamal Mohammed, *The Intellectual Origins of Egyptian Nationalism,* New York: Oxford University Press, 1960.

Antonius, George, *The Arab Awakening. The Story of the Arab National Movement,* Philadelphia: Lippincott, 1939.

Baron, Salo W., *Modern Nationalism and Religion,* New York: Harper, 1947.

Brown, Delmar M., *Nationalism in Japan,* Berkeley: University of California Press, 1955.

Brown, Donald M., *The Nationalist Movement. Indian Political Thought from Ranade to Bhave,* Berkeley: University of California Press, 1961.

Buthman, William Curt, *The Rise of Integral Nationalism in France,* New York: Columbia University Press, 1939.

Childers, Erskine B., *Commonsense about the Arab World,* London: Gollancz, 1950.

Curti, Merle E., *The Roots of American Loyalty,* New York: Columbia University Press, 1946.

Dehio, Ludwig, *Germany and World Politics in the 20th Century,* New York: Knopf, 1959.

Deutsch, Karl W., *Nationalism and Social Communication: An Inquiry into the Foundations of Nationality,* Cambridge: Technology Press, 1953.

Emerson, Rupert, *From Empire to Nation. The Rise to Self-Assertion of Asian and African Peoples,* Cambridge: Harvard University Press, 1960.

Hayes, Carleton J. H., *The Historical Evolution of Modern Nationalism,* New York: Richard R. Smith, 1931.

Hertz, Friedrich O., *Nationality in History and Politics.*

A Study of the Psychology and Sociology of National Sentiment and Character, Oxford: Clarendon Press, 1944.

Janowsky, Oscar, *Nationalities and National Minorities,* New York: Columbia University Press, 1945.

Kohn, Hans, *The Idea of Nationalism: A Study of Its Origins and Background,* New York: Macmillan, 1944.

——— *Prophets and Peoples, Studies in Nineteenth Century Nationalism,* New York: Macmillan, 1946.

——— *Pan-Slavism, Its History and Ideology,* Rev. ed., New York: Vintage Books, 1960.

——— *American Nationalism,* New York: Macmillan, 1957.

——— *The Age of Nationalism. The First Era of Global History,* New York: Harper & Row, 1962.

Linebarger, Paul M. A., *The Political Doctrines of Sun Yat-sen,* Baltimore: Johns Hopkins Press, 1937.

Low, Alfred D., *Lenin on the Question of Nationality,* New York: Bookman Associates, 1958.

Palmer, Norman D., *The Indian Political System,* Boston: Houghton Mifflin, 1961.

Pinson, Koppel S., *Modern Germany, Its History and Civilization,* New York: Macmillan, 1954.

Shafer, Boyd C., *Nationalism: Myth and Reality,* New York: Harcourt, Brace, 1955.

Silvert, K. H. (ed.), *Expectant Peoples, Nationalism and Development,* New York: Random House, 1963.

Snyder, Louis L., *Race, A History of Modern Ethnic Theories,* New York: Longmans, Green, 1939.

——— *The Meaning of Nationalism,* New Brunswick, New Jersey: Rutgers University Press, 1954.

——— *Dynamics of Nationalism, Readings in Its Meaning and Development,* Princeton: Van Nostrand, 1964.

Toynbee, Arnold, *The Western Question in Greece and Turkey,* London: Constable, 1922.

Weinberg, Albert K., *Manifest Destiny: A Study of Nationalist Expansionism in American History,* Baltimore: Johns Hopkins Press, 1935.

Whitaker, Arthur P., *Nationalism in Latin America, Past and Present,* Gainesville: University of Florida Press, 1962.

Fuller bibliographies will be found in Koppel S. Pinson, *A Bibliographical Introduction to Nationalism*, New York: Columbia University Press, 1935, and in Karl W. Deutsch, *Interdisciplinary Bibliography on Nationalism, 1935-1953*, Cambridge: Technology Press, 1955.

INDEX

Acton, Lord, 46, 121
Afghanistan, 83
Albania, 45, 90
Alexander (Macedonia), 12
Alfieri, Vittorio, 33
Alsace-Lorraine, 61
America, see United States, Spanish America
Anti-Semitism, 74, 76, 77, 165
Arabs, 76, 83, 84, 90
Argentina, 43, 80
Aribau, C., 67
Arndt, E. M., 36, 70
Austria, 44, 55, 56, 58, 60, 65, 66, 67, 70, 159

Balbo, C., 56
Barrès, M., 74, 75
Basques, 68
Belgium, 38, 40, 67, 91
Bismarck, Otto, 60, 61, 65, 173
Bolívar, Simon, 43
Bosnia-Herzogovina, 61, 65, 70
Brazil, 44, 80
Brückner, A., 66
Bulgaria, 61, 70
Burke, Edmund, 35
Burma, 90
Burschenschaft, 37
Byelorussia, 44

Calhoun, John C., 63
California, 142
Canada, 44, 91
Carducci, G., 52
Carol I (Romania), 55, 56
Catalonia, 67, 68
Cattaneo, Carlo, 56

Cavour, Count, 55, 57, 58, 60
Ceylon, 88
Chamberlain, H. S., 77
Charles Albert of Sardinia, 56
Chiang Kai-shek, 88
China, 72, 73, 87, 88, 89, 90, 179-182
Christianity, 12, 13
Class, H., 70
Communism, 78, 81, 89, 175, 176, 177, 179-182
Cosmopolitanism, 10, 151
Croats, see Southern Slavs
Cromwell, Oliver, 17
Cuza, A. I., 55
Cyprus, 91
Czechoslovakia, 39, 44, 47, 66, 72, 82, 156
Czechs, see Czechoslovakia

Dahlmann, F. C., 51
Danilevsky, N., 151
Dante, 13
Danton, G. J., 27
Davis, T. O., 43
D'Azeglio, M., 57
Deák, F., 65
Denmark, 43, 68
Dmowski, R., 66
Dostoevsky, F., 72, 160
Dreyfus, A., 74
Drumont, E., 74
Dühring, E., 77

Empire, 9, 12, 29, 34, 80, 84, 87, 89, 153
England, 16, 17, 18, 84, 90, 130
Eötvös, J., 65
Estonia, 67

188

Egypt, 83, 84, 90

Fascism, 79, 170
Federalism, 46
Fenians, 68
Fichte, J. G., 36
Finland, 66, 67
Flemish, 67
Foscolo, Ugo, 33
France, 18, 22, 23, 38, 74, 75, 76, 78, 90, 168
Franco, F., 68
French Revolution (1789), 10, 15, 22, 23, 24, 25, 27, 97; (1830), 40; (1848), 49

Gandhi, M. K., 86, 179
Gaj, L., 47
Garibaldi, G., 57
Germany, 34, 35, 36, 37, 38, 51, 54, 77, 80, 91, 104, 105, 106, 127, 132, 138, 167, 169, 173
Ghana, 90
Gioberti, V., 56
Gladstone, W. E., 68
Glorious Revolution, 17, 19
Gobineau, A., 74, 76
Goethe, J. W., 35
Gold Coast, 89, 90
Great Britain, see England
Greece, 10, 11, 12, 39, 40, 45, 61, 70, 79, 82, 91, 116
Griffith, Arthur, 69, 149
Grundtvig, N. F. S., 43
Guizot, F., 113

Haase, E., 70
Havlíček, K., 47, 155
Hebrews, see Jews
Hegel, G. W. F., 35, 60, 110
Herder, J. G., 31, 32, 46, 103
Herzl, T., 75
Hitler, A., 70, 71, 72, 77, 80
Holy Alliance, 38, 39, 44, 49
Hrushevsky, M., 67
Hungary, 45, 48, 49, 65, 66
Hu Shih, 88
Hyde, Douglas, 69, 146

Ibsen, H., 68
Iceland, 68
Illyria, 47, 157
Imperialism, see Empire
India, 85, 86, 88, 90, 149, 178
Individualism, 13, 20, 36, 174
Indonesia, 83
Iran, 83
Iraq, 83, 84
Ireland, 43, 68, 69, 147
Irredenta, 58
Israel, 76, 84, 90
Italy, 13, 14, 33, 38, 52, 56, 57, 58, 79, 80, 82, 94, 118, 119, 120, 127

Jackson, Andrew, 63
Jahn, F. L., 36, 37
Japan, 62, 72, 73, 80, 87, 89
Jews, 11, 67, 70, 74, 75, 76, 77, 165
Jinnah, Ali, 86
Jordan, 83
Jordan, W., 51
Joyce, James, 69

Kant, Immanuel, 35
Karadžić, Vuk, 47
Karamzin, Nicolai, 33
Kemal, Namik, 62
Kemal, Mustafa, 82, 83
Khrushchev, N., 90
Klein, S., 48
Kollár, Jan, 47
Kossuth, L., 49
Kuomintang, 87, 179-180

Latvia, 67, 104
Lazar, G., 48
Lelewel, Joachim, 42
Lenin, N., 72, 78, 180
Liberty, 16, 17, 18, 20, 30, 37, 51, 52, 89, 124, 125
Libya, 83
List, F., 54, 70, 129, 149
Lithuania, 44, 45, 67
Locke, John, 18, 29
Lönnrot, E., 67
Lützow, Adolf, 37

Macaulay, T., 85
Macedonia, 62, 69
Machiavelli, Niccolò, 13, 14, 93
Magyars, see Hungary
Manifest Destiny, 63, 140
Manin, D., 56
Mao Tse-tung, 181-182
Marat, J. P., 28
Marx, Karl, 78
Maurras, Charles, 74, 77
Mazzini, G., 40, 41, 56, 57, 79, 118, 123, 147, 173
Messianism, 11, 42, 72, 78, 80, 153, 160
Metaxas, J., 79
Metternich, 39, 49
Mexico, 44, 52, 89, 142
Michelet, Jules, 42, 76, 96
Mickiewicz, Adam, 42
Midhat, Pasha, 62
Mill, J. S., 51
Milton, John, 16
Minorities, 82
Müller, Adam, 34
Murat, Joachim, 33
Mussolini, B., 79, 80, 170

Napoleon I, 28, 29, 33, 35, 47, 50, 122, 126
Napoleon III, 50, 54, 55, 173
Nehru, Jawaharlal, 175
Netherlands, 61, 133
Nigeria, 89
Nikolai I, 55
Norway, 38, 68

O'Connell, Daniel, 43
O'Sullivan, J. L., 140

Pakistan, 83, 87, 90
Palacký, F., 39, 47, 71
Palestine, 75, 76
Pan-Asianism, 72, 73
Pan-Celtic Movement, 69
Pan-Germanism, 61, 70, 71
Pan-Islamism, 83
Pan-Slavism, 70, 71, 72, 152, 154, 155, 156
Papacy, 56, 57, 58
Parnell, C. S., 68

Pašić, N., 70
Peasant Problem, 42, 43
Pedro II, 44
Pétain, H., 78
Petrarch, 96
Philippine Islands, 85
Pilsudski, J., 66
Pius IX, 52, 56, 57
Pí y Margall, 68
Plato, 12, 22
Poland, 38, 42, 44, 51, 66, 67, 71, 82, 128, 157, 158
Protestantism, 14
Prussia, 31, 58, 59, 60, 62, 167
Puritanism, 16

Racialism, 73-74, 76, 109, 137, 138
Ranke, L., 60
Redmond, J. E., 68
Renan, E., 61, 76, 135
Rhee, Syngman, 88
Risorgimento, 56
Robespierre, Maximilien, 26
Roman Empire, 12, 34, 41, 79, 148
Roman Republic, 57
Romania, 45, 48, 55, 79, 82
Romanticism, 34
Rosenberg, A., 77
Rousseau, Jean Jacques, 20, 21, 22, 31
Rühs, F., 77
Rumania, 90
Russia, 33, 34, 44, 61, 66, 70, 71, 80, 90, 151, 160, 188
Russian Revolution, 78

San Martin, José de, 43
Sardinia, 55, 56, 57, 59
Saudi Arabia, 83
Schiller, Friedrich, 35
Schlegel, Friedrich, 34
Schönerer, G., 66, 70
Schurz, C., 144
Serbs, see Southern Slavs
Shevchenko, Taras, 48
Sinasi, Ibrahim, 62
Sinn Fein, 69, 149